Twentieth Century Thinkers in Adult Education

Adult education theory has developed through a number of significant thinkers this century. This book looks at thirteen major figures, bringing their ideas into one reference volume for the first time to show how each has made a unique contribution to the field of adult education.

Beginning with a general section on the development of adult education knowledge, the following chapters explore the ideas of such thinkers as Paulo Freire, John Dewey, Malcolm S. Knowles and Eduard Lindeman. Each chapter is constructed round a similar framework, and the theory is assessed in detail. Peter Jarvis's concluding chapter offers a comparison of the different figures, and asks whether the study of adult education constitutes a discipline.

The editor
Peter Jarvis is Reader in the Department of Educational Studies at the University of Surrey.

International perspectives on adult and continuing education

Edited by Peter Jarvis, University of Surrey
Consultant Editors: Chris Duke and Ettore Gelpi

Adult education in China
Edited by Carman St John Hunter and Martha McKee Keehn

Combating poverty through adult education
Chris Duke

Lifelong education and international relations
Ettore Gelpi

New perspectives on the education of adults in the United States
Huey Long

Adult education: international perspectives from China
Chris Duke

Twentieth century thinkers in adult education
Edited by Peter Jarvis

Philosophy of lifelong education
Kenneth Wain

Agricultural extension worldwide: issues, practices and emerging priorities
Edited by William M. Rivera and Susan G. Schram

Adult education as social policy
Colin Griffin

Adult education and the challenges of the 1990s
Edited by W. Leirman and J. Kulich

Alternatives in adult education
H.W. Roberts

Adult education and cultural development
David Jones

Landmarks in international adult education:
Edited by Alexander N. Charters and Ronald J. Hilton

Informal and incidental learning in the workplace
Victoria J. Marsick and Karen E. Watkins

Training adult educators in Europe
Edited by Peter Jarvis and Alan Chadwick

Education for adults: international perspectives
Karen Evans and Ian G. Haffenden

TWENTIETH CENTURY THINKERS IN ADULT EDUCATION

Edited by
PETER JARVIS

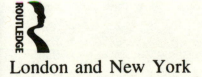

London and New York

First published 1987 by Croom Helm Ltd

First printed in paperback by Routledge 1991

11 New Fetter Lane, London EC4P 4EE

Simultaneously published in the USA and Canada
by Routledge
a division of Routledge, Chapman and Hall, Inc.
29 West 35th Street, New York, NY 10001

© 1987 Peter Jarvis

Printed and bound in Great Britain by
Mackays of Chatham Ltd, Kent

British Library Cataloguing in Publication Data

Twentieth century thinkers in adult
    education. — (Routledge series in
    international adult education)
    1. Adult education
    I. Jarvis, Peter
    374   LC5215
    ISBN 0-415-05464-8

Library of Congress Cataloging in Publication Data

Twentieth century thinkers in adult education.
    (Routledge series in international adult education)
    Includes index.
    1. Adult education — philosophy. 2. Adult education —
History — 20th century. 3. Educators — biography.
I. Jarvis, Peter. II. Title: 20th century thinkers in
adult education. III. Series.
LC5219.T85 1987   374'.001   87-5299
ISBN 0-415-05464-8

CONTENTS

PREFACE

The idea for this book took shape over a number of years of teaching the theory of adult education, during which time it became evident that there exists no single book that provided an overview of the development of the variety of approaches to the subject nor one where substantial summaries of any of the key thinkers might be easily obtained. This symposium has been designed to rectify in part these deficiencies.

Deciding upon who might be regarded as a major thinker is a difficult process and colleagues in the field might dispute the selection a little. However, it was decided at the outset that only writers whose work has been published in English would be included in this volume. Limitations of space forbade the inclusion of too many writers, unless depth was to be sacrificed. Hence, it was decided that about twelve should be the number. Consultations with one or two colleagues in the field resulted in the final selection.

The preparation of the book has not been without its hazards for the authors. Three of those who were originally approached were hospitalised within a few months of the request being made, one of those three subsequently withdrew, and so the editor was forced to write a further chapter. However, I should like to express my thanks to all those colleagues who have written the following chapters and also to those who, knowing about my intention to produce this text, have been so encouraging.

It is hoped that both students of the field of adult education and practitioners within the field will find this a useful addition to the literature of the education of adults.

Peter Jarvis
Guildford, Surrey, UK, August 1986

Part One

INTRODUCTION

Chapter One

THE DEVELOPMENT OF ADULT EDUCATION KNOWLEDGE

Peter Jarvis

Every new occupation seeking professional status has
sought to delineate its foundation in terms of its
knowledge base and it is perhaps significant as
provision to recognise that this is one of the
processes that has already begun in the education of
adults (see Jarvis, 1985). However, long before the
debates about professionalisation begin the process
of delineating of the field of practice and then the
field of study has to occur. (Bright, 1985)
    McCullough (1980, p.158) has perhaps best
described the problems of undertaking the former:

> Extracting adult education from its surrounding
> social milieu - or at least differentiating
> adult education from the social milieu - is as
> difficult as determining how many angels can
> dance on the head of a pin. Is adult education a
> practice or a program? A methodology or an
> organization? A "science" or a system? A process
> or a profession? Is adult education different
> from continuing education, vocational educat-
> ion, higher education? Does adult education
> have form and substance, or does it merely
> permeate through the environment like air? Is
> adult education, therefore, everywhere and yet
> nowhere in particular? Does adult education
> even exist?

McCullough's questions are pertinent in the light of
the observation that the British philosopher R.S.
Peters (1966, pp.23ff) made when he claimed that the
educational institution as a whole had become so
complex that it had become too difficult to define.
Rather Peters offered three criteria which he claimed
should be present in any educational activity:
education should involve the transmission of what is

3

worthwhile to those who are committed to it; must involve knowledge and an active process of understanding; must be willing and voluntary. But by specifying these three criteria Peters has merely changed the rules of definition - now definition does not seek to encompass the whole phenomenon, but to isolate a common core.

In contrast to this debate Boyd and Apps (1980) attempted to construct a three dimensional model of adult education that encompassed the whole phenomenon as they saw it. In this, they were seeking to demarcate the field of practice, a necessary and commendable exercise. Basically they sought to start with the field of practice and to build a model from their observations, claiming that adult education has: three transactional modes - independent, individual and group; three client foci - individual, group and community; three systems - personal, social and cultural. This model did not go uncriticised from the outset. For instance, Carlson (1980, p. 175) claimed that the authors had incarcerated themselves within a conceptual prison and that a great deal of adult education occurred outside of the conceptual framework which they produced (p. 178). Indeed, it is difficult to differentiate clearly some of their types; for instance, within the framework of adult education how do the social and cultural systems vary? However, perhaps their (1980, p.2) most contentious claim is that:

> we believe that it is an error to seek assistance from recognised disciplines until we have clearly understood the structure, function, problems, and purposes of adult education itself.

Boyd and Apps appear to be attempting is to isolate a social phenomenon and to interpret it within its own framework. But in order to construct the model of the phenomenon they had to employ a sociological framework and in order to interpret it they brought to it their own theories and philosophies. They were trying to isolate a social institution from the remainder of society in a manner which is both artificial and untrue to the structure of contemporary society. It is to this complex social structure with its interlocking disciplines of knowledge that recourse has to be made in order to understand the manner in which adult education knowledge has emerged, and the remainder of this chapter addresses itself to this problem; it has two main sections, the first examines the way in which the structures of knowledge change within social evolution and the second focuses upon the way that this has happened within adult education. Finally, the chapter concludes by reverting to this initial discussion.

The Changing Structures of Knowledge

Social change is itself a complex phenomenon to analyse and no attempt to isolate all of its elements will be attempted here, suffice to note that while conflict may be one element in it evolution is another. Conflict can be seen in Freire's analysis of the power structures of society and, indeed, conflict may well be necessary to change such structures in a radical manner in the great majority of countries in the world. Social evolution, on the other hand, also occurs in the process of change and this has been defined by Bellah (1970, p.21) as:

> a process of increasing differentiation and complexity of organization that endows the organism, social system, or whatever the unit in question may be with a greater capacity to adapt to its environment, so that it is in some sense more autonomous relative to its environment than were its less complex ancestors.

Hence it may be seen that as society grows increasingly complex so do most of its institutions and so does their knowledge base. Hence, it might be argued that knowledge expands in relation to the speed of social change. However, it is necessary to understand the process by which this occurs in order to relate it to the emergence of adult education knowledge. While knowledge is a personal acquisition that occurs as a result of learning, it is discussed here within its objectified sense, which is that there might be a body of knowledge that is shared by people as members of a cultural group, or a social group. This knowledge appears to be objective, even though it is actually the shared subjectivity of the group. Hence, knowledge may be regarded as related to social role within the confines of the collectivity, but because of the process of increasing complexification of society, there is a growing complexification of role and eventually of division of labour. Berger and Luckmann (1967, p.95) suggest that this occurs in the following manner:

> Given the historical accumulation of knowledge
> in a society, we can assume that, because of the
> division of labour, role specific knowledge
> will grow at a faster rate than generally
> relevant and accessible knowledge. The
> multiplication of specific tasks brought about
> by the division of labour requires standardized
> solutions that can be readily learned and
> transmitted. These in turn require specialized
> knowledge of certain situations, and of the
> ends/means relationships in terms of which the
> situations are socially defined. In other
> words, specialists will arise, each of whom will
> have to know whatever is deemed necessary for
> the fulfilment of his particular task.

The picture of social evolution painted by Bellah is
one that suggests that the growing complexification
of society is a rather linear process of sub-division
as specialists arise and coupled with this it might
be assumed that knowledge sub-divides in a similar
manner. Hence, it could be claimed there is an
emergence of a multitude of sub-disciplines within
each basic discipline of knowledge. While this claim
is not disputed here, it is suggested that the sub-
division of the disciplines is not the whole process,
since that would imply a mechanical correlation
between structure and knowledge. Again it would not
be disputed that in certain situations within certain
groups of people such a correlation does occur.
Mannheim (1936, p.2), for instance, explains this
correlation thus:

> Only in a quite limited sense does the single
> individual create out of himself the mode of
> speech and of thought that we attribute to him.
> He speaks the language of his group; he thinks
> in the manner in which his group thinks. He
> finds at his disposal only certain words and
> their meanings.

How, then, can new thoughts emerge? How can new ideas
occur if the thoughts of people are no more than
reflections of their social condition? Mannheim
himself offered an answer to this when he (1936, p.9)
wrote:

> In every society there are social groups whose
> special tasks it is to provide an interpretation
> of the world for that society. We call these the
> "intelligentsia". The more static a society is,

the more likely it is that this stratum will acquire a well-defined status or the position of a caste in that society. Thus the magicians, the Brahmins, the medieval clergy are to be regarded as the intellectual strata, each of which in its society enjoyed a monopolistic control over the moulding of that society's world-view, and over either the reconstruction or the reconciliation of the differences in the naively formed world-views of the other strata.

Mannheim goes on to argue that it is because the intelligentsia are drawn from a variety of different strata in society that they could be freed from the constraints of their location within the social structure. Perhaps today this explanation for intellectual freedom appears to be a little simplistic, since a number of learning theorists, (see Jarvis, 1987 forthcoming) have argued that there are certain kinds of reflective learning that are innovative and creative, so that individuals do not need to be a recognised member of the intelligentsia in order to be intellectually free. However, it is maintained here that certain of the specialists referred to by Berger and Luckmann within the division of labour, who might be regarded as Mannheim's intelligentsia, are able to be creative within the context of social change. Indeed, it is maintained that the innovation in their thought is not only that they are aware of the fission of knowledge into a multitude of sub-disciplines but that they straddle this continuous sub-division and draw together in new and unique constellations a mixture of these sub-disciplines relevant for the practice of new occupations and emerging professions. It is they who formulate those standardised solutions which have to be transmitted to new recruits to an occupation or a profession and which became the knowledge basis of the emerging occupation's or profession's practice.

The generation of new knowledge is both a fission and a fusion of knowledge; it is the synthesizer who draws together from a mixture of sub-disciplines and who creates new knowledge about practice. Hence, it would be quite valid to claim that until such time as the occupation or profession begins to teach its new recruits, it does not codify its knowledge in a systematic manner. But it should also be noted that this synthesis is the generation of new knowledge and it is also part of the growing complexification of society that was discussed earlier.

There is, however, another facet to social change since not everything undergoes change. For instance, the power relations in society maintain a similar function despite the changes introduced into society as a result of technological change. Indeed, while utopian ideals about an ideal society have been postulated in most ages, these are a reaction to the existing power relations in society. Hence, religious and political dreamers have all looked to a time when these relationships will change as well. Hence, some forms of knowledge, that is those relating to the continuity of power in society will remain relevant in all ages and those thinkers who include the power dimension within their analysis of knowledge will remain relevant for as long as power is still exercised by one person, or group of persons, over another person or group.

Continuity and change is a social process that happens to all knowledge and, consequently, to knowledge of education and even to the education of adults. Hence, the next section of this chapter applies this argument to the emergence of adult education knowledge.

The Development of Adult Education Knowledge

The process traced in the above discussion has occurred within the development of knowledge about the education of adults, a term which it should be noted here is used synonymously with adult education in this context only. Two points need to be made at this juncture in the argument. Firstly, that this is an on-going process that does not stop once a codified base line of knowledge about the discipline has been drawn up, but secondly, once there is a body of knowledge there is a tendency to seek to isolate it and treat it as precious so that there is resistance to the contribution that other disciplines can make to the new body of knowledge. This is, perhaps, implicit in the claim of Boyd and Apps that emphasis should be placed upon adult education interpretations rather than upon the use of other disciplines. It is even more significant in the debates about the level of knowledge/qualification in adult education it is necessary to have prior to entering the adult education professoriate or into the occupation of teaching adults generally. Since it is not the intention of this chapter to pursue this element of the discussion, it is important only to notice the manner in which boundaries are drawn around new sub-disciplines and legitimated by such processes as initial preparation and entry qualifications to the profession. This is not to deny that entry qualifications may be very important, it is merely to note the manner in which the process works in the emergence of a sub-discipline, like adult education. This argument finds some support in Bright's claim (1985, p.170) that 'adult education ... represent(s) a collection of different types of epistemologies and methods.'

It was claimed that the manner in which this synthesis occurs is on-going, so that if this claim is correct it should be possible to examine the works of any of the major thinkers in the field of adult education and to trace this process. It was also claimed that those thinkers, whose analysis related to the continuity of the power dimension in society, would also speak to the human condition in different ages and in different cultures. Throughout the following chapters then these processes should be apparent and so it is hardly necessary to illustrate this here. Nevertheless, for the sake of completing the argument it will be discussed by making reference to two writers from different historical periods in this century, both of whom in different ways have made a contribution to the development of adult education knowledge: Eduard Lindeman and Paulo Freire. Both of these demonstrate the ideas of fission and fusion of knowledge and the latter, especially, also demonstrates the manner in which he relates adult education knowledge to the power structures of society.

Eduard Lindeman: Brookfield points out that writing about adult education was but one part of the total output of Lindeman's writing and that at a testimonial dinner given for Lindeman in the last year of his life there were tributes from the American Civil Liberties Union, Adult Education Association (written by Malcolm Knowles), the American Labor Education Service, the International Ladies' Garment Workers' Union, the League for Industrial Democracy, the Society of Ethical Culture, the Planned Parenthood Association of America, the Association of American Indian Affairs, the National Child Education Committee and the Women's Trade Union League. That Lindeman never held an academic appointment in the field of adult education but he did teach in a school of social work demonstrates the breadth of his activities. Indeed,

in <u>The Meaning of Adult Education</u> there is a fusion
of the ideas that come from all of these activities
and interests, as well as Lindeman's own acquaintance
with John Dewey and his writings about adult
education. In Lindeman there is a unique combination
of humanistic philosophy and progressive education
which has both social and political concerns that
have subsequently characterised adult education,
especially that which has been labelled liberal adult
education.

Paulo Freire: Freire's work has taken longer to
become known in the English speaking world simply
because it was initially written in Portuguese and
because he has drawn upon intellectual disciplines
that are less well known to contemporary adult
educators. For instance, as a member of the Christian
Marxist movement that was strong in Brazil prior to
the military coup of 1964, Freire combined a deep
theological understanding with a radical Marxist
perspective, Freire was certainly influenced by the
theological revolution that occurred within the
Church of Rome in the late 1950s and the early 1960s,
especially the publications of Pope John XXIII, and
at the same time, he was influenced by the works of
Eduard Mournier and Teilhard de Chardin, both of whom
he quotes in his writings. But as he was influenced
by the revolutionary writing of Marx and Marxists,
such as Franz Fanon, Freire also combines these
writers with a philosophical liberal perspective and
some elements of existentialism. Indeed, writing
about Freire, Mackie (1980, p.118) calls Freire an
eclectic whose

> diversity of thought is both a strength and a
> weakness; a strength in that it creatively draws
> together many strands of contemporary thinking
> into a dynamic and challenging theory; a
> weakness, in that such a procedure makes it all
> too easy for one aspect of Freire's writing to
> be spotlighted at the expense of others.

This diversity of thought will be seen in the chapter
about Freire below in which it will become apparent
that this combination of disciplines within the
education of adults is both unique and challenging to
the theoretical perspectives of the sub-discipline
at the current time. Debates about the extent to
which Freire's ideas are relevant to the first world
are also debates about whether the theological,

philosophical and political elements are acceptable to those who seek to understand him. It is here that those whose analysis does not include the dimension of power are less likely to regard Freire's analysis of adult education as relevant to the developed world, since power is often less overtly exercised in those societies. While his educational method may be no more radical, if at all more radical, than Lindeman's or Knowles's, the formulation of his educational philosophy appears much more radical than both and more political than Knowles, because of his emphasis upon the power dimension. This, then, is the continuity of knowledge within the ever changing fission and fusion that occurs as a result of technological change and the resulting division of labour.

These two writers have been used to illustrate that at different times this century leading thinkers in the field have drawn upon a variety of sub-disciplines in order to express their understanding of the principles and practice of the education of adults. They have straddled two, or more, academic disciplines and have drawn them together in a unique manner which has inspired others to think along similar paths and to extend still further the sub-discipline.

It is perhaps significant to note within the context of this discussion that the field of the education of adults is mainly a combination of the philosophy, the social science disciplines mentioned and elements of psychology. But it is a combination, so that it might be asked if education itself is actually a discipline of which the education of adults is a sub-discipline. It is perhaps dubious to claim that education is itself an academic discipline, that is a separate sub-division of knowledge having different principles and methods of verification, although it is certain that it is a field of practice. Hence, the education of adults may also be an even more specific field of practice in which a combination of sub-disciplines from the humanities and the social sciences form its foundation. This combination, however, is neither static nor fixed, so that as society changes and evolves so other scholars add to the richness and the diversity of the field by straddling these changing areas of knowledge and producing still more permutations and combinations in an on-going process of developing adult education knowledge.

Conclusions

This chapter began by examining the extent to which it is possible to isolate adult education as a practice and concludes by questioning whether it can ever be a pure academic discipline in itself. It started by pointing to the claim of Boyd and Apps that adult education should restrict itself to adult education knowledge and concludes by claiming that knowledge about the education of adults is itself a unique constellation of those academic sub-disciplines which Boyd and Apps considered should be avoided in the first instance when analysing the field of practice. But the fact that adult education knowledge may be a combination of other sub-disciplines should not weaken the academic rigour by which that combination should be studied, only spur other scholars to seek wider perspectives, so that the field may continue to be enriched as other scholars straddle to divide between the disciplines and draw together ideas that can be incorporated into an ever-changing body of adult education knowledge.

References

Bellah R. 1970 Beyond Belief New York, Harper and Row.
Berger P.L. and Luckmann T. 1967 The Social Construction of Reality, London, Allan Lane, the Penguin Press.
Boyd R.D. and Apps J. et al 1980 Redefining the Discipline of Adult Education San Francisco, Jossey Bass Publishers
Bright B.R. (1985) The Content-Method Relationship in the Study of Adult Education, in Studies in the Education of Adults, Vol 17, No 2, pp.168-183
Carlson R. 1980 The Foundation of Adult Education: Analyzing the Boyd-Apps Model in Boyd and Apps et al, op cit.
Jarvis, P. 1985 The Sociology of Adult and Continuing Education London, Croom Helm
Jarvis P. 1987 (forthcoming) Adult Learning in the Social Context London, Croom Helm
Mackie R. (ed) 1980 Literacy and Revolution: the Pedagogy of Paulo Freire London, Pluto Press Ltd
Mannheim K 1936 Ideology and Utopia London, Routledge and Kegan Paul
McCullough K.O. 1980 Analyzing the Evolving Structure of Adult Education in Peters J. et al op cit.
Peters J. et al 1980 Building an Effective Adult Education Enterprise San Francisco, Jossey Bass

Publishers
Peters R.S. 1966 <u>Ethics and Education</u> London, Unwin
University Books

Part Two

EARLY TWENTIETH CENTURY ENGLISH THINKERS

Chapter Two

ALBERT MANSBRIDGE (1876-1952)

David Alfred

The 'Great Tradition' describes a uniquely English
form of adult education. According to Wiltshire, it
is humane, socially purposive, non-vocational, free
from intellectual means-testing and based on the
tutorial group, and its incentive is the pure love of
learning. More than anyone else, Albert Mansbridge
was responsible for popularising this type of adult
liberal education (quoted in Shaw 1959:187). Born in
1876 the fourth son of a carpenter and leaving school
at the age of fourteen to work in a succession of
clerical jobs in London, Mansbridge succeeded in
constructing a unique 'educational alliance' - the
Workers' Educational Association (WEA) - between the
working-class movement and university extension,
between Labour and Learning, and rose to that social
and educational eminence symbolised by the award of
the Companion of Honour and a number of honorary
doctorates.
    The purpose of what follows is to examine the
central elements of Mansbridge's educational thought
within its social and historical context, and to
assess briefly its influence and contemporary
relevance. An attempt is also made to bring out some
of the contradictions of his educational ideas and
practice and to show how they were conditioned by and
subtly articulated those of the society in which he
grew to maturity.
    Described as the 'prophet-founder' of the WEA,
'the biggest educational revolution of his
generation', and the 'architect of modern adult
education', Mansbridge was also responsible for many
other educational innovations, generally less well
known (Bishop of Chichester, 1952:146; J.H. Jones
and Dover Wilson, quoted in Mansbridge, 1944:xvii,
ix). They are the Central Joint Advisory Committee
for Tutorial Classes (1908), the Central Library for

Students (1916) (1), the Church Tutorial Association (1918) (2), the World Association for Adult Education (1919) (3), the Seafarers' Education Service (1919), The British Institute of Adult Education (1921) (4), and the College of the Sea (1938).

Mansbridge was also involved in British and Australian army education, participated in many official education and Church committees and commissions, notably the one that produced the 1919 Final Report which articulated the classic case for the Great Tradition, delivered innumerable sermons, speeches and lectures throughout Britain, the USA, the Dominions and on the Continent, and wrote a great deal. Mansbridge's educational thought coalesced from three sources, each with its own rich history, Christian, ethical idealism (represented by Westminster Abbey), University Extension and the Co-operative movement. Mansbridge's influence did not lie in the originality, let alone the translucence, of his ideas, but in the way he integrated them into something new and made them appealing to diverse social groups who, inspired by his sincerity, commitment and enthusiasm, then helped him to put them into action.

In his youth, Mansbridge became deeply religious and turned from the Congregationalism of his parents to Anglicanism, then 'more in harmony with the spirit of the age' than Nonconformism (Halevy, 1961:183). He was active in religious education and propaganda. Spending much of his free time in Westminster Abbey, Mansbridge heard 'the succession of great Anglican preachers' of the 1890s (1924:33). Pre-eminent among them was a Charles Gore, an Anglo-Catholic of 'radical temper (who had a) hatred of social injustice ... and whose influence on the Church of England was unequalled in his generation' (DNB:349, 352) (5). At the age of eighteen, Mansbridge had occasion to meet Gore who, until he died in 1932, became his 'friend, counsellor and guide' and the greatest of his many and varied heroes (1929:16).

Gore's main influence on Mansbridge was to reinforce the conviction he had already gained from his parents that Christian belief and practice cannot be dissociated from social issues. Gore was the exemplar of what Kelly (1983) calls 'education for civilisation', a programme which sprang from the social responsibility to working people felt by mainly the Anglican-academic section of the dominant class (6). In the 1850s F.D. Maurice and Charles Kingsley founded the Working Men's College. A generation later, the early death of Arnold Toynbee inspired the founding of Toynbee Hall, a university settlement. Kelly talks of these and others as seeking to socialise Christianity and to Christianise socialism, i.e. to preserve the existing social order by reforming it through social reconciliation. Thus Maurice's aim was to unite the classes through the sharing of higher spiritual ideals and Christian fellowship. In 'Property: its Duties and Rights' which he edited in 1914, Gore advocated moral teaching to counter 'the traditional cry of "the rights of property"' and urged Christians to be 'ready for a deep and courageous ... act of penitence and reparation' to the wrongfully dispossessed working-class (Smith 1956:39). Kelly argues that a crucial feature of 'education for civilisation' was its creation of the distinction between liberal and vocational education, commonly expressed by the slogan that 'education is a means of life, not a means of livelihood'.

Parallel with his religious enthusiasm, Mansbridge became a keen and successful student at extension courses arranged by London University. University Extension, another part of 'education for civilisation' (which might be characterised as the 'educated man's burden'), provided short lecture courses and other educational activities aimed mainly at workers in urban areas.

Mansbridge was among the quarter or so of about 60,000 extension students throughout the country who were working-class but not deterred by cost or by the largely middle-class control of extension centres. He recalled being 'entranced (when) sitting at the feet' of his lecturers at Battersea (1945:14). They 'demonstrated ... the power of trained skill and learning. Above all they opened up vistas of what the universities might mean to men and women who never by any chance could actually study in them' (1929:17). No doubt Mansbridge was thinking of his failure to get an Oxford scholarship to study for the priesthood, his great ambition. The older universities, far from being rejected, became all the more the 'land of heart's desire ... magnificent expressions of the best in human life and the foundations of inspiration and instruction', even though not always realised in practice (ibid). The extension lecturer who most influenced Mansbridge – 'the great light on my horizon' - was the legendary Hudson Shaw of Oxford who attracted huge, mainly working-class audiences in places such as Oldham and Rochdale where the Co-operative movement was most

19

active (1945:14). Indeed it was Shaw's 'rousing speech' at the 1898 Co-operative conference at Peterborough that Mansbridge claimed to be the origin of the WEA. Mansbridge's assessment of the significance of university extension was that it 'prepared the way for more effective service' in the co-operative movement' (1929:16).

Through his mother's active membership of the Co-operative Women's Guild, Mansbridge was already familiar with the ethical ideals and voluntary self-help of Co-operation that made it such a strong and distinctive working-class movement. From his father's involvement with the Amalgamated Society of Carpenters and Joiners, Mansbridge gained further understanding of the value of independent and democratic working-class organisation. In 1895, his way to Oxford and the Church barred and getting nowhere at work, Mansbridge may have faced a personal crisis (Jennings 1973:7). From the following year, when he was twenty, he began what was to prove a crucial ten-year association with the Co-operative movement. (7) While working for it as a clerk, then as a cashier, Mansbridge became involved in its educational work in his spare time. He was a teacher, a frequent contributor to its newspaper and in 1898 and 1899 attended its national conferences, a dominant theme of which was the closer collaboration between Co-operation and university extension advocated by Shaw, Robert Halstead, formerly a weaver and then Secretary of the Co-operative Productive Federation, and Michael Sadler, Secretary of the Extension Delegacy of Oxford University. Mansbridge recalled Toynbee's 'ringing challenge (in 1882) ... to meet the passion for Dividend by the passion for Education' (Mansbridge: no date:10). Co-operation thus forged the link between Mansbridge's socially activist religious faith, his admiration for university education and his conviction the working-class people, with whom he strongly identified, had as much right to education as anyone else and, furthermore, badly needed it. Combined, these elements led Mansbridge to create a secular 'field of practical idealism' that compensated for his 'frustrated vocation for the priesthood' (Jennings 1973:11).

Despite his inauspicious debut at the conferences mentioned above, Mansbridge's own passion for education was recognised by Gore, J.A.R. Marriott (Sadler's successor and, later, a Tory M.P.) and Canon Samuel Barnett, Warden of Toynbee Hall, who said of him: 'that young man has fire in his belly'

Albert Mansbridge (1876-1952)

(quoted in Smith 1956:17).

By the beginning of 1903, Mansbridge was ready
for action. An article he had been invited to write
for Oxford's University Extension Journal on 'Co-
operation, Trade Unionism and University Extension'
was published in January and aroused so much interest
that he was asked to write two further articles.
Shortly after, Mansbridge and his wife, Frances, with
two shillings and sixpence (12½p) from the
housekeeping money, set up An Association to Promote
the Higher Education of Working Men (renamed the
Workers' Educational Association in 1905) 'primarily
by the extension of university teaching, and also by
the development of an efficient School Continuation
System and the assistance of Working Class efforts of
a specifically educational character.'

The question arises as to how Mansbridge, barely
known in either the Labour movement or university
extension, managed not only to establish but make a
success of such an educational innovation as the WEA.
However formidable were his personal qualities of
commitment, energy and persuasiveness, the
explanation must take into account the pattern of
social forces at the time. Briefly put, there was
considerable class conflict and clear divisions
within both the working-class and the capitalist and
aristocratic classes. In general terms, the former
was divided between a section organised through
Nonconformism, Co-operation, craft unions and the
Radical wing of the Liberal Party, and a newer
section of mainly semi- and unskilled workers
organised in general unions which, partly through the
'socialist revival' of the 1880s, demanded either
separate parliamentary representation for Labour as
an interest in existing society or the transformation
of the existing social order. By the turn of the
century, the compromise arduously reached was that
there should be an independent and non-socialist
Labour Party. Mansbridge's WEA may be seen as the
educational counterpart of these wider political
changes. In both cases, minority revolutionary
socialist groups criticised these 'broad churches'
for being too broad and conciliatory.

Unlike the Labour Party, the creation of the WEA
would not have been possible without the active
involvement of a small but influential group of
religious, educational and social progressives from
within the dominant social class. They may be
conveniently called the Oxford Reformers, consisting
of several overlapping networks of people with whom
Mansbridge came into personal contact.

21

The largest and most significant network of
reformers was centred on Balliol College (whose
previous luminaries included Jowett and Toynbee):
Gore; William Temple, later Archbishop of York, then
of Canterbury, and the WEA's first president (1908-
1921); R.H. Tawney, later a leading economic
historian and socialist writer, the first tutorial
class tutor, and WEA president (1928-1944); and the
historian, A.L. Smith, Master of the college (from
1916), a strong supporter of WEA Summer Schools and
chairman of the committee that produced the 1919
Final Report. From New College, the group included
Alfred Zimmern, an authority on international
relations, co-author with Tawney of the 1908 Oxford
report, and sometime treasurer of the WEA; H.H.
Turner, professor of astronomy; and (later, Sir)
Robert Morant, the first Permanent Secretary to the
Board of Education (1903-1911). Other Oxford
supporters of the WEA included: Sidney Ball,
president of the Oxford Fabian Society; Sir William
Anson, Warden of All Souls, Unionist MP for Oxford,
and Parliamentary Secretary to the Board of Education
(1902-1905); John Holland Rose, historian and editor
of the University Extension Journal.

The Catiline Club was a ginger group of Oxford
dons - Gore, Temple, Zimmern, Richard Livingstone and
others - who shared Mansbridge's criticism of the way
the country's leading eudcational institutions had
unjustly excluded the 'generality of the labouring
poor' for whom they had often been wholly or partly
founded (1929:17).

Another important network centred on Toynbee
Hall, co-founded in 1884 by Samuel Barnett, a
Christian socialist, in memory of Arnold Toynbee, as
a social and cultural centre in the impoverished
district of Whitechapel. Tawney and Morant had served
as residents there and William Beveridge as Sub-
Warden (from 1903 to 1905). Mansbridge traced the
WEA's origins to the religious, social and
educational principles that had animated Toynbee's
short but active and influential life, and which he
had articulated in his 'epoch-making address' on 'The
Education of Co-operators' at the Co-operative
Congress held at Oxford in 1882 (1924:132).

The WEA-Oxford conference held in 1907 and
chaired by Gore on 'What Oxford can do for Work
people' constituted the greatest success for both the
Oxford Reformers and Mansbridge. Jennings argues
that the conference and the report which resulted
from it, 'Oxford and Working-Class Education'
(published in the following year), was part of a

planned campaign to reform the University by raising
its standards and democratising its recruitment
(1975:55). The conference was typical of those
Mansbridge had organised since the WEA had sprouted
in 1903. Amongst hundreds of 'ordinary' working-
class men and women mingled representatives of all
wings of the Labour movement, the churches,
government authorities and the universities. The
most dramatic moment of this conference was the
unexpected and electrifying intervention of J.M.
Mactavish, a Portsmouth shipwright and Labour
councillor (succeeding Mansbridge as the WEA's
general secretary in 1916) who demanded that Oxford
give 'all the best that (it) has to give to the
working-class, not for their individual self-
advancement but for the great task of lifting their
class', and rhetorically asked whether a
university's 'true function (was) to train the
nation's best men, or to sell its gifts to the rich',
to its own detriment and that of the country and the
'work people deprived of the right of access'
(1913:194).

As a result of the report, Oxford gave its
blessing to the tutorial classes that were just
starting at Longton and Rochdale, and Morant agreed
that the Board of Education would give them some
financial support. An independent Joint Tutorial
Committee of the WEA and the University was set up to
oversee this type of work, and a Central Joint
Advisory Committee for Tutorial classes was also
established to co-ordinate such courses throughout
the country (8).

Mansbridge saw the tutorial class, a sustained
course of university standard over three years, as
the pinnacle of working-class educational achievement. Together with the annual summer schools held at
Oxford, such education constituted a 'workers'
university' (Smith 1956:90).

The early success of the WEA thus owed much to
the support of Oxford, the Board of Education and the
Church, or, rather, the progressive elements within
these prestigious and influential institutions. They
cleared the space for Mansbridge and others in the
WEA who, while mostly sharing their religious,
social, and educational views, possessed the crucial
advantage over them of working-class identity. The
Mansbridgean WEA offered the perfect channel for
'clerical conscience', overcoming the inherent
limitations of the sponsorship 'from above' of
'education for civilisation' (Jennings 1973:28). The
WEA may thus be seen as an original form of

'education from above - from below'.

Freire's (1972:21) proposition that 'every educational practice implies a concept of man and the world' applies clearly to Mansbridge whose educational ideas were permeated by Christian values.

He believed that God created and sustained all matter and expressed its will or spiritual power through it. He believed that 'Real man is eternal and spiritual', and that his duty is to continue God's work of creation. Whether conscious of it or not, the power of the spirit guides all human life (1940:227). Since all human beings shared the same creator and had within them the divine spark, Mansbridge believed in the 'essential value of every human being' (1928:5). Going further, he held the view that 'every man and woman is a genius in some way' (1944:194). Mansbridge's concept of 'man' was in the tradition of Christian humanism and spiritual egalitarianism.

Mansbridge defined knowledge, not in terms of the common view of 'learning its formulae' or 'mere cleverness', but, following John Henry Newman, as a process of 'inward digestion', i.e. passing into a person's experience and so transforming their personality and bringing about wisdom (1929:32). That Mansbridge's perspective was religious, so that wisdom was interpreted as awareness of the power of the spirit, does not detract from the important principle that knowledge is of little account unless fused with experience and better action, whatever may be the criterion of 'better'. However, the way he sometimes thought of 'the pursuit of knowledge for its own sake' indicates some ambiguity if not ambivalence about the way Mansbridge viewed education (1913:1).

From his religious conviction, Mansbridge believed that the purpose of education is to help people 'in the power of the spirit, through knowledge and training, to order the material of the world for the welfare of man and the glory of God' (1929:35). Education is a 'force enabling man to develop to the furtherest limits of his powers ... of body, mind and spirit ... to reach out the work God intended that he should do' (1920:54, xv). It was thus 'an affair of the spirit', its end being a 'joyous life for all men' (1928:13, 16). Observing that spiritual influences on education were greatest in adult education, as exemplified by the work of Grundtvig, Vincent Paton and Masaryk, Mansbridge described adult education as 'a secular gospel' (1920:65-66).

Mansbridge believed that the 'educated man' was

anyone who 'fulfils his allotted task in the spirit and in the act, whether it be the digging of a trench or the writing of a poem' (1920:xv). He did not question the social processes by which people were allocated to different occupations nor why they were (as they still are) so unjustly 'rewarded'. By assuming the harmony of the existing social order and education, Mansbridge could assert that the educated person 'can do no harm to the community' because, not 'merely drifting down the streams of opportunity or aiming at (other) false purposes', he or she uses knowledge only 'for the purpose of ministering to the common good' (ibid).

So closely bound in his thought were spirituality, wisdom and knowledge that Mansbridge was convinced that the individual's desire for the latter 'is so uniform as to constitute a law of life' (1920:8). Although Thomas (1982:61) states that he looked to 'established traditional education for the model of workers' education', Mansbridge's attitude was again not unambiguous. On one hand, he praised the university tutorial class as the 'most prominent constructive work of the WEA', on the other he emphasised the need to unify the 'practical experience of students' lives with knowledge gained in class' (1920:40). Although he valued 'humanistic studies', Mansbridge criticised the way they were badly communicated to the majority of people. Hence his insistence that WEA members should say 'how, why, what, or when they wish to study' (1920:xvii-xviii). Moreover, if traditional education involved a certain practice of pedagogy as well as particular types of content, it is clear that Mansbridge was far from being conservative.

He introduced his book on 'University Tutorial Classes' in 1913 with two educational maxims: 'How shall a man learn except from one who is his friend?' (Xenophon); 'The lecture is one, the discussion is one thousand' (Arabian proverb). Generally less concerned with defining the content of knowledge, Mansbridge emphasised the importance of satisfying people's need for it, whatever it was. Not only did his research into educational history show him that working people had always produced their own scholars, but he also observed (ironically, in materialist terms) that all music, art and literature was based on or derived from the 'basic and fundamental activities of man' (1929:32). Mansbridge had a healthy disrespect for the patently false and self-serving notion that culture is confined to the dominant social class (Smith 1956:58).

The social and political aspects of Mansbridge's educational thought centre on the linked concepts of 'democracy' and 'citizenship'. He applied them to society as a whole and to education in different and sometimes contradictory ways. Mansbridge pictured society, the 'vast body of humanity', as an organism made up of different kinds of 'cells', individuals, each having its own function. Some people, like the heart, provide spiritual sustenance; some, like the brain, mental; and most, like the limbs, provide various forms of labour 'to sustain the state of the world in which the heart and brain may freely work' (1940:220). Although partly mitigated by his spiritual egalitarianism, Mansbridge's social theory exemplifies the idealist, organicist and functionalist perspective, common at the time, conditioned by the nature of contemporary British capitalism and imperialism.

Accepting that society is inherently hierarchical, Mansbridge defined democracy as a 'state of society in which every individual not only has the opportunity to make the best of his or her own individual gifts, but actually takes advantage of the opportunity' (1944:76). It was the 'Christian idea of the community', manifesting the 'co-operation of self-fulfilling individuals, each doing well in their own calling or type of work (and so achieving in the words of T.H. Green) ...'the promotion in a spirit of justice of the welfare of all classes of the citizens' (1928:10; 1940:220; undated:9). Determined by the type of Christian perspective he adopted, Mansbridge's depoliticised definition of democracy proved very acceptable to the majority of the progressive wing of the dominant class represented by the Oxford Reformers. His appeal to them was reinforced by his fulsome 'adulation of university men and university values' (Jennings 1975:58). Thus, in his 1903 articles, Mansbridge argued that only the 'deep draughts of knowledge' provided by university extension could combat the 'veneer' of elementary education that encouraged the 'unthinking absorbtion of facts (which rendered men) susceptible to flights of mere rhetoric' (1944:1). In similar vein, the Oxford report asserted that 'it would involve a grave loss both to Oxford and to English political life were the close association between the University and the world of affairs to be broken or impaired on the accession of new classes to power' (1909:48). The early success of Mansbridge's WEA therefore owed much to its being seen 'as a

politically and socially "safe" movement' and a
'sound political investment' (Jennings 1973:25,
1975:58).

Mansbridge's attitude towards individualism was
contradictory. Like socialists, he specifically
opposed utilitarian individualism and the idea that
education should be used for material advancement or
as a way of leaving the working-class. Nor did he see
education as a means of personal cultural
development. It is interesting to remember that the
WEA was based on group or federal, and not
individual, membership. However, Mansbridge was
plainly hostile to socialism as an alternative vision
and model of society. He thought that social
improvement would come about by individual, not
social or collective, transformation, because he
believed that the source of social injustice and the
conflict it generates lay in the failure of the
spirit of individuals, not in the failings of the
existing social order. Mansbridge represents the
ideology that acknowledges the existence of social
classes, and indeed criticises inequalities of
opportunities, particularly educational ones, but
denies their inherent or structural antagonism which
is rooted in relations of dominance and
subordination.

Mansbridge articulated the well-meaning but
naive belief shared by Christian socialists and some
others with a social conscience that what was
euphemistically called 'the social question' could
be overcome by Christian faith, goodwill,
reasonableness and academic reason which together
would produce 'right thinking'. He was not, therefore
an individualist in the Manchester-Liberal vein, but
rather an advocate of the New Liberalism, the
educational philosophy of which was succinctly
expressed by the 1919 Final Report (27): 'Adult
Education rests on the twin principles of personal
development and social service'. Mansbridge
specifically argued that tutorial classes were 'not
mainly about the acquisition of knowledge but a
stimulus to perform the voluntary civic work of their
(the students') associations and unions and to spread
the desire for education' (1944:61). It is thus not
wholly true that Mansbridge 'carefully eschewed any
idea of social purpose' (Smith, 1962-3:48). Of
course, it all depends on what is meant by 'social
purpose'.

Radical socialists who were concerned with
education (as they had been throughout the nineteenth
century) defined 'social purpose' quite differently

27

from the way Mansbridge did. They campaigned for 'Independent Working Class Education' under such slogans as 'knowledge for action' and 'education for emancipation'. They argued that existing adult educational provision, including that of the WEA, was tainted by ideological forms of knowledge and educational practices which blunted the spikes of increasing working-class power. When still a radical, Ramsay Macdonald (later Labour Party leader and Prime Minister) said that Oxford would 'inoculate the more intelligent sections of the working-classes ... (it) will assimilate them, not they Oxford' (quoted in Fieldhouse 1977:11). The Central Labour College (set up by the Plebs League after the Ruskin College student strike of 1908) and the National Council of Labour Colleges spent many years locked in ideological combat with the WEA (9). Mansbridge's position was clear. In his 1903 articles, he quoted the historic Taff Vale industrial dispute (which ended in punitive restrictions on trade unionism) as an example of how the lack of education or 'thinking power' can lead workers astray. He unequivocally blamed 'obstructive, poisonous and wrecking forces' for the 'unrest in British life' (1929:31). Mansbridge's attitude to the purpose of education in society well exemplifies the valuable distinction made by Williams between the motive forces of 'social conscience' and 'social consciousness' (1983:14-15).

Phillips and Putnam (1980) contrast Mansbridge's preference for 'educational uplift', as an expression of advanced Christian Liberalism, with 'education for emancipation'. Jennings (1973:30) neatly summarises the same idea by saying that Mansbridge thought that 'education is emancipation'. This did not prevent others such as Tawney, G.D.H. Cole and George Thompson from bringing to the WEA far more radical philosophical and political perspectives than those of its founder (10). Their involvement was evidence of Harrison's observation that socialism was replacing or strongly influencing Christianity as a new evangelical movement for the 'new generation of working men' (1961:229).

However, there were other aspects of 'democracy' which concerned Mansbridge and on which all in the WEA could agree. One was the indignation felt at the 'lamentable ... neglect of education for the people' and the way in which the 'ordinary working man was disinherited' (1920:55). Echoing this, Temple said (undated:13) that the 'whole purpose of the WEA is to claim for working-class people their place in the whole great national

heritage of educational culture'. Mansbridge
lambasted the idea and practice of a restricted and
ineffective 'educational ladder', which he wished to
see replaced by a 'highway' along which anyone can
travel, provided only they had the necessary 'mental
equipment and high character' (1920:31). Temple
(ibid) defended the WEA from the criticism that it
accepted without question the dominant class's
conception of what constitutes the 'national
heritage' by the example of Tawney's work in economic
history which changed its received view.
Nevertheless, Mansbridge and others tended to accept
the conventional definition of the content of liberal
or humane education, concentrating their fire
instead on the flagrant injustice of the organisation
of the educational system.

Another aspect of democracy was the belief that
education 'unites (people) and does not divide'
(quoted in Smith 1956:45). Mansbridge likened what he
called the 'WEA spirit' to a 'new Renaissance',
consisting of a 'common hope united in the common
activity of unlike people' (1924:135). He saw
education as a means of bringing together all people
in fellowship, whatever their social status or
political or religious affiliation. Mansbridge
expressed pride that the WEA's 1905 conference at
Oxford resembled 'a replica in miniature of English
life' (1920:19). However commendable his attitude,
Mansbridge avoided facing the question of how
knowledge is defined and constructed, how it is used
and what its effects are on conserving or changing
the existing social order.

The third and probably most innovative
democratic principle uniting all in the WEA related
to the organisation and practice of workers'
education, and indeed to education as such.
Mansbridge believed that the only way of overcoming
'the distrust of Universities amongst working people
in general' was to avoid the 'education "from above"
that had neutralised the good intentions underlying
the Mechanics Institutes, Working Men's Colleges and
traditional University Extension' (1913:22). He thus
flatly disagreed with Maurice's opposition to
'pupils (having) the least voice in determining what
we shall teach or not teach or how we shall teach'
(quoted in Smith 1956:17). On the contrary,
Mansbridge claimed as a fundamental principle that
the 'education of working people can never develop
unless there is frank and free intercourse on the
basis of equality between teachers and taught'
(1920:5). He exhorted WEA members to 'Discover your

own needs, organise in your own way, study as you
wish to study ... The initiative must lie with the
students. They must say how, why, what or when they
wish to study. It is the business of their colleagues
the scholars and administrators to help them obtain
the satisfaction of their desires' (1920:23).
Mansbridge's model of relations in a tutorial or any
other type of class is one in which the teacher
should be 'in real fact a fellow-student, and the
fellow-students are teachers' (1913:1).

Although he had to resign from the WEA in 1915
because of ill-health and thereafter had very little
to do with its subsequent development, Mansbridge's
influence on the course of adult education was
considerable. Tawney went so far as to refer to it as
the 'Mansbridgean revolution' and stated that its
three 'dominant conceptions' were that the majority
of ordinary people need humane education as much as
the minority, that the intimate and continuous small
tutorial group is its proper vehicle, and that the
organisation of such education should be based on the
equal participation of Labour and Learning (Tawney
1966:89). Real education thus implied both
humaneness, emphasising learning for life, i.e.
wisdom - 'a liberal as against a merely bread-and-
butter education' - and democratic organisation and
pedagogy (Manchester Guardian, quoted in 1920:19).

As already mentioned, not everyone who made a
significant contribution to the WEA's growth and
development shared Mansbridge's ostensibly apolitical interpretation of 'education for emancipation'
(of the workers) or his predilection for the company
of 'bishops and professors'.

However, the contrast between Mansbridge's
cultural purism and others' political realism is not
completely accurate because Mansbridge was concerned
with education for spiritual wisdom, and not 'for its
own sake' (Fieldhouse 1977:58). With the
acceleration of the secularisation of social life
since Mansbridge's time, much of adult liberal
education does seem to have substituted cultural for
spiritual enrichment as its main aim. Although both
emphasise education's effect on the individual
rather than on the collectivity, it should be
recalled that Mansbridge's attitude towards
individualism was contradictory.

It is impossible to calculate the impact of
Mansbridge, directly or indirectly via the WEA, on
many people of all sorts (11). Temple averred that
'he invented me' (quoted in Iremonger 1948:77).
Mansbridge recalled that George Reuben, who once

belonged to the marxist Social Democratic Federation
and later became mayor of Swindon, was 'converted to
the idea of the WEA at its 1907 conference'
(1944:191). Taylor et al (1985:176) have unearthed
evidence of the WEA's influence on some American
adult educationists in the 1920s; for example, Leon
Richardson, External Director of California
University, visited Mansbridge and the WEA in 1921.

To assess the contemporary relevance of
Mansbridge's educational thought and practice, it is
necessary to separate out some of its constituent
elements and to evaluate the way in which society has
changed since his time. As for the latter, despite
much chattering at various times about the 'quiet
revolution', the 'mixed economy', the 'post-
industrial society' and nowadays the seemingly
unending 'technological revolution', the basic
features of the social, economic and political
structures of British society are little different
today from what they were at the beginning of this
century. It is, therefore, still characterised by a
number of forms of avoidable social injustice and
oppression, even though their outward appearances
may differ in some ways from what they were before.
Despite changes in the economic, welfare and
occupational structures, most people are still
'workers' (whether currently employed or not) or
related to them. Therefore, 'education for
emancipation' of workers (of either sex and of
whatever ethnic background), is as necessary today as
it was in 1903 (12).

With the decline of the social influence of
religion, few today would share Mansbridge's
specifically Christian conception of the good
society. Nevertheless, his steadfast defence of
'liberal' education is of enduring value. Mansbridge
was not opposed to vocational education, which is
necessary if people are to do their work properly.
However, he rightly resisted the idea, often
advocated by powerful groups, that it should ever be
confused with or supplant liberal education, which
every person needs and to which all are entitled.
Mansbridge saw clearly that the aim of education is
wisdom, that is, the integration of knowledge,
understanding and action. Its process is that of
rational enquiry, which depends on the availability
of all pertinent information and the evaluation of
all contesting perspectives or theories. Its social
implications are far-reaching: mutual respect and
toleration between all those engaged in it,
acceptance of the uncertainty of its outcome (which

is not to be confused with fence-sitting) and freedom from external constraints serving to censor the process.

Mansbridge's concern with democratic education needs to be revived and redefined. The type of religiosity he espoused prevented Mansbridge from confronting the sharp political issues raised when education and democracy are mentioned in the same breath. For example, it is unrealistic to expect future and present citizens, that is, children and adults, to play their full part in a democratic political system (or one that aspires to be so) unless they experience democratic processes in their everyday lives: in their homes, places of work, voluntary organisations and other places (e.g. hospitals, government offices etc.). Unless its values are practised both within and outside educational institutions, liberal education will either fail or rightly be criticised as a sham. Described as an 'evangelical humanist', Mansbridge recognised and sought to redress the educational injustice suffered by working-class people (Smith 1965:19). Despite its expansion since his death, most formal education, or rather schooling, at all levels continues to be as competitively individual-istic, undemocratic and socially discriminatory in recruitment and in much of its curriculum content as it was before. However imperfect it is, the WEA remains a bastion of an alternative form and vision of education - cooperatively social, democratic in its organisation and pedagogy (or andragogy) and free from the distractions of certification and meritocracy. Together with other educational organisations, the WEA is also the protagonist of education for those who are nowadays euphemistically called the 'disadvantaged' or 'deprived', with the aim of maximising effective social and political participation.

What an anonymous benefactor said of Mansbridge - 'He is the most dangerous man in England. He taught the working people to think for themselves' - should be the goal and proud boast of all education, particularly adult education (quoted in Mansbridge 1944:xi). Until now, when workers and others who are oppressed have thought for themselves, they have often been attacked by those who rightly perceive a threat to their domination, however slight in practice, as subversive. If it is merely a code-phrase for habitual fence-sitting and the avoidance of what are conventionally thought to be radical or 'extreme' social and political attitudes, in the mistaken belief that knowledge and life or action are incompatible, then 'thinking for oneself' is nothing but intellectual self-deception and moral cowardice. In assessing Mansbridge's pioneering role in the development of the 'Great Tradition', it may be helpful to put forward a necessarily simplified schema of the different ways in which the idea of adult liberal education has been interpreted. The conservative view is that it is purely a self-contained process of rational enquiry, which is unrelated to specific social practices and so unconcerned with all the ways by which it is restricted by society or the state. The progressive interpretation, though recognising and ready to counteract social constraints of free enquiry, remains suspicious of the practical social consequences that would be expected to result from its widespread practice. The radical perspective acknowledges that the purpose and values of liberal education cannot be fully realised unless it actively shapes and is supported by congruent social relations, structures and processes. Whereas his interpretation tended to the second type, it is argued that the third is the logical and practical implication of Mansbridge's concept of adult liberal education.

Mansbridge's assertion that 'adult education and the claims of democratic citizenship are inseparable' was, is and always will be valid, provided education is not, as it all too often is, desocialised and thus stripped of its inherent humaneness and political relevance (Smith 1956:58). Freire put it concisely: 'education is not neutral' (1976:147). Raymond Williams said recently that adult education is not just determined by social change or is only about extending opportunities; it is about making 'learning part of the process of social change itself' (1983:9). Cole and Freeman made the same point even more clearly in 1918 when they affirmed that adult education is about the 'creation of a manhood and a womanhood capable of controlling their own destinies in a free and democratic country' (Hughes and Brown 1981:58).

Mansbridge dedicated his life to an 'adventure' in education. Today, those who think honestly and fearlessly about the nature of people, society, the world, knowledge and what their relations are and should be and, who take education, including adult and workers' education as seriously as he did, can continue to develop his work with an equal passion, enjoyment and commitment.

33

Notes
1. Established as a library for adult students in tutorial classes, it became the national Central Library in 1931, and was later incorporated into the British Library, Lending Division. Mansbridge was its chairman until 1931 and thereafter chairman of its Board of Trustees.
2. Gore, Temple and Tawney were also associated in this venture. Yeaxlee (1926:67) records that during 1923-24 there were thirteen classes and three tutors' courses in progress.
3. Mansbridge was its chairman until 1929 and thereafter its president. Jennings (1984:62) notes that, of all Mansbridge's projects, the WAAE showed the greatest gulf between aspiration and achievement. It was dissolved in 1946.
4. This was in association with Lord Haldane. The BIAE was the forerunner of the present National Institute of Adult Continuing Education.
5. Born in 1853, Gore was the first principal of Pusey House, Oxford, founded the Community of the Resurrection, was Canon of Westminster (1894-1902), then Bishop of Worcester, Birmingham and Oxford (until 1919).
6. Kelly's classification includes education for salvation, for vocation, for civilisation, for participation and for recreation. He does not mention education for emancipation.
7. Mansbridge continued to be associated with the movement for many years, when he became a director, then president, of the Co-operative Building Society (forerunner of the Nationwide Building Society), about which he wrote a book in 1934.
8. This was the first time that the universities had ever come together about anything.
9. For the views of the radical participants, see Millar and Craik. See also Corfield and Phillips and Putnam.
10. George Thompson was the first Secretary of the Yorkshire District of the WEA, serving from 1914 to 1945 (including six years in New Zealand).
11. Fieldhouse (1977:29-31) summarises some interesting data on this question.
12. The early WEA as actively involved with women's education. Frances Mansbridge helped to initiate, and was a member of, the national Consultative Committee concerned with the education of working women. There were women's sections in three Branches by 1910. Margaret McMillan, another of Mansbridge's heroes, was also involved with this

34

early radical development. Information given by
Linda Shaw.

Bibliography

Chichester, Bishop of, 1952, In Memoriam: Albert
Mansbridge, Highway 44, pp 145-8
Corfield, A.J., 1969, Epoch in Workers' Education,
London, WEA
Craik, W.W., 1964, The Central Labour College,
London, Lawrence and Wishart
Dictionary of National Biography 1931-40, 1949,
Oxford University Press
Fieldhouse, Roger, 1977, The Workers' Educational
Association: Aims and Achievements 1903-1977,
University of Syracuse
Freire, Paulo, 1972, Cultural Action for Freedom,
Harmondsworth, Penguin Books
Freire, Paulo, 1976, Education: the Practice of
Freedom, London, Writers and Readers
Halevy, Elie, 1961, Imperialism and the Rise of
Labour, New York, Barnes and Noble Inc.
Harrison, J.F.C., 1961, Learning and Living 1760-
1960
Hopkins, Philip G.H., 1985, Workers' Education,
Milton Keynes, Open University Press
Hughes H.D. and Brown G.F., 1981, The W.E.A.
Education Year Book 1918, University of Nottingham
Iremonger, F.A., 1948, William Temple, Oxford
University Press
Jennings, Bernard, 1973, Albert Mansbridge, Leeds
University Press
Jennings, Bernard, 1975, The Oxford Report
Reconsidered, Studies in Adult Education 7:1, pp 53-
65
Jennings, Bernard, 1976a, Albert Mansbridge and
English Adult Education, University of Hull
Jennings, Bernard, 1976b, New Lamps for Old?
University Adult Education in Retrospect and
Prospect, University of Hull
Jennings, Bernard, 1979, 'Knowledge is Power': A
Short History of the WEA 1903-1978, University of
Hull
Jennings, Bernard, 1984, Albert Mansbridge and the
First WAAE, Convergence 17:4, pp 54-64
Kelly, T., 1973, Two Reports: 1919 and 1973, Studies
in Adult Education, 5:2, pp 113-123
Kelly, T., 1983, The Historical Evolution of Adult
Education in Great Britain, in Opportunities for
Adult Education, (ed.) M. Tight, Milton Keynes, Open
University Press

Mansbridge, Albert, 1906, A Survey of working-class Educational Movements in England and Scotland, (from CWS Annual), Publication No. 10, WEA

Mansbridge, Albert, 1913 University Tutorial Classes, London, Longman, Green & Co.

Mansbridge, Albert, 1920, An Adventure in Working-Class Education, London, Longman, Green & Co.

Mansbridge, Albert, 1923, The Older Universities of England, London, Longman, Green & Co.

Mansbridge, Albert, 1924, The Beginning of the W.E.A., Highway 16:3

Mansbridge, Albert, 1928, The Educated Life, London, Ernest Benn Ltd.

Mansbridge, Albert, 1929, The Making of an Educationist, London, Ernest Benn Ltd.

Mansbridge, Albert, 1932, Margaret McMillan: Prophet and Pioneer, London, J.M. Dent & Sons Ltd.

Mansbridge, Albert, 1934, Brick upon Brick, J.M. Dent & Sons Ltd.

Mansbridge, Albert, 1935, Talbot and Gore, London, J.M. Dent & Sons Ltd.

Mansbridge, Albert, 1940, The Trodden Road, London, J.M. Dent & Sons Ltd.

Mansbridge, Albert, 1944, The Kingdom of the Mind: Essays and Addresses 1903-37 of Albert Mansbridge, London, J.M. Dent & Sons Ltd.

Mansbridge, Albert, 1945, W. Hudson Shaw, Highway 37 (October)

Mansbridge, Albert, 1948, Fellow Men; A Gallery of England 1876-1946, London, J.M. Dent & Sons Ltd.

Mansbridge, Albert, no date, Arnold Toynbee, London, C.W. Daniel

Millar, J.P.M., undated, The Labour College Movement, London, NCLC Publishing Society Ltd.

Ministry of Reconstruction, Adult Education Committee, 1919, Final Report, Cmd 321

Oxford and Working-class Education, 1909, Oxford, University Press

Phillips, A. and Putnam, T., 1980, Education for Emancipation: the Movement for Independent Working Class Education 1908-1928, Capital and Class, 10

Shaw, Roy, 1959, Controversies, in Trends in English Adult Education (ed.) Raybould, S.G., London, Heinemann

Smith, H.P. 1956, Labour and Learning: Albert Mansbridge, Oxford and the W.E.A., Oxford, Basil Blackwell

Smith, H.P., 1962-3, Adult Education in History: A Review, Rewley House Papers, 4:1

Stocks, Mary, 1953, The W.E.A.: the First Fifty Years, London, Unwin

36

Tawney, R.H., 1952, Mansbridge, <u>Highway</u> 44, pp 42-5
Tawney, R.H., 1966, <u>The Radical Tradition</u>, Harmondsworth, Penguin Books
Taylor, R., Rockhill, K. and Fieldhouse, R., 1985, <u>University Adult Education in England and the USA</u>, London, Croom Helm
Temple, W., 1924, the W.E.A.: A Retrospect, <u>Highway</u> 16:3
Temple, W,. undated, <u>The Place of the W.E.A. in English Education</u>, W.E.A. N.W. District
Thomas, J.E., 1982, <u>Radical Adult Education: Theory and Practice</u>, University of Nottingham
West, L.R., 1972, The Tawney Legend Re-examined, <u>Studies in Adult Education</u> 4:2, pp 105-119
Williams, Raymond, 1983, Adult Education and Social Change, <u>Adult Education and Social Change: Lectures and Reminiscences in Honour of Tony McLean</u>, Rochester, Workers' Educational Association, South Eastern District
Yeaxlee, B.A., 1926, <u>Spiritual Values in Adult Education</u>, Oxford, Oxford University Press

Chapter Three

BASIL YEAXLEE AND THE ORIGINS OF LIFELONG EDUCATION

Angela Cross-Durrant

Introduction

Lifelong education is generally thought to have
emerged as a result of the United Nations'
International Education Year (1970), during which
the concept was offered for discussion. The United
Nations Educational, Scientific and Cultural
Organization (UNESCO) adopted the notion in 1972 and
decided to clarify the concept, and to pose it as a
potential alternative to existing educational
principles, envisaged as being better able to prepare
people to maintain and improve the quality of life
amidst change and uncertainty. Shortly thereafter, a
comprehensive study was undertaken to form a well-
constructed, logically sound and authoritative base
of descriptive guidelines for the introduction of a
system of lifelong education. The study relied upon
the synthesis of philosophical, historical,
sociological, psychological, anthropological, ecolo-
gical and economic considerations, and resulted in a
comprehensive collection of studies edited by Dave
(1976). The ideas of (amongst others) Lengrand (1975)
and of the Faure Report (1972) set the pattern of
thought for this 'European' concept.

The idea of lifelong education is generally
regarded, therefore, as being attendant upon modern
technological and societal changes, and as such, as
being 'new'.

However, although usually associated with
UNESCO, the concept first found expression half a
century earlier in England, through the vision and
intellectual effort of Basil A Yeaxlee (1929). His
was the original English twentieth century
publication which sought to establish a way of seeing
education in toto; to

attain ... unity of spirit and purpose amidst

differentiation of functions, (Yeaxlee, 1929: 124)

recognize the educational value of the unorthodox, and perhaps unsuspected, means of education to which thousands ... respond, (ibid: 121)

express that activities and organizations "recreational or ... connected with livelihood ... must play their part." (ibid:122)

point out that "To ask whether a man should be a student for the sake of the knowledge he acquires or for the sake of the qualities he develops in the course of particular studies is to raise a false dilemma. Each has its own importance but neither is separable from the other." (ibid:146)

and to assert that "While ... the case for lifelong education rests ultimately upon the nature and needs of human personality in such a way that no individual can rightly be regarded as outside its scope, the social reasons (i.e. democracy and responsibility) for fostering it are as powerful as the personal." (ibid:311)

Yeaxlee's publication represents the first formal attempt this century to combine the whole of the educational enterprise under a set of guiding principles with each phase or agency (formal, informal and non-formal) enjoying equal esteem. His idea of lifelong education rested upon integrating learning and living, both horizontally across work, leisure and community 'life spaces'; and vertically from virtually the cradle to the grave. Its area of concern was different from either university tutorial, mainly liberal educational classes, appended to the end of secondary, further or higher education; and from compensatory education for adults. The kind of integration he advocated demanded a degree of co-operation, co-ordination and sharing of philosophy and resources, which the emergent educational provision (and current provision) was not wont to do.

The backcloth of envisaged social reforms after the First World War and of major changes in secondary education provided the scene for the first major, fully articulated argument for lifelong education in England. Although the 1919 Report had expressed

dissatisfaction with the concept of technical and
vocational training, and had seen such activity as
outside of the province of education for adults, one
of the contributors to the Report saw the
possibilities for new technical and vocational
preparation as part of a reinterpretation of
education and its relationship to industrial,
social, community, professional, private and family
life - to the whole of life itself. This was Basil A
Yeaxlee, who remained optimistic about the
possibilities which he perceived emerging from the
great post-war educational debate, and the
prevailing 'mood' of social reconstruction after the
war. He was as interested in the education of the
young as he was in that of the adolescent and the
adult.

The Context
Basil A Yeaxlee, CBE, MA, B Litt (Oxon), BA, PhD
(London), was born in 1883 and died in 1967. He was
deeply involved in adult education and religious
education, as is manifest by the following posts
which, amongst others, he held during his working
lifetime: 1915-18 Editorial Secretary of the
National Council of Young Men's Christian
Associations; 1917-19 Member of the Ministry of
Reconstruction Adult Education Committee; 1920-28
Secretary, Educational Settlements Association;
1930-35 Principal, Westhill Training College, Selly
Oak; 1933-57 Editor of "Religion in Education"; 1935-
49 University Reader in Educational Psychology, and
Lecturer and Tutor in the Department of Education,
Oxford; 1940-48 Secretary, Central Advisory Council
for Adult Education in HM Forces; 1949-51 Secretary,
Education Committee, British Council of Churches.
    It is clear from some of his published work,
viz, "An Educated Nation" (1920), "Spiritual Values
in Adult Education" Vols I and II (1925), "Towards a
Full Grown Man" (1926), and "Religion and the Growing
Mind" (1939), that Christianity was the spring from
which he drank, the source of his interpretation of
life, and the vehicle he used to convey his views
about the meaning and purpose of education.
    But it is his book entitled "Lifelong
Education", published in 1929, which is one of the
earliest expressions of a vision of regarding all of
life's resources and experiences (personal, social
and work) as playing a related and meaningful part in
an individual's education, and of education as being
seen as truly life long. Yeaxlee viewed education at

school as merely the start of the process, and projected subsequent education for adults beyond an exclusively compensatory, occupationally expedient, abstractly liberal or politically led activity. He did not subscribe to the notion that tutorial classes and university education were the only means of education for adults.

> Neither 'the university of the people' nor 'nightschool' is a sufficient description of what adult education really is. Both ideas may be included, but many other names will be needed as well. One man may be seeking the philosophic key to the meaning of existence: another may be concerned with political or economic questions: another may be discovering some hitherto unsuspected aptitude for using his hands artistically and skilfully. Each is attaining a new understanding of himself and enriching the values of his world. (Yeaxlee, 1929:45)

> adult education must be more comprehensive than university education. It must teach many things which a university would not include ... and by methods which (it) would never dream of adopting ... and yet ... must maintain the ideals ... which we so naturally associate with university traditions. (ibid:152)

Much of education for adults, he argued, should be practical in terms of its relationship to students' experiences and interests, whilst at the same time it ought to be concerned with 'intellectual authority', so that it would help adults to continue to reflect and to think rationally.

> No man is free so long as he remains ... in bondage to intellectual authority, however venerable, or to his own crassness and ignorance, however absorbed he may be in the practical service of his kind. (ibid:50)

He also exhorted his readers to consider new, informal and non-formal methods of learning and teaching, to

> look about them for new and promising forms of educational life and activity among men and women, and perhaps themselves to take some share in adding to the number. (ibid:100)

41

In this context, he acknowledged and applauded the educational work carried out over the wireless by the British Broadcasting Corporation. He also looked to "all kinds of community organization" to play their parts in the educational enterprise, "Recreational or controversial, connected with livelihood or wedded to leisure". (ibid:122) He also wished to unite the efforts of the various 'realms' of education (elementary, secondary, technical, university, adult) in order to embark upon the joint enterprise of education for, through, and throughout life.

By the time Yeaxlee had published most of his books, intensification of class consciousness and espousal of a joint cause provided the main impulse for educational reform. Yeaxlee, however, preferred to look to the evolutionary development of each citizen, rather than to a mass, politically led, strategy. His religious beliefs convinced him that respect and responsibility emanated outwards from the individual's spirit. On the other hand, however, disillusionment in the (Anglican) Church had, however, resulted from the inescapable recognition of the implications of Christian fighting Christian during the First War. Some Christian educators recognised and acknowledged the supremacy of the 'humanistic socialism' pervading the day, e.g. R H Tawney.

> We have to revise the work not of four years but of a century and a half. The quarrel is not merely with the catastrophic changes of 1914-1919, but with the economic order of the age which began with the spinning-jenny and ended with the great war ... Social Reconstruction either means Social Revolution, or it means nothing. (Tawney in Hinden, 1964:103)

These men sought to legitimise large-scale economic and social transformation (which would include education) for economic and social liberty and responsibility.

Yeaxlee, on the other hand, argued for transformation of education to prepare everyone for, and provide everyone with, continued, lifelong education, so that having thereby given man his intellectual and, consequently, his spiritual freedom, man would find his way back to the Christian fold, better acquainted with himself, his fellows, the world and the metaphysical. He saw education as clarifying the image of man for man; that image not

being simply a passive victim of his condition, but
rather a vital, responsive, interactive agent
capable of generating the right attitudes and future
conditions for the flourishing of self-fulfilment
and perpetual growth of harmony and of love, until
all were united in a 'wholeness' of humanity and
Christianity. By concentrating on the full
development of individuals whilst celebrating
collective life, he argued, could man hope to seek
freedom and claim responsibility. "The aim, then, is
a philosophy and a way of living, an insight and a
joyous purpose, with some power of achieving it."
(Yeaxlee, 1929:165) He would have everyone develop

> his own individuality to the utmost, no longer
> as a separated and conflicting being but as a
> part and contribution to one continuing whole.
> (H G Wells in Yeaxlee, 1929:164)

When referring to Robert Peers' similar views,
Yeaxlee wrote,

> There all the distinctive notes of lifelong
> education are struck - knowledge experience,
> wisdom, harmony and the giving of self in
> service. All of them are rooted in the practical
> affairs of ordinary men and women. Each of them
> reaches out into the infinite. They are
> meaningless apart from the growth and the
> activities of the individual personality. They
> are impossible unless that personality is in
> perpetual living relationship to the whole - the
> whole of truth and the whole of life, immediate
> reality and ultimate. (ibid:165)

It is here that Yeaxlee's concern with the 'ultimate'
and 'the whole', of which he would have claimed we
are all a part, comes to the fore. Whilst some
educators (e.g. Tawney and Dewey) with strong social
consequences and commitment looked to social,
politico-economic and educational reform or
revolution for the betterment of the human condition,
Yeaxlee sought to use educational reform to lead
people back to Christian values, thereby putting
themselves at the (social) service of their fellows.
In his book "Lifelong Education", Yeaxlee
looked to the education of adults to help the whole
nation to 'grow up', to seek the twin ideals of
freedom and responsibility.
"We begin to seek quality in living - more life
and fuller." (Yeaxlee, 1929:23) Based on a notion of

"knowledge as the mother of understanding and thus of creative enjoyment" (ibid:24), he saw the adult education movement as a means of achieving a harmonized world and a more democratic lifestyle. He would have all adults aware of and responsive to

> industrial disputes and social crises, rather than subject to crass ignorance and culpable narrowness of outlook ... They are the fruitful irritant sources of malignant disease in the body politic. The less we are conscious of them the more, like repressions and complexes in the individual personality, they work desperate mischief. (ibid:22)

He pointed to improved, and prolonged, education for children and young adults as an optimistic and positive step in achieving the wherewithal to generate such understanding and behaviour, and shared the view that "a great increase in the facilities for higher education given as a right of citizenship, independently of social status or financial circumstances" (ibid:26) should form part of the new educational structure. He then addressed himself to a question which, it seems, even today has considerable currency - a view which has long influenced the paucity of resources trickled into adult educational provision.

> Shall we not then grow out of the need for adult education - and perhaps sooner than we anticipate? Ought we not to avoid exaggerating the importance of it, and to recognise that it is a transitory social phenomenon, a medicine for a social weakness which we are rapidly overcoming rather than a part of 'human nature's daily food'? (ibid:26)

This was followed shortly afterwards by what could be viewed as the linchpin of the concept of lifelong education in its modern guise also, as outlined, for example, by Dave et al (1976).

> We discover more, and not less need of adult education as we make progress. It will not have a fair chance until better preparation is made for it during the years of adolescence. On the other hand, we are unlikely to achieve a thoroughly sound and complete system of primary and secondary education until the adult members of the community, by continuing their own

education, realize how mischievous a thing it is
to abbreviate or mishandle the school-education
of boys and girls. But adult education, rightly
interpreted, is as inseparable from normal
living as food and physical exercise. (Yeaxlee,
1929:28)

He argued that in as much as people are all involved
in political and social strife, changes and re-
interpretations,

it becomes obvious that we all stand in need of
much wider and fuller lifelong education.
(ibid:34)

The enjoyment of expansion, of growth and
exercise (he claimed), was to be found in the
love of sport, exciting music, dancing, and so
on. Education does not imply any extraction of
the sparkle and the sting from these expressions
of vitality. It sends them on fresh ... voyages
of discovery, with more reliable compasses and
with better charts - which they are to take
their share in completing. ... When, therefore,
we interpret adult education in terms of life
and people, and not merely in those of books and
subjects of formal study, we shall see fresh
opportunities and stimulating challenges
everywhere ... The distinction between
'highbrow' and 'lowbrow' ... will no longer
possess meaning. (ibid:39)

As he saw it, because everyone had the capacity to
continue to grow intellectually, (and he cited
Spearman's and Thorndike's work to support his claim)
long after leaving, and outside, formal education, he
was at pains to establish the view that adult
education ought not to be regarded as compensating
for earlier deficiencies, or as a rival to technical
education, or as the poor sister of higher education.
Nor did he accept that people received all the
education they were ever likely to need or want by
the time they left formal education. (Incidentally,
he was also one of M Knowles' (1978) precursors in
drawing attention to motivating factors in adult
learners. "It is largely in order that he may answer
the questions or satisfy the hungers stimulated by
the experience of daily life that he (the adult
learner) turns to the resources of class, lecture-
room, or library." (Yeaxlee, 1929:44))
He also faced the long held assumptions,

45

prejudices and differential esteem regarding
vocational and liberal education.

> Clearly, it is not a matter of superiority or
> inferiority ... The two are simply different –
> but also complementary ... The consideration of
> motive and aim is relevant and helpful only when
> we agree that in both fields the governing
> impulse may and should be a worthy one, and that
> in the complete personality, fulfilling a
> proper function in society, the two will blend
> harmoniously. (ibid:129)

The solution to this enduring dualism, he argued, was
for the agencies of education to "attain this unity
of spirit and purpose (i.e. the full bloom of
personality and growth) amidst differentiation of
functions." (ibid:14) He urged society to keep in
mind that in a democratic community, everyone has a
distinctive contribution to its well-being and
progress; and that difference is not to be equated
with inferiority. But he did support the claim that
humane studies formed the foundation for all
education.

> Humanistic studies ... must surely include all
> that for them lends living a deeper significance
> and a more abiding joy, whichever of the senses
> or of the areas in the grey matter of the brain
> may happen to be the gateways whereby it finds
> entry. (ibid:153)

'Humanistic studies', he claimed, can have no
finality.

> If we ask ... 'When is his (a person's)
> education complete?' the only true answer is
> 'Never while he lives.' ... There all the
> distinctive notes of lifelong education are
> struck ... (ibid:164)

Yeaxlee made the claim that self-realization (the
achievement of continually developing personality as
a result of on-going learning) and social idealism
had always been presented as conflicting aims of
adult education. This he argued, was a fallacy,
because it was possible to combine both. A lifetime
of education, he maintained, would provide mastery of
ascertaining relevant fact, the ability and courage
to distance and analyse "one's own views and
prejudices, or those of one's party, as well as those

of differing or opposed groups." (ibid:50) lest any
group cared overmuch for the immediate success of its
cause, at the expense of care for its members. "At
once more critical and more tolerant our corporate
life would become more imaginative and creative,
because more scientific in its quality." (ibid:148)
The best preparation for this practice, he argued,
was an early and then on-going liberalising education
(alongside any vocational needs) conducted in a
democratic spirit, and he embraced recreational
learning activities for adults as well as for
children, such as painting and other hobbies, carried
out at Working Men's Institutes, for example, as a
"not less important or fruitful" nor "less truly a
part of the adult education movement." (ibid:114/5)

> To stereotype adult education is to arrest, if
> not to kill it. But the real issue is whether we
> shall be sufficiently alert to recognize the
> educational value of the unorthodox, and
> perhaps unsuspected, means of education to
> which men and women respond in thousands –
> books, plays, music, the cinema, wireless, the
> Press, travel, political and religious
> activities, and a dozen others. If we recognize
> their potentialities in self-education by such
> means, are we going to help them to strive for
> high standards and encourage them to maintain a
> level of excellence which does not depend upon
> being academic and conventional.
> Moreover, no aspect of community life and
> human growth must be overlooked or excluded.
> Recreational or controversial, connected with
> livelihood or wedded to leisure, all the forms
> of community organization must play their part.
> (ibid:121/2)

For the construction of a bridge between technical
and liberal education, he suggested that "sociology,
broadly interpreted, is the proper bridge"
(ibid:130) since it could so readily be made part of
both technical and liberal education. To cement the
connection, he suggested that not only fundamental
connections between the two be made via "technique
and leadership" (ibid) in teaching and learning, but
also through physical contiguity (thus providing an
early suggestion of comprehensive education). It is
interesting to compare this notion with that of
Tawney who, with the backing of the Labour Party,
advised different types of secondary education in
quite different schools, though, of course, enjoying

parity of esteem. It is highly debatable which of the two approaches was the more idealistic in its assumptions. Yeaxlee made the point that what was needed was some common ground or meeting place (for adults particularly)

> where every kind of liberal study and educative activity may be pursued, and where all sorts and conditions of men may interchange knowledge and opinions, experience and ideals. ... the struggle for freedom and self-government, for a social and international order which will ensure creative and joyous peace, must be carried to a victorious issue in the minds and spirits of men before it can be happily resolved in their political and social organization. More than this, there must be achieved a keenness of insight ... as only a constructive clash of minds and temperaments in the frankest friendship can give. (ibid:116/7) and constraining them to judge and choose between the ultimate values by which their lives shall be ordered. (ibid:125)

His vision clearly spanned a much wider horizontal canvas than did that of some other advocates of education for adults; for example, those who leaned towards university 'content and style'.

These few extracts serve to illustrate that so far as Yeaxlee was concerned, education was a means of developing personality, of establishing a unity of purpose - a 'wholeness'; each person at one with himself, his society, the universe and ultimately with God. He ended his book on lifelong education with a quotation from Middleton Murray, which included the following:

> The soul is simply the condition of the complete man. And to this completeness in the man, which is his soul, there corresponds a completeness and harmony of the world of his experience; it also, without abstraction or denial of any of its elements, suffers a like transformation and becomes organic, harmonious - it becomes God. (ibid:166)

Yeaxlee's thesis was based upon the premise that the fully actualised individual, immersed in a lifetime of learning, was bound to be self-propelled towards Christian values, and it was the resultant quickening of human sympathies that would lead to harmonious, egalitarian social and Christian life. He had not, it seems, fully appreciated the extent of both social and religious dis-spiritedness.

It is as well to remember, however, that the origins of the WEA were equally 'spiritual', rooted in recognisably Christian socialism. Although Albert Mansbridge allied himself particularly to the immediate condition of the working class;

> The appeal of the hour to trade unionists and co-operators is that they make political strokes, promote Bills, register protests, and send deputations to responsible ministers. The true appeal is that they lift themselves up through higher knowledge to higher works and higher pleasures, which, if responded to, will inevitably bring about right and sound action upon municipal, national, and imperial affairs; action brought about without conscious effort - the only effectual action. (Mansbridge, 1964:2)

> the ground of his hope was spiritual, not political or economic. (Harrison, 1961:263)

Mansbridge himself had written

> It was quite clear in my mind at that time, (when the ideas of the WEA occurred to him) that education was a reaching out of the soul towards the divine. (Mansbridge in Harrison, 1961:262)

His meeting with the Canon of Westminster, Charles Gore, was significant in the formulation of his ideas of education for working men and women, and as Harrison has noted, it is an interesting feature of the conception of these ideas that Mansbridge was, to a very large extent, self-educated, a Christian, and that the likemindedness of Anglican bishops and Oxford dons, provided the foundation for the WEA. Also, Mansbridge did succeed in bringing together under his educational banner, personalities from the religious, political and educational fields. There may yet be some important lessons to be learned from such an (originally) holistic effort, especially now in these times when there is much professing of supposed harmony, while the actual practice is polarisation. Mansbridge had intended class reconciliation. Gradually, however, the ideology of the workers' educational movement determined that education was to be used explicitly to aid the struggle for a classless society. Yeaxlee's concept

49

of lifelong education supported the potential held in knowledge and education for personal fulfilment and with all subjects considered as equal in value. The workers' movements, on the other hand, decreed that some subjects were of more use than others in the bid for social and industrial emancipation. Thus, the social sciences were placed in highest position and consequently all subjects were not given equal value. Those which were deemed relevant to the class struggle emerged as most important, and a strongly utilitarian or political ethos hung around the education of all those participating. The Labour movement was growing, and since the WEA had become more closely and explicitly allied to Labour's plans, touching as they did upon everyone's day-to-day physical and material conditions, it is not difficult to understand why such a movement should overshadow, if not stifle, notions such as those of Yeaxlee.

Religious ideals had, of course, also given rise to Adult Schools in earlier years. These Schools, because of their intellectual distance and, therefore, their less intellectual and literary approach, from the universities, and indeed from "leftwing political overtones" (Harrison, 1961:301) once again began to appeal to many ordinary working people. They placed great emphasis on community activity and the spirit of fellowship. By 1930, the Settlement ethos found its way to the Adult Schools, which eventually became local 'Centres', catering now for somewhat higher academic achievement but coupled with semi-educational and semi-recreational activities. The presiding ethos changed from the religious to the secular (partly due no doubt to the influence of the Board of Education's inspections which were necessary for financial support) but nonetheless still encouraging a corporate life ideology. In this instance, what began as a religious enterprise, gradually became humanistic in design and practice. (see Harrison, 1961, Chap VIII)

Nonetheless, the argument for a liberalizing, university-style education found impressive support. For example, writing in an article in "Political Quarterly" in 1914 Tawney pointed to the inescapable fact that most people lived by working, and for different kinds of work specialised kinds of preparation were necessary. He turned roundly upon the notion that 'humane education' was suitable preparation only for some who entered a restricted group of professions (e.g. doctors, lawyers, business managers, "but that it is a matter with which the manual working classes have nothing to do."

(Tawney in Hinden, 1964:71). The following extract is self-explanatory.

Such a misinterpretation of the meaning of educational specialisation is felt to be intellectually an imposture. If persons whose work is different require, as they do, different kinds of professional instruction, that is no reason why one should be excluded from the common heritage of civilization of which the other is made free by a university education, and from which, ceteris paribus, both, irrespective of their occupations are equally capable, as human beings, of deriving spiritual sustenance. Those who have seen the inside both of lawyers' chambers and of coal mines will not suppose that of the inhabitants of these places of gloom the former are more constantly inspired by the humanities than are the latter, or that conveyancing ... is in itself a more liberal art than hewing.

It is certainly not the case that the only avenue to humane education of the kind ought to be that which consists of a career of continuous school attendance from 5 to 18 ... To suppose that the goal of educational effort is merely to convert into doctors, barristers, and professors a certain number of persons who would otherwise have been manual workers is scarcely less unintelligent than ... to regard the existence of freed-men as making tolerable the institution of slavery. ... Universal provision is wanted because society is one, ... because no class is good enough to do its thinking for another. ... It is not enough that a few working class boys and girls should be admitted to universities, and that many more will be admitted in the future. We want as much university education as we can get for the workers who remain workers all through their lives. The idea of social solidarity which is the contribution of the working classes to the social conscience of our age has its educational as well as its economic applications ... Perhaps our educationalists have not hitherto allowed sufficiently for the surprising fact that there is no inconsiderable number of men and women whose incentive to education is not material success but spiritual energy, and who seek it, not in order that they may become something else, but because they are what they

51

are. (ibid:71-3)

These magnificently articulated sentiments also serve to illustrate that there was considerable agreement with Yeaxlee's notions of spiritual gain from education in adult years. They were both concerned with the quest for self-fulfilment. Tawney, however, preferred the tellurian idiom. He had looked to the specifically human condition first, and clearly to 'university type' education, rather than to Yeaxlee's expansive, 'pluralistic' notions of educational activities.

Yeaxlee's proposal was to induct children into metaphysical thinking (i.e. to direct them away from just the 'here and now', and the obvious and physical), and to make explicit the metaphysical or spiritual enquiry in adult education. He claimed that what was wrong with the world was that it had 'lost sight of spiritual values' (Yeaxlee, 1925:8); that "we have not found, or even set ourselves to find, that philosophy which sees everything as part of one harmonious whole', using education to help young people and adults alike to develop personalities "rightly and consciously related to society and the universe" (ibid:7). This philosophy, or metaphysical quest, he argued, was a natural goal of every person - "In the depths of every mind there is a philosophy" (G Gentile, in Yeaxlee, 1925:9).

According to Yeaxlee, then, philosophy or seeking answers to metaphysical questions about the purpose, meaning and value of life, was not beyond the "shop and market place", nor "beyond the ken of the common people". (Yeaxlee, 1925:8-9) In psychological terms he spoke of this capacity as an integral part of personality.

> The problem of knowledge, the problem of thought, the problem of unified moral action, are all problems that spring out of the greater problem of the nature of personality. How do we remain ourselves and yet go out of ourselves? How can we retain our identity and yet enter into innumerable relationships with others? To this Bergson offers an answer: 'Obviously there is a vital impulse ... something which ever seeks to transcend itself, to extract more from itself than there is - in a word to create. Now a force which draws from itself more than it contains, which gives more than it has, is precisely what is called a spiritual force.' (Yeaxlee, 1925:21)

It is this immanent force which Yeaxlee sought
to uncover and develop throughout life (in the way
that Dewey (1964: Chap 4) explored 'growth'; in order
to have it propel mankind toward values which would
interpret and ennoble all of life, and place each
individual, society and nation in a universal
setting, thus enabling understanding of what makes
life worth living.

Why should we make any leap (in any one
particular direction) at all, why not confine
ourselves to the little bit of reality we have
seen? The answer is that we are not only
spectators of reality, we are also makers of
reality. When we act, we create a new bit of
reality ... The movement of time compels us,
whether we want to or not, to act. But for
action we need to form some hypothesis as to the
universe in which we act, as to what lies beyond
the range of previous experience. (Mackenzie in
Yeaxlee, 1925:35)

Yeaxlee argued that education could not escape
the universal, the metaphysical dimension to the
quality and meaning of life: questions, he argued,
such as: What is personality? How is each person
related to other persons and to the universe? What is
the meaning and purpose of human life? Where can we
find a scale of values that is ultimate and
universal? (He did not question that there was such a
universal and ultimate 'scale'.) Education, he
claimed, "being inevitably concerned with them,
should both implicitly and explicitly direct enquiry
and thought towards them". (Yeaxlee, 1925:54) On this
point, he further argued that adult education could
be appropriately envisaged as a kind of spiritual
activity because earlier schooling had failed to
remove most people from the 'here and now'. Adults
were capable of re-evaluating their lives.
"Education as a weapon, or as an elevated form of
recreation, appeals readily to many a man who has
never conceived it as integral to life itself. The
revelation of spiritual values and the adjustment of
personal and social life to them" had not been seen
as the "supreme gains" of education. (ibid:57)
However, as adults, bringing with them wider
experience of the rigours and practical wisdom of,
say, adult social and working life, such enquiry
acquired relevance and perhaps urgency.

For Yeaxlee, citizenship was not merely an
expression of Christian life, it was the Christian

53

life. By comparison, "Tawney never sought to blend socialism and Christianity together into a civic religion. ... A just social order, Tawney implied, will be a ... better garden for the flowering of Christian life. But a just social order is not itself the Kingdom of God." (Terrill, 1973:178) "In Tawney's terminology the 'vacant throne' of religious authority was occupied by totalitarian power theories and the secular messiahs who incarnated them." (ibid:140)

Tawney was more interested in "right relationships" than in control and saw himself as socialist rather than proletarian. (ibid:193)

Both men proclaimed an innate spirituality of humankind, both began with the individual; "the individual is an end in himself" (Tawney, in Terrill, 1973:215). Tawney could not agree that socialism was predicated on saintly conduct, though he fully assented to the importance of 'spiritual edification'.

Opportunities for spiritual edification are more important than mere material environment. If only the material environment were not itself among the forces determining men's capacity to be edified (Tawney, ibid:164)

There are those today who, to an extent, would echo Yeaxlee's sentiment with regard to 'religious studies' forming an important part of individual cognitive development. See, for example, Jarvis' exposition of man's questions of meaning changing as he advances from childhood to youth to adulthood, and the way that changed circumstances or 'biography' can produce a situation "in which the individual recommences his quest for meaning." (Jarvis, 1983a:22)

Since man's religious quest begins with the individual, then the aims of an adult education course (in religious studies) should relate to the facilitation of the growth of the ... participants and to assist them in discovering or re-discovering beliefs and ideas that they regard as relevant to their questions of meaning. In no way should the educator seek to inculcate ideas ... Finally, this approach recognizes no conflict between the process of exploring knowledge discovered in different disciplines and exploring beliefs articulated by various religions ... Hence the more we

> explore the meaning of life the more we may grow
> and develop - and that, surely, is an aim of
> adult education. (ibid:22-3)

Yeaxlee went further and said that the

> relationship between adult education and
> religion is not only close, but organic ...
> Either the relationship follows directly from
> the nature of personality, the meaning of
> spiritual values, and the necessities intrinsic
> to the educational process, or it is indeed
> negligible. (Yeaxlee, 1925:60)

> On the other hand, it is equally indisputable
> that a spiritual attitude towards life and the
> universe does not necessarily imply possession
> of definite religious faith ... (ibid:62)

He did claim, however, that Christianity may be used
as a vehicle for formalising the relationship between
education and religion, because, he argued, it was
less open to superstition and misunderstanding than,
say, Stoicism or Buddhism.

Thus Yeaxlee claimed that by reflecting
purposively upon man's own nature, the purpose of
life "and the nature of the power that controls the
universe" (1926:27) each individual would become
"full-grown", by having "felt desperately the
necessity and gained some glimpse of the possibility
of such a view of life - nay, until he has begun to
test it, and found that he can live by it. His
philosophy must become his religion." (ibid:28) This
could be achieved, he argued, by referring to gestalt
psychology. Perceiving outward objects, action, etc,
in patterns "each part of which owes its significance
to its relationship to the other parts, while the
whole is more than the sum of the parts" (Yeaxlee,
1952:x) was the start. "Furthermore, we are
constantly aware of incomplete patterns and we find
ourselves impelled to try to complete them ... by
insight." (ibid) This is how a person might perceive
the 'wholeness' or the 'universal'. This process, he
argued, should begin in childhood, with education
aimed at developing to the full the sentient and
sentimental (in the truly psychological sense)
personality or disposition of every child, and was
best achieved by including Christian religious study
in the school curriculum to provide the best model
for understanding and for behaviour.

This, then, was the religious inspiration of

Basil Yeaxlee. In a world far more secularised now than at the time of his earlier writing, his inspiration might appear somewhat confined. On the other hand, there are those who would commend a 'philosophical' stance (as opposed to a religious one) in education, on the grounds that "Philosophy ought to transform those who pursue it. People ought to be better, by being philosophical". (Sprague, 1978:5) The point might be said to be made, admittedly grandiloquently, by Sir Thomas Browne: "The world was made to be inhabited by beasts, but studied and contemplated by man." Contemporary philosophers might enlarge upon this by explaining the world, philosophically, at any rate, as all that

> anyone might perceive. The effect ... is to bring out that we can expect to get in touch with the sum of all that is, by perceiving what we can of it, and understanding that there is still more to it than we can perceive at any one time. These considerations will lead one to say that we do not see the world, but only bits of it; so the world is not a perceptible thing, but a notion we have that there is a system that contains all we have seen, and can see, and more. (Sprague, 1978:84)

This enquiry and perception has then to be made meaningful.

> Generally, things become meaningful to us as we attach values. Family, community, church, nation are meaningful to us because they represent certain values. Would that be equally true of mankind? Is not mankind meaningless to most of us because we do not attach any particular value to it? This may be a matter of indifference rather than intent. Some may also question whether the survival of mankind is worth the effort involved. But suppose we had determined that civilization must not perish, that we want to make a better world for our children if not for ourselves, that through education we must try to create a better understanding of our world. Would mankind not then become meaningful? (Hirschfield in Ulich, 1964:viii)

> Unfortunately, the irrational behaviour of man is caused not only by his psychological limitations; it has its cause also in our

intellect itself. For purposes of clarity, the
intellect has to isolate the object of its
attention from the whole within which it stands.
Even when we try to extend the span of our
interest as far as possible, the whole is beyond
our grasp; it exists only in our vision, or
intuition. Yet without a picture of the whole we
cannot even comprehend the single ... behind
every person is also his society, his nation,
and its history, mankind, and finally the
universe. It is good to remind ourselves from
time to time of all this infinity in order to
acquire this healthy relativism, which should
prevent us from idolizing ourselves and our
nation, our creeds, our truths, and our little
knowledge. (Ulich, 1964:22-23)

Though secularised sentiments, there is much in these
views which is in sympathy with Yeaxlee's ends.

Whereas Kekes (1980) looks to philosophers to
interpret, criticise, defend or develop 'world
views', Yeaxlee would have argued that, with
appropriate education, everyone could contribute to
that process. Others might well point to the fact,
however, that "In the face of violence and
destruction that have come upon us this century, a
philosophy based on the fundamental goodness of man
seems altogether naive." (Kitwood, 1970:86) It is
salutary to reflect that the quest for meaning and
purpose has endured throughout time, in all segments
of the globe. Sometimes it has been conveyed or
interpreted through myths, through religions or
through philosophy. The questions remain; they
remain unanswered yet seemingly pertinent to each
generation. (Perhaps the reason we are now,
particularly, failing to answer questions about our
humanity is because, tied as we are to 'the
scientific method' and to 'objectivity', we cannot
cope with questions which concern us most, and in
which we are inextricably and deeply involved.
However, "We must ... try to understand what is human
for the very simple reason that we have a human life
to live." (Kitwood, 1970:8)

Religion as an educative vehicle gradually lost
its supremacy as secularization increased and the
State gained more control over educational
provision. Perhaps this is why a writer so committed
to religious inspiration and design was lost to a
society increasingly looking to man and 'humanness'
as opposed to 'superman' and the religiously
metaphysical. Nonetheless, a metaphysical perspect-

57

ive on human life still has currency - albeit largely
but not exclusively in the philosophical realm. Many
people would, perhaps, prefer to use the term
'philosophical' rather than 'religious', but Jarvis
(1983b) makes the point that religion is one element
in man's response to the process of questioning, that
the questioning endures, and has endured throughout
time. In his sociologically slanted discussion on
religiosity, he makes a case for regarding any
process of the questioning for meaning as
'religious':

> Religion is, therefore, regarded as an element
> in man's response to this fundamental process of
> questioning ... the provision of answers to
> questions of meaning suggests, at the very
> least, that the person has pondered upon the
> problem of human existence and may thus be
> described as being religious. (Jarvis,
> 1983b:55)

Human beings have always sought universal meaning
beyond merely detailed, documented knowledge. The
language or medium of religion, once popular and
arguably misused, employed to convey the collective
and personal search may seem inappropriate now, but
the process - as argued for example by Jarvis - when
analysed, can offer great insight into personal
development and the realisation and nourishing of
'self'.

Yeaxlee attempted a plan to draw upon man's
inherent quest (in a process of lifelong education),
to help to equip him with the intellectual and
affective instruments to guide him to a truly
democratic, benevolent society, committed to
Christian values. Whilst some looked to government
and political activity for potentially sweeping
changes in society, Yeaxlee focused his attention on
each individual in a universal setting. He would have
had everyone understand him/herself and the concept
of the universe, in order to unite collective effort
towards an ultimate goal. He was not alone in
expecting that each individual could reach out beyond
his/her inheritance to seek out the question of
meaning and quality of life and explore their
possibilities.

Whether a religious, philosophical or
ideological perspective is used to 'examine' life,
the one linking strand is that education sets the
sights, and that a lifetime of education ensures
continuous examination.

Conclusion

It needs to be borne in mind that Yeaxlee's views were being published at a time when the Board of Education was strengthening its control over Church schools, because, it was argued, religious dogma adversely influenced the standards in these schools; as highlighted by Simon;

> that other lion in the path of educational advance, the interest of the Churches in many elementary schools and in most of the worst of them. (Simon, 1974:149)

There was general dissatisfaction with Church elementary schools on the part of many local education authorities. It was recognised, also, by Labour Party supporters, that unless the Church improved the standards of teaching and learning conditions, and the buildings, many children would be doomed to failure regardless of the proposed secondary schools because of inadequate earlier learning opportunities. In this climate, when the general public and many educators were disenamoured of the Church's relationship with education and suspicious of religion generally, there was probably only a minority who would have accepted all that Yeaxlee had to suggest. Also, a disastrous general strike had recently occurred in a desperate bid to improve, materially, the lot of the workers. To these exhausted, and probably hungry, people, it could be argued, the ethereal, metaphysical or spiritual, assumed low priority in their pressing concerns.

Whereas Yeaxlee was wise in seizing the opportunity of asking that education for adults be considered at the same time as secondary education for all was being established (for he saw the one being inextricably linked to the other), he was clearly fighting a losing battle. It is hardly surprising that government policy concentrated first and foremost on establishing national secondary education. The organisational task involved was obviously of immense magnitude, and it seems likely that the Board of Education was only too happy, for that moment, to allow the universities and voluntary bodies to continue the major overseeing of education for adults - such as it was.

In any event, by 1924, the Board of Education agreed to 'separate' liberal adult education from technical and evening classes. The decision was reached after consultation with the Advisory Committee on the Liberal Education of Adults, and this effectively cemented the gap between liberal adult education from all other forms of education. Thus, for another fifty years the idea of integrated lifelong education lay dormant and almost forgotten. The concept and its practice are beginning to be found in some of the initiatives of community and tertiary colleges, in new means of accreditation, access, mature student programmes in Polytechnics, Colleges and Universities, taught-collaborative degree schemes, flexistudy and open learning. Its future rests in the intellectual and active efforts of those who acknowledge that the late twentieth century manifests features which demand complex and systematic reappraisal of the nature, purpose and duration of education - a reappraisal begun in the 1920s by Basil Yeaxlee.

Bibliography
Dave R H (ed) 1976 Foundations of Lifelong Education; Paris, UNESCO
Dewey J 1964 Democracy and Education (first publ 1916); New York, Collier-Macmillan
Faure E (Chairman) 1972 Learning to Be; Paris, UNESCO
Harrison J F C 1961 Learning and Living 1790-1960: A Study in the History of the English Adult Education Movement; London, Routledge & Kegan Paul
Hinden R (ed) 1964 Tawney: The Radical Tradition; London, Allen & Unwin
Hirschfield G 1964 The Council for the Study of Mankind, in Ulich, op cit
Jarvis P 1983a 'The Lifelong Religious Development of the Individual and the Place of Adult Education'; in Lifelong Learning: The Adult Years, May; vol. 5, No. 9, pp 20-23
Jarvis P 1983b 'Religiosity - a theoretical analysis of the Human Response to the Problem of Meaning'; in University of Birmingham, Bulletin for the Institute for the Study of Religious Architecture, pp 51-66
Kekes J 1980 The Nature of Philosophy; Oxford, Blackwell
Kitwood T M 1970 What is Human? London, Intervarsity Press
Knowles M 1978 The Adult Learner: A Neglected Species; Houston, Gulf Pub Co
Lengrand P 1975 An Introduction to Lifelong Education; London, Croom Helm
Mansbridge A 1964 The Kingdom of the Mind - Essays and Addresses; London, Dent
Ministry of Reconstruction 1919 Final Report of the Adult Education Committee; (reprinted 1980),

University of Nottingham
Simon B 1974 <u>The Politics of Educational Reform</u>;
London, Lawrence & Wishart
Sprague E 1978 <u>Metaphysical Thinking</u>; New York,
Oxford University Press
Terrill R 1973 <u>R H Tawney and His Times</u>; London,
Andre Deutsch
Ulich R (ed) 1964 <u>Education and the Idea of Mankind</u>;
University of Chicago Press
Yeaxlee B A 1925 <u>Spiritual Values in Adult Education</u>
(2 vols) Oxford University Press
Yeaxlee B A 1926 <u>Towards a Full Grown Man</u> (The John
Clifford Lecture); London, The Brotherhood Movement
Yeaxlee B A 1929 <u>Lifelong Education</u>; London, Cassell
Yeaxlee B A 1952 <u>Religion and the Growing Mind</u> (first
publ 1939); London, Nisbett & Co

Chapter Four

R. H. TAWNEY - 'PATRON SAINT OF ADULT EDUCATION'

Barry Elsey

This short biography of Richard Henry Tawney (1880-1962) deals mainly with his extensive and significant contribution to the 'heroic age' of adult education. This means making only passing reference to the many other important activities of Tawney's creative and crowded life. But for him adult education was a matter of great personal commitment, where he worked out his values and used his position as a teacher, organiser, executive, advocate, reformer and writer to give expression to the many other avenues of academic life and social affairs where he excelled.

It has to be acknowledged that it is virtually impossible to say anything new about him for Tawney has been canonised in at least six biographies, which amply testify to the volume, scope and significance of his impact on adult education, economic history, social and political philosophy, government policies in education and industry, educational journalism and the development of the Labour Party (see bibliography at end of the chapter). Nonetheless, from the standpoint of the gloomy and cynical 1980s it is difficult to be objective, but possible to attempt some assessment of his continued influence on British adult education.

Before detailing Tawney's contribution to adult education it is necessary to outline the origins and destinations of his life and career. Tawney was born in Calcutta into the folds of the privileged upper class where his progress in life was mapped out by private education, first at Rugby and later to Balliol College, Oxford. His father was a distinguished Sanskrit scholar and after service in the Indian Education Service became a professor and head of Presidency College. Such a background would have moulded most into a comfortable acceptance of privilege but Tawney was made of different metal.

Tawney's early life has been described as a mixture of the breeding of a gentleman fired by the instincts of a social democrat and the leaning towards service to the community as a duty of the high born. It seems that Oxford made sense of these strands embedded in Tawney's life for during his undergraduate days a view was emerging that the right to influence the values of society should be based on an individual's contribution and service to the community, not just from the ownership of property or high social status. This led Tawney to run his back on the 'call of India', characteristic of his Oxford contemporaries, and seek instead an understanding of poverty by becoming a social worker at Toynbee Hall in the East End of London. It should be noted, though, that Tawney learnt his trade as a professional scholar at Oxford, as well as an abiding taste for social reform through active involvement. His subsequent career is marked by an outstanding capacity to combine scholarship with practical actions on a wide variety of educational and political fronts.

Today some of the work Tawney did at Toynbee Hall would be regarded as non-formal adult education, closely allied to the ideas and practices of community development. In his time university settlement work was seen as a mission to the poor, by providing a taste of edifying culture laced with a strong sense of paternalism under the leadership of Canon Samuel Barnett (Preston 1985:27-32). Tawney made his own special contribution by emphasising the importance of social investigation and giving regular classes on literature, religious topics and political economy. These were the embryonic beginnings of Tawney as an adult educator. His view that the purpose of his lectures was to help the workers gain political power through knowledge put him at odds with Barnett's cultural vision of adult education. Tawney's views attracted the notice of Albert Mansbridge, founder of the Workers' Educational Association (WEA), and therein began a very long partnership. (See the second chapter of this book for a full discussion on Mansbridge).

In 1903, the year Tawney took up residence at Toynbee Hall, the WEA was founded, a movement pioneered by Mansbridge to promote the higher education of working people. Tawney met Mansbridge at the instigation of Canon Barnett. Mansbridge was impressed by his enthusiasm and energy. Soon afterwards William Temple was attracted to the WEA by Tawney, cementing the Balliol-Toynbee Hall connection and bringing together three illustrious figures which gave the Association such an impressive early start (see Styler 1985:590-591). As Terrill (1974:37) remarks: "For Tawney it began half a century of institutional connection (he was on the WEA executive for 42 years, and president, 1928-1945) that for many years meant more to him than even his connection to the Labour Party, the London School of Economics, or the church. He had come to think that education, not charity, was what workers needed. And he chose the WEA, rather than academia, as the arena for his first sustained phase (seven years) of teaching and research. Life in the WEA made him a socialist; work in the WEA made him an economic historian. In turn, he gave tutorial classes in England the spirit of comradeship in study which was their genius."

The decisive development for the WEA, and for Tawney, was the setting up of university tutorial classes. For Mansbridge the cultural enlightenment of the working classes depended upon the acquisition of properly taught and rigorously learnt knowledge. Tawney shared the same view, except for him the road to working class power and socialism lay through political education. These two outlooks sometimes led to clashes between Mansbridge and Tawney but this emerged sometime after university tutorial classes were fairly well established. The real achievement of the WEA was to bring together in a working partnership traditionally conservative, yet socially conscious, universities with the trade unions and cooperators, representing working class educational aspirations. Thus in 1908 these interested parties gathered together in an historic assembly to consider the prospect of a university level adult education for the working class. The tutorial class movement that sprang from the conference and report 'Oxford and Working-Class Education', which was largely written and inspired by Tawney, was founded on the idea that a sound education was more than the outpourings of occasional lectures. Mansbridge believed passionately in the virtues of sustained and regular study involving class discussion, private reading and essay writing in the manner of the highest education of university standards. These were the highways to individual development, cultural emancipation and class equality. Tawney worked within the broad framework of these ideas and provided the additional dimension of a scholarly based education into the ideas of political theory and economic history. He also put into effect the idea of adult education as 'the spirit of comradeship in study'. This contribution warrants more detailed description.

Tawney had accolades heaped upon him in just about every avenue of his glorious career, especially as an adult educator. It was Mansbridge who described him as the 'best tutor in England' in offering to provide Rochdale with the first university tutorial class, on the understanding that 30 worker-students pledged themselves for two solid years of study under Tawney's tutorship. Longton in Staffordshire soon became the base for the second tutorial class under Tawney and the sponsorship of Oxford University.

Tawney's workload would cripple most WEA and University Extension tutors today. Tawney would set off by train from Glasgow (where he was a part time lecturer at the university), and later from his marital home in Manchester, for Longton on Friday for an evening class. Spending the night at a local pub he would travel to Rochdale for an afternoon class, returning on Sunday. Tutorial classes by modern standards were large, between 30 and 40 hungry and relatively untrained adult minds. A lengthy lecture was followed by an hour of discussion which often spilled over in an informal and relaxed way to free ranging exchanges over matters of philosophy, history, religion, politics and literature. Over tea and biscuits Tawney showed himself as more than just a teacher and he revelled in the unique opportunity to rub shoulders with ordinary men and women fired with the thirst for knowledge. It was an experience that opened doors of the mind for those special few who shared the fellowship of learning. Tawney acknowledged the benefits of this experience in some of his later writings. In the meantime he slaved over the essays laboriously produced by students. In one session of nine weeks he marked and made elaborate comments on over 500 essays.

The images of Tawney as a lecturer are well worth quoting.

> To all students he was a fine lecturer. He always had a script, done in his cramped handwriting, all loops and hooks, sometimes on the back of notepaper picked up in hotels, and he would declaim its rolling phases with quiet intensity. He would steer gargantuan sentences to harbour because he had an unerring sense of the geography of a sentence, revealed in his meticulous punctuation. At the lectern, ash would drop onto his papers, and sometimes he would, when transported, thrust his still

burning pipe into a pocket of his tweed jacket.
(Terrill 1974:65)

The admiration of his biographer is obvious but even
more so is the image of Tawney as an adult teacher,
in the days when the didactic style of lecturing was
considered quite normal and credit was given for
knowledge distributed and lubricated by clever
phrases and learned wit. Such a style has all but
disappeared from adult education and although there
might be some regret at the passing of the
scholarship that went with it few would wish to
resuscitate such an old fashioned method of enabling
adults to learn. In Tawney's day it was the accepted
and admired method of teaching adults.

Tawney was probably a better teacher when he was
off the pedestal of the lecturn and the formally
prepared lecture. Indeed biographers have noted his
liking of questions from students and the opportunity
to talk over ideas in an informal manner. Tawney,
like all good adult educators, learnt from his
students and in recognition of their valuable
insights into everyday economic and social life he
readily acknowledged their wisdom and contribution
to his own thinking. It is held that Tawney's
excellent contribution to economic history as an
academic subject grew out of his involvement with
working class adult education and his classic book
"The Agrarian Problem in the Sixteenth Century" is
dedicated to the WEA. Tawney (1912:ix) wrote paying
tribute to

members of the Tutorial Classes conducted by
Oxford University, with whom for the last four
years it has been my privilege to be a fellow-
worker. The friendly smitings of weavers,
potters, miners, and engineers, have taught me
much more about the problems of political and
economic science which cannot easily be learned
from books.

Tawney's career as a teacher, in the narrow
sense of being involved in conducting university
tutorial classes, was a relatively short seven years.
Of course, he taught for many years at the London
School of Economics (LSE) but that was not the same
experience as the education of working adults, which
was his first calling. In a wider sense Tawney
continued as an adult educator throughout his long
life. His involvement was cemented throughout half a
century with the WEA. For over 40 years he served on

the WEA executive and was President for 17 years. During those years Tawney undoubtedly stamped his mark on the educational and social ideals of the WEA. He once claimed that his experience of the WEA made him a socialist and economic historian. In return Tawney insisted that the WEA honour, in form as well as spirit, its commitment to high intellectual standards and to working class education. This insistence sometimes put him at odds with Mansbridge who occasionally resented Tawney's sharp criticisms about declining standards and demands for better facilities to enhance the 'tutorial' side of classes.

Good teaching and high intellectual standards were for Tawney essential complements to the ideas of equality of opportunity for workers and the use of education for political ends. Tawney spent his life teaching these ideas at a time when the dark forebodings of totalitarianism were gripping the world and suffocating democracy. Intelligent citizenship had to spring from a sound education of adults and a slackening of intellectual standards was regarded by Tawney as a disservice to the ideals of social democracy and moral reasoning. It was Tawney's moral passion and academic respectability that played such a decisive part in building solid foundations for the WEA and their partnership with the universities. Tawney sustained and advocated these beliefs on a much wider and significant canvas thereafter.

In later years Tawney expressed some disquiet about the WEA fearing that it had lost sight of its original purpose. He was critical of the WEA's attempt to broaden and popularise its programme and lamented the decline of the tutorial class movement. Tawney was caught out of step with the times as his vision of workers being challenged by education was being superseded by a cafeteria diet of more easily digested fare. More significantly, the idea of education for socialism had all but vanished as a moving force in the WEA and adult education generally.

During his zenith as the WEA President Tawney devoted great energy to its executive affairs and was in every sense a working leader. His involvement ranged from political in-fighting within the executive of the WEA to the details of staff appointments. His main struggles were to keep the WEA's commitment to working class education and avoid splinter groups forming for the purposes of serving wider, apolitical cultural interests. This line of thought reflected the earlier version of Mansbridge and was taken up by Richard Livingstone who in 1941 wrote the definitive account of liberal adult education ideals and values. Tawney was in these matters an astute strategist and a ruthless side to his otherwise generous nature showed through. By skilled manipulation Tawney successfully shunted the idea into a harmless non-providing role. His attempts were in the long run only partially successful for the WEA was turning itself into two organisations. The traditional commitment to an intellectual education service for working class adults was giving way to provision for recreational and leisure time pursuits. Tawney was witness to the gradual waning of his ideas but for most of his active years he maintained a strong stand between adult education and the social emancipation of the working class.

Alongside his executive role and an earlier teaching one with the WEA Tawney lubricated its ideas and development through the power of his writing. He wrote frequently for the WEA journal "Highway" and essays in other publications of the organisation. His writing output for the WEA is modest compared with his enormous contribution to educational reform and ideas as a correspondent for the then 'Manchester Guardian'. Through his writings Tawney was in turn advocate, critic and teacher. Simultaneously he continued to produce a steady stream of high quality academic scholarship on economic history, social and political philosophy and other matters. This output was combined with membership of government committees of inquiry where both his ideas and writing skills were deployed.

His reputation as a teacher, organiser and charismatic leader drew him into the ambit of policy making, mainly in education but also in other spheres of government activity through committees, commissions and quango bodies. In adult education Tawney is best known, in this particular context, for his membership of the Ministry of Reconstruction which produced the famous 1919 Report (reprinted in 1980), still regarded as the foremost document produced for its philosophical and practical insights into the provision of an education service deliberately designed for adult purposes and needs. The report has served as a model for other official committees which periodically examines the nature and future directions of adult education. Tawney undoubtedly exerted his influence throughout the committee's proceedings, as he did with so many others (notably the Royal Commission on the Mining Industry). He wrote two sections of the 1919 Report;

on the supply of teachers and the organisation and finance of adult education. Even with the driest subject matters Tawney had the literary skills to elevate thought to a high level of lucidity and comprehension.

This short biography has dwelt on Tawney's life in general and his involvement with adult education in particular. Attention shifts now to his visionary philosophy and moral values which underpinned his actions throughout his life and career. Indeed it is the bequest of his ideas which he gave to adult education that warrants his inclusion as a great contributor to the movement. The testament of Tawney is the greatness of his ideas. It is the abiding good fortune of adult education, certainly in the past and to a considerable extent today, that his ideas reached, permeated and were consistently expressed through his teaching, writing and organising in a movement which grew into a significant range of learning opportunities for millions of adults throughout the twentieth century. Undoubtedly adult education today would be poorer, both as a service and a movement of ideas, without the continuing influence of Tawney's thinking which he so vigorously stamped during the long years of his reign.

There are four pillars of thought which Tawney inscribed onto the heart of British adult education. The first may be termed the fellowship of learning, reflecting the humanitarian spirit of adult education. The second is the idea of liberal education expressed through the great art of teaching adults. The third is the belief in adult education as a purposeful means of ensuring the survival of a democratic citizenship based on educated and critical minds. Finally there is the link between adult education and the values of socialism. These ideas are, and were for Tawney, inter-related values that he so eloquently expressed through adult education.

With regard to the idea of fellowship of learning, passing mention has been made of Tawney's impact on the adult students attending university tutorial classes. The key idea is the belief that in all other regards other than knowledge and scholarship the relations between the tutor and adult students is based on mutual respect. Adult education offers little comfort to pundits or tyrants, which are the temptations inherent in the teaching and control of compulsorily educated schoolchildren. Tawney, along with other early adult educators, established the legacy that teaching is founded upon

informal and friendly relations. This idea is just as
valid today in teaching adults, most of whom in
returning to learning experience the feeling of
uncertainty about abilities and other self doubts. At
its best adult teaching is a delicate balance between
sympathetic empathy, the skills of the adult tutor in
communicating knowledge and the capacity to enable
students to learn. Through his example set in
university tutorial classes Tawney has handed down a
model for teaching and learning which is more than
trained skills and academic knowledge and is just as
much about rapport and understanding of adults as
learners and individual people. It is to Tawney's
credit that he related education to ordinary adults
and broke through the pomp and arrogance of
university teaching. Reduced to essentials adult
education is a profoundly humane experience and
Tawney was amongst those who demonstrated this simple
value.

Closely related to the legacy of Tawney's idea
of the fellowship of adult learning is the ethos of
liberal education. Tawney was a passionate advocate
of the liberal ideal at a time when adult education
was still struggling for a place in the educational
system, and during the dark years of encroaching
fascism and precarious democracies. Given Tawney's
scholarly erudition and socialist beliefs it would
have been easy to slip from education to
indoctrination in pursuit of his political views.
Tawney steadfastly avoided that pitfall into arid
polemic without compromising his passionate zeal for
social reform and equality. Instead Tawney stuck to
the practice of examining ideas from different
perspectives and treating them to a fair minded yet
critical analysis. He upheld the virtues of
dispassionate inquiry and was reportedly very stern
with adult students, some of whom in their conversion
to left wing views, were impatient with him for his
moderation and tolerance.

Liberal education is more than a balanced
approach to rival political ideas. It is also a
belief in the value of knowledge for its own sake,
without regard to its vocational purposes and means
of occupational and social mobility. It is not clear
where Tawney exactly stood in relation to this idea.
As suggested earlier he was sometimes at odds with
Mansbridge and his cultural view of the purpose of
adult eduation. Tawney regarded adult education as a
means to working class political power. In that sense
education was not just for personal cultivation but
for political emancipation. Thus Tawney's view of

liberal education was focused on an approach to learning and an emphasis upon a knowledge of political economy as an avenue of class liberation. But that does not mean he was against the exploration of religious ideas, the arts and literature. Clearly not, for Tawney was a man of learning and religious conviction. Liberal adult education was for him the pursuit of knowledge for social purposes and personal development based on an ideal of intellectual excellence and the inquiring mind. His struggle was against blind beliefs and trivial pastime learning masquerading as adult education in the corridors of the WEA. His views of recreational learning in the developing adult education services provided by local education authorities in inter-war years is less well known. It is likely that he viewed it as irrelevant to the really important task of education as a means of political consciousness. But this is mere speculation.

It is clear that Tawney passionately believed in adult education as an arm of democracy. This belief goes beyond his partisan political values expressed through his educational activities and involvement with the Labour Party. Tawney's brand of socialism fused with his religious values, humane sympathies and liberal education practices made him an ardent social democrat. On that basis he regarded adult education for working class people as a vehicle for various forms of emancipation - intellectual, cultural and political. But this was not to create an hegemony of the working class, replacing one tyranny of class domination with another, but as a means of fostering a genuine pluralist society founded on secure democratic principles. Tawney's adult education work testifies to the practice of sharing knowledge and ideas through reasoned argument and discussion with people of mixed abilities and background. This is the stuff of a basic 'grass roots' democracy, equipping adults with the tools and knowledge for a fairer society. This kind of social democracy arises from real experience rather than an imposed version handed down by political leaders. In its essence democracy is built upon adult education and active involvement in learning experiences which are meaningful to ordinary people.

This idea certainly took root, surprisingly, during the second world war with the setting up of the Army Bureau of Current Affairs. ABCA, as it was known, established the principle and the practice of the open minded discussion of political ideas and invited under-educated service men and women to pool

71

their thoughts about the social reconstruction of Britain after the war. This was the practice of the idea of democratic citizenship through discussion. The antecedents of this approach to adult education can be traced to the splendid example set by the WEA and university tutorial classes, which Tawney so indelibly stamped with his values.

Tawney's ideas have certainly been an inspiration to many people in adult education, without necessarily sharing his political beliefs. As a practitioner, through the several avenues of creative expression in adult education, Tawney has been a shining example. Few could fail to be inspired by his teaching, scholarship, humanity and capacity to lead a major adult education provider of this century. Of course, he is not the only inspiring example, as this book and 'The International Biography of Adult Education' (Thomas and Elsey, 1980) amply testify.

It is Tawney's political beliefs and the communication of these through adult education which is for me his abiding contribution. Therein lies the nature of his inspiration. Adult education like other branches of the educational system is so easily dominated by the passion for bureaucracy, matters of technique, regulation of behaviour, allocation of resources and all the other tedious (but necessary) elements of the everyday business of management and organisation. Tawney's work is a constant reminder of the vitality of far-reaching ideals and political vision in adult education which gives the movement its dynamic thrust and wider social purpose.

The heroic age of adult education is just about spent. Today adult education is managed, little enough by inspiration and too much by careerists. Adult education with a fiery will is a thing of the past and with each year beginning to radiate a romantic glow. Tawney is part of the romantic heritage of adult education and a British style of socialism that has long since faded into glorious memory.

It would be foolish to expect adult education and the socialism of Tawney to make a comeback. In any case his style of teaching would be old fashioned and his liberal, democratic beliefs largely unheeded in the scramble to survive through the contingencies of vocational training and cafeteria style programmes. Nonetheless, if only for the sake of history some explanation of Tawney's socialism and its relation to adult education is useful.

The socialism of Tawney was based on two ideas.

First, Tawney was a man of deep religious conviction and Christianity was in his view founded on a belief in a common humanity. This common humanity derived from a recognition of God as the Father of Man. It does not matter whether Tawney's God was 'out there' or an internal spiritual force which men and women discover for themselves in the light of life experiences. For Tawney, God represented a moral basis to the human condition which had to be achieved through personal awareness and collective action. The means to establishing a social order properly recognising the moral basis of our common humanity is the idea of equality of worth.

Man has qualities which go beyond individual differences. These qualities of humanity express the potential for individual contributions for the common good. This idea is underpinned by a belief in the ultimate moral goodness of mankind and, in more concrete terms, the capacity of people to freely recognise their obligations towards others. The route to this essentially moral view of mankind is through a proper recognition of the equal worth of people and the need for equal treatment. By such means social relations and social order rest on a commonly accepted consensus of values.

Tawney in his role as an adult educator gave expression to the idea of treating people equally, as he did in his personal life too. He crossed the boundaries of a class ridden society, with its deep, inbuilt inequalities of a material and cultural kind, through the simple act of treating others as equals and raising their self-esteem. He enabled teaching adults with the moral principle of regarding students as worthy people with skills to unfold and valuable contributions to make to a more just society. Equality is more than the distribution of power and wealth in this approach for it demonstrates the humane quality of egalitarianism through social relationships. This is socialism as fellowship, just as there is morality through fellowship, and these constitute the bedrocks of our common humanity.

The second dimension of Tawney's socialism, closely linked to the first, is the idea of equality as a means of personal freedom and development. This is not the same thing as greedy, self-seeking individualism for it involves a sense of obligation and the urge to do one's duty for the common good. Again, this is an essentially humane aspect to socialist beliefs, not slide-rule socialism with its concern for distributional equality.

Freedom arises from within people who are given

the opportunity to explore their capabilities and develop themselves. This is the ideal ethos of liberal adult education and the pursuit of knowledge and learning for its own sake, that is, without regard to vocational or certification purposes. Adult education was for Tawney an inalienable right and a means of self-fulfilment through the struggle for knowledge by sustained learning. But adult education used in that way is also the route to a more equal society. In this regard adult education enables talents to develop and become available for the common good of society. The socialism in this view rests on a belief in the desire of those who have benefited from access to educational opportunities to service the community through their abilities. Self-fulfilment, therefore, is linked to the ideal of service which in the long run reduces inequalities in society.

Central tenets in Tawney's socialism are the belief in morality and serving the needs of a common humanity. It is an essentially human doctrine derived from the experience of fellowship. The allusion to basic Christian doctrine expressed through the ideas of morality, service and fellowship is very strong. His classic book on the subject of equality (Tawney, 1952) is rich with the thinking of a socialist guided by a concern for the quality of social relationships as much as political and economic analysis. Tawney's ideas of common humanity and fellowship were formed in part from the experiences of his high born family background. Just as significant, though, were the deep impressions derived from the experiences of mixing with ordinary working people in the East End of London and, undoubtedly, through the exchanges and insights of teaching adults in university tutorial classes. In this sense Tawney's experience of adult education provided a real basis for his personal convictions and political beliefs.

An assessment of Tawney's standing today is bound to be subjective. He is still a shining beacon for a particular kind of British socialism with its leaning towards Christian morality and community service. In my early years as a mature student at the LSE the ghost of Tawney stood behind the earthly powers of people like Richard Titmuss who combined academic intellectualism with a real concern to help adult students come to grips with social policy and administration. Titmuss and others like him impressed upon idealistic adult students destined for careers in social welfare the need to combine the rigours of the intellectual-rational traditional with humane feelings and practical commonsense. This is the spirit of Tawney and a legacy of British socialism and social welfare that has largely faded, just like fond memories of the past always do.

Adult education as a form of social welfare in the widest sense has just about let go of the Tawney legacy. There are still faint echoes, as in some of the romantic enthusiasm for the fellowship of learning through some aspects of community based adult education. In small measure too the liberal adult education ethos lives on through some forms of university education and WEA teaching. But time is not on the side of Tawney's kind of adult education. Undoubtedly adult education is a more professional service than in his days and it is much better resourced and established, in spite of prevailing policies of financial restriction. Yet somehow the moral passion and sense of purpose, the idealism of adult education, has given way to a far less spirited form.

Acknowledgement

I am indebted to Professors Gammage, Stephens and Thomas of the University of Nottingham for their valuable comments on earlier drafts of this chapter.

Bibliography

Brooks J.R. 1974 R.H. Tawney and the Reform of English Education. (unpublished Ph.D. Thesis) University of Wales

Hinden R. (ed) 1964 The Radical Tradition London, George Allen and Unwin

Jennings B (1985) Mansbridge Albert in Thomas and Elsey (eds) op cit

Livingstone R.W. 1941 The Future of Education Cambridge, University of Cambridge Press

Preston P. (1985) Barnett S.A. in Thomas and Elsey (eds) op cit

Ryan A. 1980,'R.H. Tawney - a socialist saint', in New Society 27th November

Smith H.P. 1962 R.H. Tawney Rewley House Papers, Oxford

Styler W.E. 1985 Temple William in Thomas and Elsey (eds) op cit

Tawney R.H. 1912 The Agrarian Problem in the Sixteenth Century London, Longmans

Tawney R.H. 1952 (4th ed) Equality London, George Allen and Unwin Ltd

Terrill R. 1974 R.H. Tawney and his Times: a

socialism of fellowship London, Deutsch
Thomas J.E. and Elsey B. (eds) 1985 <u>International Bibliography of Adult Education</u>. University of Nottingham. Dept of Adult Education
Williams J.R. <u>et al</u> 1960 <u>R.H. Tawney: a Portrait by Several Hands</u> London, Shenval Press
<u>The 1919 Report</u> 1980 republished by Dept of Adult Education, University of Nottingham

Part Three

EARLY TWENTIETH CENTURY AMERICAN THINKERS

Chapter Five

JOHN DEWEY AND LIFELONG EDUCATION

Angela Cross-Durrant

Introduction

John Dewey, born in Vermont in 1859, was one of
America's foremost pragmatists. Pragmatism as a
philosophy emerged in the early nineteenth century in
America at a time when many opposing views pulled
public opinion and action in different directions.
The new scientific world view opposed the religious;
romanticism faced positivism; democratic ideals
challenged the aristocratic reactionary stance.
Pragmatism developed as a unifying or mediating
philosophy (Scheffler 1974), trying to link science
and religion, speculative thought and analysis,
knowledge and action, and to highlight the
responsibilities for the initiation and the
consequences of such a unifying theory or philosophy
of life. Dewey wrote profusely on 'traditional'
philosophical problems of ethics, metaphysics,
aesthetics, etc, and on 'applied philosophy', such as
that expressed in his educational writing. He also
published comments and analyses on prevailing social
conditions and on politics. His holistic and unifying
philosophical ideals may be readily traced in any of
his works.

So far as his educational writing is concerned,
Dewey is primarily associated with the education of
the very young, but he has been described as the
"major philosophical founder father" of the
'alternative' ideas found in the lifelong or
recurrent learning movements (Flude and Parrott,
1979:21). This is because the movements propose
reform of education to allow a new way of perceiving
education, in toto, with each phase as one small step
in a longer co-ordinated lifelong journey, and they
all advocate an holistic view of learning and living.

Before proceeding with the discussion,
something needs to be said about 'alternatives' to

79

the prevailing educational enterprise.

Recurrent education is one of several potential alternatives, born of adult educators, and is usually synonymous with a way of seeing education in toto, with learning occurring at intervals throughout life, alternating with normal life activities; the unifying of all stages of education; accepting formal and non-formal patterns of education; and embracing education as an integral - not peripheral or separate - part of life. It also subscribes, to a significant extent, to 'de-schooling' (OECD, 1973). It differs from, say, éducation permanente, continuing education or the notion of alternance, in that these latter ideas suggest refresher and 'topping up' programmes (semantically, more of the same, so-to-speak, implying former education to a particular standard as a prerequisite for continuing) and retraining; whereas recurrent education, or Boshier's learning society, or lifelong education, suggest a complete "shift of paradigm" (Houghton and Richardson, 1974:ix). The approaches of éducation permanente and of continuing education, even when they mean different things to different people, usually imply a considerable expansion of existing services which form part of the general adult education provision, and as such are concerned primarily with post-compulsory (or post-initial) education. They may be viewed as tinkering with an existing engine.

The approaches of recurrent education, a learning society or lifelong education, on the other hand, involve the fitting of an entirely new engine to drive the educational bus. Implicit in these notions is the view that reform in compulsory education is more significant to post-compulsory learning than any reform or improvement of, addition to, or financial injection into, adult education could be, and this is in harmony with Dewey's thinking.

However, proponents of recurrent education, rather than of lifelong education, suggest that a "certain amount of 'deschooling'" is required (OECD, 1973:25), which denotes a significant departure from Dewey's adherence to schooling - though very much reformed in terms of methodology and curriculum - as an important vehicle for education. Thus, Dewey's ideas may be seen as closer in spirit to lifelong education in that this latter concept is radical in re-appraisal, but reformist in stratgey.

Each of the alternatives has its own nomenclature, criteria, principles and strategies, and using the various terms interchangeably (e.g. Flude and Parrott, 1979:16) can throw the differences out of focus. They all aim to maintain and improve the quality of life; to help the individual contend with a kaleidoscopic future – though some concentrate on a 'working' future more than a 'personal' future. But lifelong education, as will be discussed, most clearly reflects John Dewey's vision of education.

Although he did not write specifically about adult education, Dewey did explicitly refer to adults learning, and to the fact that all adults would continue to learn throughout life if their earlier education had sown the seeds for continuity of the learning process, thus giving everyone "a fair chance to act as a trustee for a better human life." (Dewey, 1922:97) According to Dewey, this continuity, or lifelong learning, would be achieved through his notion of growth.

This chapter briefly discusses Dewey's theory of growth as it appears in a selection of his works during the period 1886-1938, the latter being the year in which his publication "Experience and Education" appeared, in an attempt to view his educational philosophy (culminating in this publication) from a lifelong education perspective.

Lifelong Education and Dewey's Theory of Growth
Because Dewey is so closely associated with the earliest phase of the educational enterprise, his views and potential influence in later phases are rarely given the attention they deserve. Yet pervading his works is the belief that education, being concerned with growth, is truly lifelong since humans are capable of 'growing' intellectually throughout life, and that whereas schooling is a prerequisite for efficient and effective early learning, all of life's experiences and resources, from pre-school to old age, in and outside the school, could play meaningful part in an individual's education. As a pragmatist he emphasized the empirical basis of knowledge. He believed that continuity involved connectedness and that it was folly (in educational and humane terms) to separate a phase in life from the whole of life itself:

> education should not cease when one leaves school ... The inclination to learn from life itself and to make the conditions of life such that all will learn in the process of living is the finest product of schooling (Dewey,

1964:51)

Underpinning this sentiment is a recognition that we cannot receive all the education for life during the few years traditionally devoted to compulsory schooling, and a belief that there is immanent in everyone an ability to grow personally, intellectually and, as a result, socially, during and well beyond school years.

Dewey wrote over 700 articles, books, abstracts and lectures on philosophy, democracy, learning and education during his lifetime and it is generally agreed that during the period 1882-1939 he revised and restated more clearly some of his ideas in the form of 'rejoinders' (Schilpp, 1939). This revision of his ideas is often referred to. However, an all-pervading and unchanging theme running through his educational writings is that of growth as a result of educative experiences, which enables an individual to assimilate something from each new experience, add it to the next, and thus change and improve his views and actions as a result of this on-going, lifelong process. Experience and Education, for example, published in 1938, is a result of being personally aware of this process plus a response to critical analysis which distanced and revealed the strengths and weaknesses of his ideas. In 1938 the idea of growth is still central to his theory of education, and rather than being a complete reconstruction of his earlier ideas, the publication is a logical evolution of his thinking. He practised what he preached.

> I seem to be unstable, chameleon like ...; struggling to assimilate something from each (influence) and yet striving to carry it forward in a way that is logically consistent with what has been learned from its predecessors (Dewey, 1979e:22)

> It is less important that we all believe alike than that we all alike inquire freely and put at the disposal of one another such glimpses as we may obtain of the truth for which we are in search.

> Criticism by means of give-and-take of discussion is an indispensable agency in effecting (this) clarification. (Dewey, 1939b: 607)

Lifelong Education

The lifelong education movement is usually associated with the United Nations Educational, Scientific and Cultural Organization (UNESCO). It makes a plea for regarding all of life's resources and experiences, from pre-school to the grave, as playing a meaningful part in an individual's education. This education, it claims, should be lifelong since we face a lifetime of novelty and uncertainty as a result of the 'knowledge explosion' and its effects, not only on the role but on the number of roles an individual will have to adapt to in order to contend with its resultant rapidly accelerating social change. It is an all-pervading theme running through each phase of an unfolding educational process. The theme originates in the adult education phase, but it is not envisaged as that part of the present educational enterprise devoted to the correction of earlier educational deficiences; nor to the carrying of a few forward from the educational point reached, in "chaste isolation" from the rest of the educational enterprise (Paterson, 1979:38); nor indeed as a movement established to solve problems of access to existing provision, as, say, continuing education is largely expected to do (Griffin, 1979:81-85). It is a (speculative) idea for a completely different way of educating not only adults but children and young adults too. It offers a unifying philosophy for education to be seen as a whole, with each phase working in collaboration with another. This does not, however, imply uniformity of strategy but rather unity of purpose, since much will depend upon local and individual circumstances. Its ultimate aim is to maintain and improve the quality of life - in the face of change and uncertainty - and it wholly recognises that such a process cannot but be begun during school years. Lifelong education does not, therefore, seek to provide a service appended to the main educational provision as an

> intermittent peripheral activity only engaged in by people with the necessary time, money and energy. ... The major purpose of education cannot remain the inculcation of knowledge and skills, but should become the development of intellectual and psychological capacities which enable people to learn continuously for the rest of their lives. (Boshier, 1980:2)

Lifelong education is thus opposed to the

isolated development of the academic mind, of abstract intellectualism to the exclusion of virtually all else. Unlike the Greek school, advocates of lifelong education are concerned with the potency of mind - all minds - with the directive, regulative and disciplinary aspect of intelligence. It does not begin with absolutes nor end with ultimate truths. It does not seek separatist educational and social aims. It is in the business of affording everyone the power to achieve a sense of self-actualization, a strong sense of identity, and recognizes fully that the intellect does function effectively throughout life (vertical integration).

> As a result it is seen as serving to facilitate psychological development throughout life, and lifelong education is proposed as the organizing principle which will make it possible for education to function in this way. (Cropley, in Dave 1976:196)

On the other hand, lifelong education does not abandon the purely 'academic', but rather embraces it, as for some it will be the means or end of self-actualization. It recognizes the legitimacy, for any individual, of academic, vocational, professional, recreational, community pursuits, etc, with parity of esteem, regarding them all as potentially instrumental in achieving the goal of identity and self-actualization. It demands equality of access to a fully horizontally and vertically integrated process of education throughout the whole of life.

The concept of lifelong education embraces the basic notion of relating school (and later, college, university, etc) learning to the whole sphere of life, but, of course, makes the significant leap of recognizing all of life's situations, institutions, professions, etc, as strategically potential educational agencies (horizontal integration), thus formalising the notion.

The concept, says Suchodolski, is based "on the idea that the continuous development of man forms an integral part of his existence" (in Dave 1976:65). This is in complete harmony with Dewey:

> To prepare him (the child) for future life means to give him command of himself: ... so that he will have the full and ready use of all his capacities. (Dewey, 1966a:27)

> a living creature lives as truly and positively

at one stage as at another, with ... the same absolute claims. Hence education means the enterprise of supplying the conditions which ensure growth, or adequacy of life, irrespective of age. (Dewey, 1964:51)

Although the notion of lifelong education has been embraced by adult educators, the problem of dissatisfaction with the quality of compulsory education, because it breeds difficulties for later learning, is the same problem over which Dewey took issue. He, however, viewed it from the early end of the life spectrum.

Growth

Growth, according to Dewey, is the reward of education. "The criterion of the value of school education is the extent to which it creates a desire for continued growth and supplies means for making the desire effective in fact." (Dewey, 1964:53). His definition of growth was "a general and persistent balance of organic activities with the surroundings, and of active capacities to readjust activity to meet new conditions. The former furnishes the background of growth; the latter constitute growing" (ibid:52). This concept rested on forming the disposition - through democratic teaching methods based on sequential problem-solving rather than on isolated subjects - to be ever ready for new (educative) experience, able to learn from it and from life itself. This disposition was to be established for every child. An educative experience, selected responsibility by teachers, produced a situation of 'undergoing', and 'trying to transact' (practical and active solving) a problem. Reflecting upon these two aspects of a problem (the one passive and the other active), then perceiving relationships, recognizing significance and being changed by the whole experience, enabled the individual to be prepared to bring the findings of that experience to the next. (This, he asserted, was the way to establish meaning). Thus, he saw a kind of chain reaction set up which, in his view, ended only when life ended, since the habit or disposition would have been set in motion, propelling the individual to go on learning indefinitely from, and modifying, subsequent experiences. If it had been educative, previous experiences would change the objective conditions under which subsequent experiences would occur. At school the experiences would have been contrived by teachers but linked to life outside school also, and others would occur naturally in everyday life, throughout life.

Dewey's notions of growth have been criticized because some would argue that whereas growth is taken as the basic value and result of education, Dewey did not specify the direction or ultimate goal of growth - save itself. But, as Scheffler has pointed out,

> the ideals of intelligence, growth, and freedom, open-ended as they are, are not amorphous or directionless; ... they make the most stringent of demands upon those who would embody them in human institutions and strive to rear their young by their light. (Scheffler, 1974:247)

It is clear that Dewey would judge any institution or process according to how far it had succeeded in enabling individuals to develop their innate powers of awareness and analysis. These powers might well differ, depending on each individual's capacity, but the disposition to continue their exercise, indefinitely, in order to bring past experience to bear upon new experience, conditions or problems, was never to be abbreviated. Since this disposition could and should be activated throughout life, something would, Dewey insisted, be learned as a result of each activation. Thus, experiences become educative, and individuals can learn from life, throughout life. In this way, growth becomes a means and an "end-in-view" (Dewey, 1930:225). In other words, growth as a process or means becomes growth as an end, and is called into play again each time this process is required to contend with different (problematic) aspects of life. These would include those associated with personal, vocational, leisure and social life, or with disinterested interest. (There is much to bind Dewey's philosophy and pedagogy to Knowles' andragogy (1978), and perhaps further comparisons might well illuminate the similarities found in the methodology of elementary education and in education for adults.) This is not to say that life would consequently be perfect - he well recognized life's hazards which have to be confronted, as well as the enrichment which life's experiences can bring.

> The more an organism learns ... the more it has to learn, in order to keep itself going; otherwise death and catastrophe. If mind is a further process in life, a further process of

registration, conservation and use of what is conserved, then it must have the traits it does empirically have: being a moving stream, a constant change which nevertheless has axis and direction, linkages and associations as well as initiations, hesitations and conclusions. (Dewey, 1979c:20)

According to Dewey, therefore, armed with the capabilities for intelligent enquiry and solution, (which are the properties of effective growth) no one would be debarred from being intellectually and personally developed to act confidently, discriminating and acting from a position of wisdom, at every phase of adulthood, and to learn "from life itself" (Dewey, 1964:51). This was necessary in order to negotiate life's contingencies, and on a grander scale, so that man would be able to select that which contributes to the quality of (all) life. Elitist education for the few was, therefore, dismissed by Dewey. To him, the 'educated person' was one whose innate analytical powers were developed sufficiently to enable him or her to be effective in all aspects of life and work. "This is what Dewey meant when he said that habits, which are the outcomes of educative experience, are ways or arts for dealing with the environment." (Wingo, 1974:173). Thus, 'ways of knowing' rather than 'states of knowledge' were of primary importance to Dewey.

These views are similar to those expressed by advocates of lifelong education. For example, Cropley says: "What is needed is a system in which adult and school learning are seen as part of a continuous fabric" (in Dave 1976:209). And "Lifelong education squarely recognizes that learning occurs throughout life." (ibid:196) Similarly, Janne writes: "In lifelong education, learning ... becomes a normal, constant dimension of man's entire life" (in Dave 1976:129). Not only are these writers describing lifelong learning, they are arguably describing Dewey's view of growth.

To understand Dewey's faith in growth, intelligence and behaviour (all inter-connected) they have to be seen in terms of power to reason, which underpins Dewey's insistence on problems or practice or tensions to be resolved. "It (reasoning) begins in tensional situation, and its validity is tested by the pertinency of the plans it develops for the resolution of the conditions that create the tension, or problem (Dewey, 1939a:430). Reasoning, Dewey claimed, "as such, can provide means for

effecting the change of conditions but by itself
cannot effect it. Only execution of existential
operations directed by an idea in which ratiocination
terminates can bring about the re-ordering of
environing conditions required to produce a settled
and unified situation" (ibid:430). He wished to
acknowledge that there is an active as well as a
passive dimension to reasoning and intelligence. It
is suggested that the controversy is not so much over
whether Dewey belittled the 'intellectual' or
'educated' person as over the nature of intellect or
intelligence and the method for its nurture. For
Dewey it was relative, not fixed, and therefore
education was not simply in the business of realizing
pre-existing abilities, but rather the reaching out
of minds to points which they had not previously
touched. It rested on a belief that a person's
intellectual power and practice could continue to
grow throughout the whole of life, so long as the
'habit' of reasoning, or of intelligent appraisal, or
of exercising intellect, or whatever other name is
given to clear, potent thinking, was formed and
nurtured through applicative learning in early
schooling.

Dewey has sometimes been criticised for on the
one hand expounding the theory and virtues of
limitless growth, and on the other for apparently
contradicting himself by seeming to confine his idea
of growth through learning experiences to those which
concentrate more on the practical and utilitarian
than on the intellectual or academic. But it needs to
be borne in mind that Dewey suggested that practical
and active occupations should be adopted as only the
first stage in the learning process. Familiarity and
practical pursuits may then lead on to social
communication; the exchange of ideas in a social
content, guided or facilitated by a teacher, for
example. The third stage is a growing ability to
organize, analyse and to synthesize, all of which
underpin mastery of knowledge - however defined (see
Dewey 1964). It is not so much 'subject matter' that
Dewey rejected as the manner in which it was used or
communicated - usually in terms of the teacher's
experience. This meant (and to an extent still means)
that children have to identify themselves and their
activities in terms of other people, associations,
and so on. Children were regarded as 'inexperienced',
and particularly because of the American
essentialist tradition, this largely remained so for
much of their learning lives. Common practice was to
begin with the teacher's experience in order to

broaden (vicariously) the pupil's experience. The pyramid process in the United Kingdom has long been designed to introduce, at the age of about 11 years, probably the widest subject based curriculum that learners are ever likely to meet. It is gradually whittled away until 'interest' or 'ability' is discovered in a number of subjects to be taken at, say, General Certificate of Secondary Education Ordinary Level examinations. Those who are 'unmotivated' are led back to what does interest them (hardly surprisingly, the quickest way out of the pyramid) and to find an exit at the top by way of employment, a Youth Training Scheme or a college vocational course. It is perhaps salutary to reflect upon the possibilities of turning the traditional pyramid over, resting it on a corner, and beginning with a pupil's interest and allowing other interests to develop out from there. There may be a case for gradually widening rather than reducing the angle of the pyramid.

Dewey's critics would claim that by confining his idea of growth to practical pursuits he narrowed his field of vision to the parochial whilst professing the adoption of a very wide, universal vision. He did indeed advocate a practical, scientific and active approach to learning, which was consistent with his pragmatic philosophical stance. Also, his critics might argue that unless lifelong education is purely utilitarian or vocational in direction (which, since it embraces all kinds of education it is not), Dewey's notion of growth would not bear comparison with the ideas found in lifelong education.

Poole (1975:138-149), for example, has criticised Dewey for his remark that "The simple facts of the case are that in the great majority of human beings the distinctively intellectual interest is not dominant. They have the so-called practical impulse and disposition." (Dewey, 1966c:98). However, Dewey qualified this by highlighting the fact that most American children left school as soon as they had acquired the rudiments of learning sufficient to get them employment, because they had to. "While our educational leaders are talking of culture ... as the ... aim of education, the great majority of those who pass under the tuition of the school regard it as only a narrowly practical tool with which ... to eke out a restricted life" (ibid:98). He did not, however, advocate the removal of all that is cultural but rather the marriage of both 'cultural' and 'technical' in the curriculum, with parity of esteem. His practical approach to learning may be translated into a 'relating' or horizontally integrating approach - as found in lifelong education.

> To realize what an experience, or empirical situation, means, we have to call to mind the sort of situation that presents itself outside of school ... And careful inspection of methods which are permanently successful ... will reveal that they depend for their efficiency upon the fact that they go back to the type of situation which causes reflection out of school in ordinary life. They give the pupils something to do, not something to learn; and the doing is of such a nature as to demand thinking, or the intentional noting of connections; learning naturally results. (Dewey, 1964:154)

> if we were to introduce ... the activities which appeal to those whose dominant interest is to do and to make, we should find the hold of the school upon its members to be more vital, more prolonged, containing more of culture. (Dewey, 1966c;99)

Poole also claims that Dewey decried the use of textbooks because of the non-active process of acquiring knowledge therefrom. Poole argues: "Is thought inactive? ... What is wrong with absorbing through a book accumulated knowledge? ... Books can engage a reader actively giving him a knowledge of things which his own practical experience cannot provide" (Poole, 1975:143). However, Dewey has again qualified what he meant by such statements as: "Most objectionable of all is the probability that ... the book or the teacher, will supply solutions ready-made" (Dewey, 1964:157-8). What Dewey is at pains to point out is that the content of a book should not necessarily be an end in itself, but rather used for "suggestions, inferences, conjectured meanings, suppositions, tentative explanations; - ideas, in short ... The data arouse suggestions ... Inference is always an invasion into the unknown, a leap from the known" (ibid:158). He censured the use to which books were put, i.e. meaningless regurgitation, particularly rote learning for "Pupils who have stored their 'minds' with all kinds of material which they have never put to intellectual uses are sure to be hampered when they try to think" (ibid:158). "A book (or a letter) may institute a more intimate association between human beings separated ... from each other than exists between dwellers under the same roof" (ibid:5). And it can be argued that there is an instrumental aspect to the study of literature, for example. As Dewey said in "Lectures for the First Course in Pedagogy":

> Literature as a key to life behind it, or as a mode of interpretation, deserves all that has ever been said in its favour ... It is the record of his consciousness of the value contained in that (social) experience. There comes a time when experience is so laden with meaning, that ... this meaning breaks through the outer form in which that meaning is bound up. It becomes possible for men to see that their experiences have a value which goes beyond momentary occurrence. (Dewey, 1979a:172-3)

Then there is Peters' (1977) point that much is lost in the purely theoretical sense if our cultural heritage is introduced to children only by stressing its relevance to current practical and social situations. He claims that what is not immediately relevant is deemed by Dewey to be unworthy of inclusion in the educational experiences designed to help people to grow. Dewey did say, however, "Culture is also something personal; it is cultivation with respect to application of ideas and art and broad human interests." (Dewey, 1964:121) What Dewey was pointing to here was the application, rather than just the passive storing, of the ideas and interests introduced through education. As a humanist he was primarily interested in what education could actually do in "liberating human intelligence" (Dewey, 1964:230).

> social efficiency as an educational purpose should mean cultivation of power to join freely and fully in shared or common activities. This is impossible without culture, while it brings a reward in culture, because one cannot share in intercourse with others without learning - without getting a broader point of view and perceiving things of which one would otherwise be ignorant. (ibid:123)

He argued for a synthesis, for reflection on human methods and interests; that the present should be reflected upon by recapitulating the past and anticipating the future.

By 1925 Dewey said; "Those who start with a coarse, everyday experience must bear in mind the findings of the most competent knowledge, and those who start from the latter must somehow journey back to the homely facts of daily existence." (Dewey, 1979c:21). Dewey's view of culture was a personal one as opposed to one of 'ism'. "And there is perhaps no better definition of culture than that it is the capacity for constantly expanding the range and accuracy of one's perception of meanings." (Dewey, 1964:123). It is a matter of common sense that this cannot be achieved by ignoring the 'theoretical'. All that Dewey is doing is to couch his definition in an active rather than a passive context. "Learning is active. It involves reaching out of the mind" (Dewey, 1966b:127). And in response to the accusation that there is little room for the speculative and imaginative in Dewey's practical approach, by 1938 he was able to say, "The environment, in other words, is whatever conditions interact with personal needs, desires, purposes, and capacities to create the experience which is had. Even when a person builds a castle in the air he is interacting with the objects which he constructs in fancy" (Dewey, 1971:44). Thus, imagination and creativity, as well as utility, have a meaningful place in Dewey's theory.

The foregoing sentiments signify a far wider perspective on Dewey's part than he has been suggested by either Poole or Peters. They also emphasize his view that mastery of the learning process - 'learning to learn' - is more important than the 'encyclopaedic' content of learning, and is complete accord with lifelong education's call for reform of compulsory education, as outlined by Janne (in Dave, 1976:152-3).

Dewey's idea of growth emerges also in his views on secondary and further/higher education.

> After all, the period from, say, fourteen to twenty-two is a comparatively short portion of a normal lifetime. The best that education can do during these years is to arouse intellectual interests which carry over (Dewey, 1979b:212)

He called for education to "awaken some permanent interest and curiosity" (ibid:212). So far as the quality of the educational experiences during those years is concerned, he had this to say:

> Its freshness and vitality may be restored by making it what it should be, the renaissance of

the individual mind, the period of self-consciousness in the true sense of knowledge of self in relation to the larger meanings of life. (ibid:225)

It could be argued that it is precisely because this has not materialized that few are able to 'learn from life itself', and that a significant part of adult education is beleaguered by the need to fulfil a remedial rather than an augmentative and enhancing role.

Dewey is not, of course, unique in his view that early education 'sets the scene' for effective learning throughout adolescence and beyond, but most comparable theories (e.g. those of Rousseau, Pestalozzi or Froebel) associate an end of education with mature adulthood. It is this (seemingly) generally accepted view today that weakens the case for adult education provision. Implicit in Dewey's idea of growth, however, is the notion that curiosity and a disposition to learn can carry over into adult life, and that people would want to learn more as their lives progressed once that disposition had been established. Thus he claimed that "Education as growth or maturity should be an ever-present process" (Dewey, 1971:50).

Whereas this may not lay the only foundation for lifelong learning and education it is clear that in spirit there is a very strong affinity between Dewey's philosophy and that of lifelong education. Dewey's notions do more than suggest that a mature adult, having experienced appropriate early education, has received all the education he will need for his future. In the late 1980s, Dewey's earlier ideal of promoting on-going learning has now changed to an imperative, if only in socio-economic terms. It becomes clear, therefore, why he is regarded as the philosophical founder-father of lifelong education.

Dewey's wish that an adult would no longer review his life and see it as a "scene of lost opportunities and wasted powers" (Dewey, 1964:51) is pertinent to any discussion about adult education. His plea for a reformed educational enterprise to equip its wards with the capability to fashion for themselves (through growth) a way of life for which they have respect and conjoint responsibility, his belief in the continuity of learning, his acceptance of a wide spectrum of educational activities cutting across the traditional academical-vocational divide, his faith in the educational value of a broad

93

horizontal integration of school and community, his egalitarian outlook and strongly pragmatic, holistic philosophy, stamp his educational works clearly with the spirit of lifelong education.

Conclusion
It is argued that Dewey's theory of growth could have been written for lifelong education.

> What he has learned in the way of knowledge and skill in one situation becomes an instrument of understanding and dealing effectively with the situations which follow. The process goes on as long as life and learning continue. (Dewey, 1971:44)

> In a certain sense every experience should do something to prepare a person for later experiences of a deeper and more expansive quality. That is the very meaning of growth, continuity, reconstruction of experience. (ibid:47)

This is in complete accord with Suchodolski:

> man can find his vocation and his happiness only by constantly exceeding the boundaries of what he has already achieved. New horizons of cognition and new spheres of activity are made the source as well as the consequences of lifelong education. (Suchodolski, 1976:64)

The spirit of lifelong education may be traced in Dewey's thought from the late 1890s through to 1939. (Leaders in the adult schools movement, in the co-operative colleges, mechanics' institutes, people's colleges, working men's colleges, etc, had religious, philanthropic and/or intellectual ideals for adult education, but tended to express them either in compensatory terms, or as extra to the main provision. They tended not to demand reform of all education - as does lifelong education).
References to the growth of the individual can, of course, be found in earlier writings, e.g. Comenius, Kant, Pestalozzi and Froebel. Dewey's view of growth, however, was not the same as Pestalozzi's, or as Froebel's 'unfoldment'. Earlier views of development or growth were finite. The seedling grew into a plant (a popular analogy) and there the process eventually ended - in full-bloom adulthood.

For Dewey, however, growth was not finite; his philosophical stance was pragmatic but humanist rather than Christian-idealist, and his psychological outlook was organic but non-finite. For him, development and learning was able to continue throughout adult life.

Dewey's thorough analysis, and call for reform, of the nature, purpose and methodology of initial education, found especially in <u>Democracy and Education</u> can, it is posited, be regarded as the trans-Atlantic origins of twentieth century lifelong education thought. (Yeaxlee, 1925, may be regarded as his British, spiritual/Christian counterpart). His pragmatic philosophy with its unifying and mediating perspective, striving to weld theory and practice, to hold an holistic view of the problems posed by human life, continually informed and influenced his educational theory, and is easily traced in his attempts to integrate learning and living, school and life, and in his views on learning throughout life. It is impossible in a brief space to do more than suggest that Dewey's thinking is as important to lifelong education as it is to initial education. His writings certainly bear comparison with the many descriptive details, strategies, analyses and discussions of lifelong education.

As R J Roth has expressed it, "Future thought in America" (and for the purpose of this discussion, in lifelong education) "must go beyond Dewey ..., though it is difficult to see how it can avoid going through him." (in Scheffler, 1974:190)

Bibliography

Boshier R (ed) 1980 <u>Towards a Learning Society</u>; Learning Press, Vancouver

Cropley A J 1976 '<u>Some Psychological Reflections</u>'; in Dave R H (ed) op cit

Dave R H (ed) 1976 <u>Foundations of Lifelong Education</u>; London, Pergamon Press

Dewey J 1922 <u>Human Nature and Conduct. An Introduction to Social Psychology</u>; New York, H Holt & Co

Dewey J 1939a '<u>Logic: The Theory of Inquiry</u>' (first pub 1938); in Schilpp P A, op cit

Dewey J 1939b '<u>Experience, Knowledge and Value: a Rejoinder</u>'; in Schilpp P A, op cit

Dewey J 1964 <u>Democracy and Education</u> (first pub 1916); London, Macmillan

Dewey J 1966a '<u>My pedagogic creed</u>' (first pub 1897); in Garforth F W, op cit

Dewey J 1966b 'The child and the curriculum' (first pub 1902); in Garforth F W, op cit
Dewey J 1966c 'The school and society' (first pub 1915); in Garforth F W, op cit
Dewey J 1971 Experience and Education; London, Collier-Macmillan
Dewey J 1979a 'Lectures in the first course in pedagogy'; (first pub 1896); in Wirth A G, op cit
Dewey J 1979b 'Are the schools doing what people want them to do?' (first pub 1901); in Wirth A G, op cit
Dewey J 1979c 'Experience and nature' (first pub 1925); in Wirth A G, op cit
Dewey J 1979d 'The Way out of Educational Confusion' (first pub 1931); in Wirth A G, op cit
Dewey J 1979e 'From absolutism to experimentalism' (first pub 1930); in Scotland J, op cit
Flude R & Parrott A 1979 Education and the Challenge of Change; Milton Keynes, Open Univ Press
Garforth F W 1966 John Dewey: Selected Educational Writings; London, Heinemann
Griffin C 1979 'Continuing education and the adult curriculum'; in Adult Education, 52, 2, pp 81-5
Houghton V & Richardson K 1974 Recurrent Education; London, Ward Lock
Janne H 1976 'Theoretical foundations of lifelong education'; in Dave R H, op cit
Knowles M 1978 The Adult Learner: A neglected species; Houston, Gulf
Organisation for Economic Co-operation & Development/CERI 1973 Recurrent Education: A Strategy for Lifelong Learning; Paris, OECD
Paterson R W K 1979 Values, Education and the Adult; London, Routledge and Kegan Paul
Peters R S (ed) 1977 John Dewey Reconsidered; London, Routledge and Kegan Paul
Poole R H 1975 'The real failure of John Dewey'; in Education Review, 23, pp 138-149
Scheffler I 1974 Four Pragmatists; London, Routlege and Kegan Paul
Schilpp P A (ed) 1939 The Philosophy of John Dewey; Wisconsin, George Banta
Scotland J 1979 Doctrines of the Great Educators; London, Macmillan
Suchodolski B 1976 'Philosophical Aspects'; in Dave R H, op cit
Wingo G M 1974 Philosophies of Education: An Introduction; Massachusetts, D C Heath & Co
Wirth A G 1979 John Dewey as Educator; New York, R E Krieger
Yeaxlee B A 1925 Spiritual Values in Adult Education; Vols I & II, Oxford University Press

Yeaxlee B A 1929 <u>Lifelong Education</u>; London, Cassell

Chapter Six

E.L. **THORNDIKE**

W.A. Smith

Introduction

There are few theories of learning that have had as
marked an effect upon American educational practice
as Thorndike's. Much of this was due to his
prodigious volume of writing. An unusually creative
scholar, he was author or co-author of more than 500
books and articles. His influence on psychological
and educational thinking has been worldwide. Much of
his time and attention was devoted to theoretical
aspects of learning, but even more to the applied
aspects and classroom situations. The specificity of
Thorndike's theory contributed much to its
applicability.

Thorndike suggested that the learner was an
individual ready to make certain responses, capable
of varying those responses, and attempting to respond
to the aspects of a stimulus situation which appeared
familiar to previously successful responses in
similar situations. In order to develop the learner's
potentials efficiently, he suggested the following
teacher tasks: (1) to determine the particular
response desired to a given stimulus, (2) to develop
an orderly progression of the parts of the task from
simple to complex, and (3) to identify the specific
elements of a learning task and present them in a way
providing the most favorable opportunity for
eliciting the correct response, which could then be
rewarded. (Thorndike, 1917:7-10) As the learner
experienced repetition and reward to the correct
responses, he would cleave to those which were
desired and gradually eliminate those which were
inappropriate.

While Thorndike did not deny that insightful
learning occurred, he believed it to be a most
infrequent form of learning. Therefore McClusky has
suggested that his theory of learning is a much

98

better explanation of the quasi-mechanical learning of early childhood than it is of the more complex learning of the adult years. (Grabowski, 1970:80-95)

Brief History

Edward Lee Thorndike was born at Williamsburg, Massachusetts, U.S.A. on August 31, 1874. He was educated at Wesleyan (Conn.), Harvard, and received a Ph.D. from Columbia University. His career, of 42 years, save for one year at Western Reserve University, Cleveland, Ohio, was spent at Teachers College, Columbia University. James E. Russell, then dean of Teachers College, brought him to the faculty at Columbia, where Thorndike remained until his death. His two brothers were also professors at Columbia: Ashley Horace Thorndike (1871-1933) was an authority on Elizabethan drama, Lynn Thorndike (1882-1965) a medieval historian. Thorndike died at Montrose, New York, on August 9, 1949.

The emphasis upon the scientific method at the beginning of the twentieth century resulted in making Thorndike a transitional figure in the history of education. He represents a transition from the philosophical approach in the association of ideas to the experimental approach in association through physiological stimulus-response observations.

Thorndike was responsible for many of the early applications of psychology to such fields as arithmetic, algebra, reading, handwriting, and language. Other major contributions include works on the theory of psychological tests and compilations of the words occurring most frequently in English reading matter.

Best known in his three-volume work Educational Psychology (1913-1914). For our purposes, his work Adult Learning (1928) is of major importance. Additional works of special interest treat the behavior of animals; prediction of vocational success; wants, interests, and attitudes; and principles of education. Some of the better known publications include The Psychology of Arithmetic (1922), The Measurement of Intelligence (1926), The Fundamentals of Learning (1932), A Teacher's Word Book of 20,000 Words (1921, later revised), and Thorndike-Century Junior Dictionary (1935).

Early Influences

The events of the late nineteenth century and the early twentieth century which led to the "new

99

psychology" movement greatly influenced Thorndike. Darwin published his <u>Origin of the Species</u> (1859) just fifteen years before Thorndike was born. Thorndike was five years old when the first experimental laboratory for the study of psychology was established at Leipzig by William Wundt. Ebbinghaus was just a young man when Thorndike was born. G. Stanley Hall established the first psychological research laboratory in America to Johns Hopkins while Thorndike was a teenager. By the time Thorndike was doing his early work there were only twenty-six of these laboratories in the United States.

The journals which were to carry Thorndike's reports were just beginning to be published. Hall founded the <u>American Journal of Psychology</u> in 1887. Cattell, Thorndike's professor at Columbia, founded <u>Psychology Review</u> the year he left Wesleyan and went to Harvard. The American Psychological Association was founded in 1892. This was one year before Thorndike entered college. Thorndike himself helped establish the <u>Journal of Educational Psychology</u> in 1910.

He became identified as an experimenter in psychology at the time in which philosophical associationism of Hobbes, Locke, Hume, Hartley, and Mill was accepted. The more scientific studies of Wundt, Ebbinghaus, Morgan, Hall, James, and Cattell were just beginning to gain attention. Though he was influenced by both streams of thought, he preferred to be identified with the latter. He (1917:164) said, "It is the vice or misfortune of thinkers about education to have chosen the methods of philosophy or of popular thought instead of those of science."

Evolution as stated by Darwin was one of the strongest influences from the historical tradition upon the thinking of Thorndike. Joncich (1962:5) observes that it was through Darwin's influence that Thorndike placed man "squarely in the animal world" making psychology an important avenue in the study of human behaviour and learning. As early as 1909 Thorndike (1909:65-80) stated that Darwin had shown psychologists that the mind has a history of thousands of years. The mind could be understood only when one understands its past.

Evolutionary views form the basis of his descriptions of mental life. This can be found in the summary work <u>Selected Writings from a Connectionist's Psychology</u> published in 1949, the year of his death. Thorndike (1917:77) suggests that the intellect is developed in the same way the animal or plant kingdom has developed. The difference between animal and human learning is a matter of quantity. (Thorndike, 1931:168). He (ibid:181) compares human and animal learning by saying "No new kind of brain tissue is needed ... nothing save a mere increase in the number of associative neurones." Man is considered nothing more than a superior animal.

At the point of acceptance of evolution and the scientific method the old associationism of the earlier philosophical associationists ends and the new physiological associationism begins to influence Thorndike. Perhaps William James influenced him more than any of the others. He encountered the work of James as a student through reading Principles. He (Thorndike, 1935:263) later acknowledged this to be the most stimulating book he had read. Indeed, he used the James home for his early chick experiments. He consistently followed the James approach. He freely acknowledged this in The Human Nature Club. (1901:vi)

Thorndike emerged from the early period of his life as a part of the "new psychology" movement. He pioneered in extending the descriptive method of research from animal experiments to human learning thus applying the new psychology to education.

Connectionism

In an abbreviated account of Thorndike's approach, the impression could be given that Thorndike was a very systematic writer. His "system", with the exception of a few persistent preferences, is in fact a rather loose collection of rules and suggestions. What Thorndike called a "law" at any one time was a statement which at the time appeared to have some general application. "No effort was made to retain internal coherence among the concepts used, or to establish any genuine relationship of coordination or subordination among the laws." (Hilgard, 1956:21)

The physiological nature of man underlies the psychology of connectionism and forms the basis for Thorndike's pedagogy. Thorndike (1914:199) said the mind is the "sum total of the connections between situations which life offers and the responses which the man makes." Physiological motivation and satisfaction of human wants become of primary importance in the system. (Thorndike, 1913:309) Purposiveness in learning is explained as a matter of man's superior connection system. He (1931:122) said "Purposes are as mechanical in their nature and action as anything else."

Thorndike's S-R formula is derived from this view of the nature of man. The changes which occur in behavior become a matter of changes in the neurones bonds. He (1913a:) said,

> A man's nature and the changes that take place in it may be described in terms of the responses - of thought, feeling, action, and attitude - which he makes, and of the bonds by which these are connected with the situations which life offers. Any fact of intellect, character or skill means a tendency to respond in a certain way to a certain situation - involves a situation or state of affairs influencing the man, a response or state of affairs in the man, and a connection or bond whereby the latter is the result of the former.

The primary and secondary laws of learning follow from this physiological view of situation-response-connection.

Humans do not possess at birth all the connection systems they will have later in life. They do have the potential for these connection systems, however. (1917:2) Individuals are born with certain connections which form a fund of learned tendencies found in the "original arrangement of the neurones in the brain." (1913a:3) These original connections form the reflexes, instincts, and inborn capacities which are classified by Thorndike as unlearned human behavior.

The unlearned human behavior systems are then classified. From these classifications he (1913a:123) concludes that the "basic aim of human life" is the "improvement and satisfaction of wants." Mankind changes his environment by eliminating those things which fail to give him satisfaction and by developing those things which give him pleasure. The satisfaction of wants becomes the basic aim for education (1920:11), the ultimate source of value (1929:19), and forms the point from which the laws of learning are developed.

The Law of Readiness. Thorndike (1913a:123) says the first guides of learning are certain original satisfiers and annoyers. He (1913b:11) identifies the most characteristic form of learning of both lower animals and man as trial-and-error learning, or as he preferred to call it later, learning by selecting and connecting. Satisfaction and annoyance as principles of learning were observed in the animal experiments.

Thorndike (1913a:124) said a satisfying state encourages the development of a "conduction unit (but) an annoying state prevents the development of a conduction unit." A conduction unit is whatever makes up a path which is ready for conduction. Hilgard (1956:18-19) argues that Thorndike did not pay much attention to neuroanatomical details and that he talked about neurones to be clear that he was talking about direct impulses to action and not about "consciousness" or "ideas". Hilgard also suggests that it should be remembered that Thorndike's system antedated behaviorism and that physiological language was the most available vocabulary for the objectivist prior to the rise of behaviorism. Actually Thorndike's "conduction units" have no precise physiological meaning. If the term "action tendency" were substituted for "conduction unit", the psychological meaning of Thorndike's law of readiness would become clearer. "Readiness thus means a preparation for action". (Hilgard, 1956:18)

The law of readiness is stated in terms of satisfaction, annoyance, and conduction units:

1. When a conduction unit is ready to conduct, conduction by it is satisfying, nothing being done to alter its action.
2. For a conduction unit ready to conduct not to conduct is annoying, and provokes whatever response nature provides in connection with that particular annoying lack.
3. When a conduction unit unready for conduction is forced to conduct, conduction by it is annoying. (Thorndike 1913a:128)

Thorndike (ibid:124) was careful to point out, "To satisfy is not the same as to give sensory pleasure and to annoy is not the same as to give pain." Among humans satisfaction and annoyance may be emotional and subjective. Also, it should be pointed out that Thorndike's law of readiness was a law of preparatory adjustment, not a law of growth.

The Law of Exercise. The law of exercise has a history as old as learning. The early associationist thought repetition had something to do with fixing ideas in the mind. The work of Ebbinghaus on memory indicates this approach.

At first Thorndike (1917:166) called this law the law of habit. In 1911, he (1911:244) changed the wording of his statements and called it the law of exercise. In 1913, the law of exercise was subdivided into the laws of use and disuse. (1914:70)

The law of use is stated in relation to a situation. Thorndike (ibid) says, "A modifiable connection being made by him between a situation S and a response R, man responds originally, other things being equal, by an increase in the strength of that connection ..." The law of disuse is similarly stated in relation to a situation. He (ibid) says, "A modifiable connection not being made by him between a situation S and a response R, during a length of time T, man responds originally other things being equal, by a decrease in the strength of that connection."

Hilgard (1956:25) suggests that Thorndike in two volumes under the titles The Fundamentals of Learning (1932) and The Psychology of Wants, Interests, and Attitudes (1935) renounced the law of exercise as a law of learning in his later revisions. However, Thorndike had much earlier stated that he did not believe that frequency alone would produce improvement and retention. As early as 1912 he (1914:11) said, "Mere practice does not make perfect." He (ibid:12) continued to say that repetition must be accompanied with interest and zeal.

The Law of Effect. Alexander Bain is credited with having first formulated a law of effect in 1877. (Pax, 1937:117) James (1893:549) modified the view of Bain by relating the pleasure-pain principle to idea-motor action. Thorndike (1911) developed his own conclusions from the experiments done on animal intelligence.

Satisfaction and annoyance combine with the idea of the possibility of human modifiability in their relation to the law of effect. The original satisfiers and annoyers provide the source of human desires and aversions furnishing the guides for learning. Satisfaction and annoyance also lead to the development of reflexes, instincts, and capacities in humans. (Thorndike, 1914:69) These form the basis for human modifiability.

Human behavior, like animal behavior, is modifiable because bonds between a situation and a response grow stronger when accompanied by satisfaction. They weaken when accompanied by annoyance. (Thorndike, 1913b:11-12) Thorndike (ibid:4) stated the law of effect in these terms:

> When a modifiable connection between a situation and a response is made and is accompanied or followed by a satisfying state of affairs, that connection's strength is increased: when made and accompanied by an annoying state of affairs, its strength is decreased. The strengthening effect of satisfyingness (or weakening effect of annoyingness) upon the bond varies with the closeness of the connection between it and the bond.

When he published his major work on educational psychology in 1913 these three primary laws of learning were considered as being complete. He (1913b:21) said, "One form of misunderstanding these laws consists in supposing the necessity of additional factors." He also felt the law of effect was primary and irreducible to the law of exercise. The two together were considered the moving force in all learning. (1913a:192)

One of the major events in the Thorndike career was the revisions he made in his laws during the later period. He launched a series of experiments in the second decade of the twentieth century on the modification of human behavior. When he announced the results of this work, some significant revisions in the statement of the laws came forth.

Thorndike claimed at the Ninth International Congress of Psychology in 1929 that he had been wrong about the law of effect. Materials written from 1932 to 1935 indicate this revision, plus others regarding the influence of punishment upon connections.

He (1949:37) no longer considered satisfaction and annoyance as being a complete and exact parallelism. He (ibid:56 and 38) said,

> In general, punishment compares very unfavorably with reward in dependability. Unless it is a means of inducing a person to shift then and there to a right connection which is then and there rewarded, it may involve waste or worse.

> Rewards in general tend to maintain and strengthen any connection which leads to them. Punishments often but not always tend to shift from it to something else, and their educative value depends on what that something else is ...

These statements on punishment indicate quite a revision of the earlier statements made in connection with the law of effect. Thorndike interpreted his findings when he (1932:58) suggested, "The results of all comparisons by all methods tell the same story. Rewarding a connection always strengthened it substantially; punishing it weakened it little or not at all."

While doing these later experiments in human behavior, Thorndike derived a new principle which relates to the law of effect. He called it the principle of belongingness.

Belongingness. Thorndike (1949:63) asked the question, "In particular, what results in respect to the probability that A therefore will evoke B? He concluded that mere sequence and repetition would not cause A to evoke B.

These later experiments led him to believe that sequence should be accompanied by belongingness. He decided that the sense of belonging need not be "logical or essential, or inherent, or unifying." He (ibid:68) said, "Any 'this goes with that' will suffice." According to this principle, a connection is more easily learned if the response belongs to the situation, and an after-effect does better if it belongs to the connection it strengthens. The belongingness of a reward or punishment depends upon its appropriateness in satisfying an aroused motive or want in the learner, and in its logical or informative relationship to the activities rewarded or punished. (Thorndike, 1935:52-61)

Thorndike also developed secondary laws of learning which were derived from the study of animals. He (1913b:12) says they are "secondary in scope and importance only to the laws of readiness, exercise, and effect."

Secondary laws of Learning. Five secondary laws of learning are stated. They are: (1) multiple response to the same situation; (2) multiple response to varied reaction; (3) set, attitude, or adjustment, or determination; (4) the law of assimilation or analogy; and (5) the law of associative shifting. (Thorndike, 1913b:12-15)

The first law relates to the multiple responses made by animals in a pen. The law of multiple response and varied reaction relates to human learning. When a learner faces a new situation he will try one thing or another. The response which brings satisfaction or success will eliminate the other responses.

The law of set, attitude, or adjustment, or determination suggests that the total set of the learner serves as a guide for learning. Thorndike (1914:144) says, "Consequently it is a general law of learning that the change made in a man by the action of any agent depends upon the condition of the man when the agent is acting."

The law of partial or piecemeal activity states that the learner can pick out the element of a situation and base his response on it. Humans are better than other animals at eliminating features of situations which do not relate to the desired response. (ibid:145) This law explains analytical and insightful learning, according to Thorndike. (Hilgard, 1956:23)

Explanation of how man reacts to a novel situation is set forth in the law of assimilation or response by analogy. New responses can be explained in terms of past learned experiences plus man's original nature. He (ibid:148) says, "To any new situation man responds as he would to some situation like it, or like some element of it."

The law of associative shifting relates to the idea of conditioned response. Thorndike (ibid) said that a response series may change to a new stimulus by successively dropping and adding new elements to it.

Thorndike's connection model of education begins with the human organism in a situation. The primary and secondary laws of learning were developed from the principle of the organism being placed in a situation to respond originally from its satisfiers and annoyers. The satisfaction of human wants provides the basis for motivation leading to both motor and mental activity.

Learning is Connecting

Thorndike views mental functions as biological connections. When human biological wants are satisfied, biological connections are formed in the brain. He (ibid:174) says that learning is connecting, and man is a great learner, because he can make so many connections.

Connections account for the range of learning from the most concrete to the most subtle and abstract. This view of learning led to the early development by Thorndike of a connectionist description of the cognitive process.

He outlined much of <u>Principles of Teaching</u> in terms of the cognitive process. Thorndike (1917:105-164) said one learned through instinct, attention, habit, memory, correlation, reasoning, and ideation.

A few years later he described the cognitive process in somewhat different terms. Two general principles were introduced at that time. They are analysis and selection. Thorndike (1914:138) stated,

> We roughly distinguish in human learning (1) connection-forming of the common type, as when a ten month-old baby learns to beat a drum, (2) connection-forming involving ideas, as when a two-year old learns to think of his mother upon hearing a word or to say candy when he thinks of the thing, (3) analysis or abstraction, as when the student of music learns to respond to an overtone in a given sound, and (4) selective thinking or reasoning, as when a school pupil learns the meaning of a Latin sentence by using his knowledge of the rules of syntax and meanings of the word-roots.

Regardless of the level of learning the major characteristic of it is connecting. Thorndike held this view to the end of his career. As late as 1931 he (1931:120) said expectations, intentions, purposes, interests, and desires are explained by the same type mental connection system as hearing four times five and thinking twenty.

Thorndike (ibid:122) says,

> I read facts which psychologists report about adjustments, configurations, drives, integrations, purposes, tensions, and the like, and all of these facts seem to me to be reducible, so far as concerns their powers to influence the course of thought or feeling or action, to connections and readiness. Learning is connecting. The mind is man's connection-system. Purposes are as mechanical in their nature as anything else.

Mental connections in the brain provide the necessary equipment in the organism for analysis and selection of common elements in a situation.

Adult Learning

The descriptions of learning as found in the

connectionist model of Thorndike hold true for his concepts of adult learning. During the decade from 1925 to 1935, Thorndike did a great amount of research on adult learning. Most of the work was done for the Carnegie Corporation as recommended by the American Association for Adult Education.

Irving Lorge (1940:778) summarizes the thinking about the adult learning processes before the Thorndike research.

> Previous to 1925, much of the theory for adult pedagogy either was transferred from the known facts about learning established by studies of children, adolescents, or college students, or was based upon anecdotal evidence from the learning experiences of able and successful older men and women. Thorndike's <u>Adult Learning</u>, in a sense, was a pioneering effort to determine how and how much adults learn.

Thorndike compared adult with youthful learning. He also compared adults of superior and inferior intellect. His conclusion was that adults can learn. Concerning the modifiability among adults he (1928:106) said:

> On the whole, it seems reasonable to state the case concerning sheer modifiability as follows: The general tendency from all our experiments is for an inferiority of about 15 per cent as a result of 20 years from twenty-two on. Learning representing an approximation to sheer modifiability unaided by past learning shows considerably more inferiority than this. Actual learning of such things as adults commonly have to learn shows considerably less.

Later Thorndike modified this indicating that adult learning ability decreased slowly after age twenty-five at the rate of about one per cent per year. The relationship of learning ability to age is summarized by Thorndike: (ibid:124)

> In general the testimony of this group indicates (1) that almost anything is learnable at any time up to age fifty, (2) that the experience of these individuals leads them to expect more difficulty in learning from forty on than from thirty to thirty-nine, except with making and breaking food habits, (3) that the difficulty expected from thirty up to forty is no greater

E.L. Thorndike

than for childhood or adolescent years in the
case of intellectual acquisition pure and
simple, and (4) that, in general, age seems to
them to influence the power of intellectual
acquisition very much less than it influences
motor skill. There is evidence also that (5) the
difficulty expected in learning at late ages is
in part due to a sensitiveness to ridicule,
adverse comment, and undesireable attention, so
that if it were customary for mature and old
people to learn to swim and ride bicycles and
speak German, the difficulty might diminish.
(1928:124)

Intelligence loss, he (1928:158-59) found to be
slight from age between twenty-two to forty-two in
the case of strength, speed, and skill. (1928:158-59)

Intelligence. There have been two types of data used
to deal with the issue of adult intelligence, one is
cross sectional and the other is longitudinal. The
research that supported the everyday notion that
"what goes up must come down" was cross sectional in
nature. The researcher administered intelligence
tests to people of various ages at a given point in
time, and compared the performance levels of the
different age groups. The first of the cross
sectional type was administered by Thorndike and the
results of the research was reported in his volume on
Adult Learning (1928). Numerous studies of this type
were conducted following the work of Thorndike. All
led researchers to believe that intelligence
increases up to early adulthood, reaches a plateau,
and begins to decline in a regular fashion around the
fourth decade of life. (Baltes and Schaie, 1974:35)
    The first doubts about these intelligence
studies arose when the results of longitudinal
studies began to be available. In this type of study,
the researcher observes a single group of subjects
for a period of time, often extending over many
years, and examines their performance at different
ages. Longitudinal studies suggested that intelligence during maturity and old age did not decline as
soon as people had originally assumed. In contrast to
Thorndike's view that aging is equated with a decline
in intellectual capacity is the following 1971
Recommendation to the White House Conference on Aging
from the American Psychological Association Task
Force on Aging:

Many studies are now showing that the intelligence of older persons as measured is typically underestimated. For the most part, the observed decline in intellectual functioning among the aged is attributable to poor health, social isolation, economic plight, limited education, lowered motivation, or other variables not intrinsically related to the aging process. Where intelligence scores do decline, such change is associated primarily with tasks where speed of response is critical. (Eisdorfer and Lawton, 1973:1x)

Baltes and Schaie (1974:35-36) found that longitudinal test scores reflected four general, fairly independent dimensions of intelligence: (1) Crystallized intelligence which encompasses the sorts of skills one acquires through education and acculturation, such as verbal comprehension, numerical skills, and inductive reasoning; (2) Cognitive flexibility which measures the ability to shift from one way of thinking to another; (3) Visuo-motor flexibility which measures a similar, but independent skill, the one involved in shifting from familiar to unfamiliar patterns in tasks requiring coordination between visual and motor abilities; and finally, (4) Visualization which measures the ability to organize and process visual materials, and involves tasks such as finding a simple figure contained in a complex one.

There was no age-related change in cognitive flexibility. For the most important dimension, crystallized intelligence, and for visualization as well, there was a systematic increase in scores for the various age groups, right into old age. Even people over 70 improved from the first testing to the second. The only decline on the four measures was visuo-motor flexibility.

Thre results of longitudinal studies indicate little, if any, decline in intellectual abilities with age. (Botwinick, 1973; Knox, 1977)

Memory. Thorndike conducted memory experiments among adults. He (1928:160) found that adults' immediate memory ability is much better than young children's. The ability for memory over longer periods was less conclusive. He (ibid:159-165) also felt his experiments in retention among adults were to be considered inconclusive.

Recent research on short-term memory and long-

term memory, as summarized by Botwinick (1973) and
Woodruff and Birren (1975), indicates that young
people and old people do not differ in short-term
ability. However, there is apparently a decline with
age in the rate at which information can be retrieved
from short-term memory. With regard to long-term
memory, recent investigations have found that older
adults perform more poorly than young adults in this
ability.

The results of recent research also suggest that
loss of speed is one of the most important factors
affecting learning. Older adults do poorly on rapidly
paced learning tasks because of insufficient time to
respond rather than as a result of learning ability
that is impaired (Knox, 1977; Woodruff and Birren,
1975). Knox (1977) states that older adults tend to
do best when they set their own pace, and also that
they tend to reduce speed of learning and to give
greater attention to the accuracy of their response.

In summary, age differences in learning
performance can be reduced by giving older adults
more time and by slowing the pace.

Theoretical Approaches to Adult Education. Theoretical approaches to learning can be divided into two
main groups, those which can be classified as
objective theories and those which can be classified
as relational theories. The connectionism of
Thorndike falls within the objective classification. Objectivism sees the man as a passive organism
governed by stimuli which are produced by one's
environment. Based on this assumption, the
objectivists feel that man can be controlled or
manipulated by structuring his environmental
stimuli. Therefore, strict objectivism is only
interested in the observables of behavior (i.e.,
stimuli and responses). It avoids any attempted
speculation about the internal complexities of man.
(Dubin and Okun, 1973:3-19)

Some of the behaviorists (also objectivists)
criticized Thorndike, saying his language was too
subjective. On close examination, however, one finds
that Thorndike said nothing about the feelings of
learners; he concerned himself only with what the
learners did (i.e., their overt behavior). When
addressing this particular point, Hill (1979:59)
stated, "His language may sound subjective, but his
meaning is as objective as Watson's."

Goble (1971:17-18) states that:

Nearly all American behavioral scientists since 1920, and frequently much earlier have adopted their study of human behavior to the 'scientific' model. Their basic assumption was that the scientific approach, so tremendously successful in the solution of physical and technical problems could be equally successful in the solution of human problems. The behavioral scientist has believed he must study man as an object - an object to be observed but not questioned.

Subjective information, man's opinions about himself and his own feelings, desires, and wants were to be ignored.

Alonzo, LaCagnina, and Olsen (1977:137) have suggested that even though the individual objective theories might differ somewhat, there are common identifiable characteristics which are associated with and incorporated into each particular theoretical variation, be it Watson's, Thorndike's, Hull's, Dollard's, Skinner's or any of the others.

In contrast to the objectivists who choose to study only extrinsic or external and environmental determinants the relationalists believe a comprehensive theory of behavior must also include the internal or intrinsic determinants. The relationalists feel that learning theory has to be much more than just an objective science. To understand completely human behavior, they believe, the subjective must also be considered (i.e., man's feelings, desires, hopes and aspirations). "To them everyday phenomena of life such as experiences, feelings, meanings, and humor are psychologically relevant." (Milhollan and Forisha, 1970:82)

It is important to note that the relational orientation considers the whole greater than the sum of its parts. Relational psychology is extremely critical of objectivist scientists who utilize the atomistic approach attempting to isolate independent drives, urges, and instincts, and study them separately. The relationalists indicate that each individual part of man is related to the other, and unless you study them as a whole, the answers will be insufficient. Consequently they "desire a science which considers the whole person and which elevates this prerequisite over any particular concern for method". (Milhollan and Forisha 1970:97)

The relational approach rejects the objectivist's strong dependence on animal psychology. Although animal psychology can be useful in describing those learning characteristics man shares with all primates, in their view, it ignores those unique characteristics of man. Therefore, rather than studying cats, rats, pigeons, or other lower animals, the relationalists have chosen to deal with humans themselves.

Parker J. Palmer (1983:34-5), writing about adult education, has said:

> In the conventional classroom the focus of study is always outward - on nature, on history, on someone else's vision of reality. The reality inside the classroom, inside the teacher and the students, is regarded as irrelevant; it is not recognized that we are part of nature and of history, that we have visions that are of our own ... If we believed that knowing requires a personal relation between the knower and the known (as some new epistemologies tell us) our students would be invited to learn by interacting with the world, not by viewing it from afar. The classroom would be regarded as an integral, interactive part of reality, not a place apart. The distinction between "out there" and "in here" would disappear; students would discover that we are in the world and the world is within us; that truth is not a statement about reality but a living relationship between ourselves and the world. But such an epistemology is rarely conveyed by our teaching; instead, objectivism is.

Maslow (1970:150), one of the most distinguished relational scholars, determined that the goal of learning or education should be self-actualization, that is, "the full use of talents, capacities, potentialities, etc."

Rogers found from his experience in psychotherapy that when the human being is functioning freely, he is constructive and trustworthy. And it is when the human being is in closest touch with the bedrock of himself that he is functioning most freely. It is Rogers' (1969:290) contention that if a learning climate conducive to trust and openness has been successfully created, the learner will make decisions most appropriate to his particular stage of growth as a learner.

McClusky mapped out directions for the development of a "differential psychology of the adult potential" in which the concepts of margin (the power available to a person over and beyond that

114

required to handle his load), commitment, time perception, critical periods, and self concept are central. (Knowles, 1973:34-5) McClusky suggested that "the mistake of the original S-R formula has been its reductionist oversimplification of the highly complex nature of the learning process. By overemphasizing both stimulus and response as well as their external character, it has reduced, if not ignored, the unique importance of the person as the agent receiving and often originating the stimulus as well as the one giving the response. (Grabowski, 1970:80)

The andragogical model of Knowles, in <u>The Adult Learner: A Neglected Species</u>, is a process model, in contrast to the content models employed by most objectivists. Knowles (1973:45) speculates "with growing support from research (see Bruner, 1951; Erikson, 1950, 1959, 1964; Getzels and Jackson, 1962; Bower and Hollister, 1967; Iscoe and Stevenson, 1960; White, 1959) that as an individual matures, his need and capacity to be self-directing, to utilize his experience in learning, to identify his own readinesses to learn, and to organize his learning around life problems, increases steadily from infancy to pre-adolescence." Adults are seen as much more problem-centered in their orientation to learning.

While the relational approaches to learning can be applied at any level of learning, they are especially applicable to adult education. (Rogers, 1969; McClusky, 1971; Knowles, 1973)

The distinction made between these two major approaches might seem to suggest that one should (1) pick one approach over the other, (2) pick one approach for training and one for education, or (3) take the best from each approach and structure teaching around the one most successful for particular kinds of learning. (Knowles, 1973:93-101)

It is suggested here that the two basic approaches are really two expressions or modes of a singular human learning process and this is depicted in the following diagram.

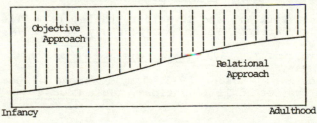

The speculation is that children predominantly work out of the mode of objectivism while having some tendency (though less than adults) to learn through relational approaches. As the child moves toward maturity, it is speculated that a shift occurs so that the adult learner works predominantly out of the mode of relationalism while retaining a tendency (though greatly diminished) to learn through the mode of objectivism. If this is true, then an integration of methods for both modes should be developed as one progresses from childhood education to adult education.

Thorndike would have great difficulty with this type of integrated thinking. For him (1931:122) all of these thoughts could be "reducible, so far as concerns their powers to influence the course of thought or feeling or action, to connections and readiness. Learning is connecting. The mind is man's connection-system." For Thorndike purposes are as mechanical in nature as anything else.

Conclusion

Indeed it may be said of Thorndike that he offered the psychological world of education the first miniature system of learning. This system, however loosely organized, has had a profound influence on the course of learning theory even until this date. His pioneering efforts rank among the greatest in the history of learning. Whatever the ultimate status of Thorndike's basic laws, his theory of learning inaugurated the rise of modern learning theory. His objective approach has generated many questions for the adult educator therefore giving rise to much research in adult learning.

Bibliography

Alonzo, Thomas M., and Giulia R. La Cagnina, and Bob G. Olsen. 1977 "Behaviorism vs. Humanism: Two contrasting Approaches to Learning Theory", The Southern Journal of Educational Research. Vol. 11, (Sum), 135-151.

Baltes, Paul B., and K. Warner Schaie, 1974 "The Myth of the Twilight Years", Psychology Today. (March), 35-40.

Botwinick, J. 1973 Aging and Behavior. New York: Springer.

Dubin, S.S. & Okun. 1973. "Implications of Learning Theories for Adult Education", Adult Education, 24 3-19.

Eisdorfer, C., and M.P. Lawton, (eds). 1973 <u>The</u>
<u>Psychology of Adult Development and Aging</u>.
Washington, D.C.: American Psychological Associat-
ion.
Goble, F.G. 1971 <u>The Third Force: The Psychology of</u>
<u>Abraham Maslow</u>. New York: Pocket Books.
Grabowski, S.M. (ed.). 1970 <u>Adult Learning and</u>
<u>Instruction</u>. Syracuse: ERIC Clearinghouse on Adult
Education.
Hilgard, Ernest R. 1956 <u>Theories of Learning</u>. New
York: Appleton-Century-Crofts, Inc.
Hill, W.F. 1979 <u>Learning: A Survey of Psychological</u>
<u>Interpretations</u>. (Rev. ed.). Scranton: Chandler
Publishing Co.
James, William. 1893 <u>Psychology</u>. New York: Henry Holt
Co.
Joncich, G.M. (ed.). 1962 Selected Writings of Edward
L. Thorndike, <u>Psychology and the Science of</u>
<u>Education</u>. New York: Teachers College Columbia
University.
Knowles, Malcolm. 1973 <u>The Adult Learner: A Neglected</u>
<u>Species</u>. Houston: Gulf Publishing Company.
Knox, Alan B. 1977 <u>Adult Development and Learning</u>.
San Francisco: Jossey-Bass.
Lorge, Irving. 1974 "Publications from 1889 to 1940
by E. Thorndike," <u>Teachers College Record</u>, XLI (May)
778-788.
Maslow, A.H. 1970 <u>Motivation and Personality</u>. New
York: Harper & Row.
Milhollan, F., and B.E. Forisha. <u>From Skinner to</u>
<u>Rogers: Contrasting Approaches to Education</u>.
Lincoln: Professional Educators Publication, Inc.,
1970.
Maclinson C (ed). 1936 <u>History of Psychology in</u>
<u>Autobiography - E.L. Thorndike</u>. Worcester Clarke,
University Press.
McClusky, H.Y. 1971 <u>Education: background and</u>
<u>issues</u>. Washington D.C., the Fourth White House
conference on aging.
Palmer, Parker J. 1983 <u>To Know as We are Known</u>. San
Francisco: Harper & Row.
Pax, W.T. 1937 <u>A Critical Study of Thorndike's Theory</u>
<u>and Laws of Learning</u>. Washington: Catholic
University of America.
Rogers, C.R. 1969 <u>Freedom of Learn</u>. Columbus, Ohio:
Charles E. Merrill Publishing Co.
Thorndike, E.L. 1901 <u>The Human Nature Club</u>. New York:
The Chautauqua Press.
Thorndike, E.L. 1909 "Darwin's Contributions to
Psychology," <u>University of California, Chronicle</u>,
XII.

Thorndike, E.L. 1911 Animal Intelligence. New York: Macmillan & Co.

Thorndike, E.L. 1913(a) Educational Psychology, Vol. I: The Original Nature of Man. New York: Columbia University.

Thorndike, E.L. 1913(b) Educational Psychology, Vol. II: The Pscyhology of Learning. New York: Columbia University.

Thorndike, E.L. 1914 Educational Psychology, Vol. III: Mental Work and Fatigue and Individual Differences and Their Causes. New York: Columbia University.

Thorndike, E.L. 1914 Educational Psychology, A Briefer Course. New York: Columbia University.

Thorndike, E.L. 1917 The Principles of Teaching based on Psychology. New York: A.G. Seiler.

Thorndike, E.L. 1920 Education, A First Book. New York, Macmillan & Cox.

Thorndike, E.L. 1928 Adult Learning. New York: Macmillan & Co.

Thorndike, E.L. 1929 Elementary Principles of Education. New York: Macmillan Co.

Thorndike, E.L. 1931 Human Learning. New York: Century Co.

Thorndike, E.L. 1932 Fundamentals of Learning. New York: Columbia University Press.

Thorndike, E.L. 1935 The Psychology of Wants, Interests and Attitudes. New York: Appleton-Century-Crofts

Thorndike, E.L. 1949 Selected Writings from a Connectionist's Psychology. New York: Appleton-Century-Crofts, Inc.

Woodruff, D.S. and J.E. Birren, (eds.) 1975 Aging: Scientific Perspectives and Social Issues. New York: D. Van Nostrand.

Chapter Seven

EDUARD LINDEMAN

Stephen Brookfield

At the occasion of a testimonial dinner for Eduard
Lindeman in 1953, the last year of his life, a letter
of tribute from the American Civil Liberties Union
declared that "a catalogue of Dr Lindeman's
activities during his first seventy years might lead
a careless visitor from Mars to believe that he was
not a man but a syndicate". On the same occasion a
letter on behalf of the Adult Education Association
of the United States written by Malcolm Knowles, then
the Association's administrative coordinator,
addressed the Association's tribute to Lindeman with
the words "you have been the one 'elder statesman' in
the field to whom the younger organizers of the new
Adult Education Association have consistently and
confidently turned for inspiration, moral support,
and wise guidance". Letters of tribute for this
dinner were also received from organizations as
diverse as the American Labor Education Service, the
International Ladies' Garment Workers' Union, the
League for Industrial Democracy, the Society for
Ethical Culture, the Planned Parenthood Federation
of America, the Association on American Indian
Affairs, the National Child Labor Education
Committee, and the Women's Trade Union League.

The breadth of interests represented in these
tributes, and the fact that Lindeman never held an
academic appointment as a professor or lecturer in
adult education, make it all the more surprising that
he should still be regarded as the major philosopher
of adult education in the United States. He wrote,
after all, only one major work on the field, The
Meaning of Adult Education (Lindeman, 1926a) and that
in the early stages of his career. Yet though his
writings on adult education (scattered through these
may be and representing only a fraction of his total
work), and through his active involvement in adult

education committees, associations and programmes, he both articulated and implemented a vision of adult education which still constitutes the conceptual underpinnings of the field of theory and practice in the United States. This can be interpreted both as a testament to the accuracy and power of his vision and as a depressing verdict on the paucity of philosophical analysis which has characterized the American field since his death.

Life

Eduard Christian Lindeman was born in St. Clair, Michigan, on 9th May, 1885, one of ten children of Danish immigrant parents. Orphaned at an early age he worked in a series of laboring jobs in agriculture, shipbuilding, and construction attending formal schooling only intermittently. At age twenty-two, however, he managed to gain admittance to a special program for "sub-freshmen" at Michigan Agricultural College, later Michigan State University, in East Lansing. Biographers such as Gessner (1956), Konopka (1958) and Rielly (1984) all agree that on his entry to college Lindeman was, if not illiterate, at least well below the average in terms of reading and writing abilities. With the help of a sympathetic college secretary, and a series of jobs on the college farm, however, Lindeman persevered with his studies to the extent that while an undergraduate he authored essays, poetry, editorials for the college newspaper and a four act play. While at the college he met and married (in 1912) Hazel Taft, the daughter of the Chair of the Horticultural Department at the college.

For nine years after his graduation, from 1911 to 1920, Lindeman was employed in a series of different jobs. For a time he was editor of a Michigan agricultural journal, The Gleaner, in which some of his earliest published writings are contained. He was assistant to the minister of the Plymouth Congregational Church in East Lansing, 4-H Club extension director based at Michigan Agricultural College, and instructor at the YMCA George Williams College in Chicago. In 1920, however, he obtained his first university teaching post (at the North Carolina College for Women) and he was to stay in university life, apart from the interruption caused by World War Two, until his retirement. Moreover, he was to serve nearly all his time as a professor at only one institution, the New York School of Social Work (later the Columbia University

School of Social Work) which he joined as professor of Social Philosophy in 1924.

It was soon after joining the New York School of Social Work that in 1926 he published his major work on adult education (actually his fourth book) titled The Meaning of Adult Education. According to Rielly's (1984) biographical sketch, in the twenty-four years between the The Meaning of Adult Education and his retirement in 1950, Lindeman published approximately 204 articles (of an average length of three to four pages), 107 book reviews, five books, sixteen monographs, and seventeen chapters in other works. He edited four books, shared joint authorship of another, and gave at least 44 talks of which some written record remains. He was a close friend and advisor of Leonard and Dorothy Elmhirst during their establishing of Dartington Hall in Totnes, the progressive experimental school; in fact the Elmhirst's held the mortgage on the Lindeman's home in New Jersey where the family lived until 1942.

Rielly (1984) records that Lindeman served on the National Child Labor Commission, was Education Director of the Workers' Education Bureau (of America) from 1926 to 1937, and editor of the journal Workers' Education. He was both a lecturer and trustee at the New School for Social Research in New York City, and held visiting professorships at Temple University (1934-1935), the University of California (1936 and 1938), Stanford University (1941), Columbia University (1941-1942), the University of Wisconsin (1943) and the University of Delhi, India (1949-1950). He was advisory editor to Mentor books (a series he conceived), educational advisor to the British Army of Occupation in Germany (1946), and Chair of the American Civil Liberties Union Commission on Academic Freedom (1949). After retirement from the New York School of Social Work in 1950, he undertook numerous speaking engagements in locations as far afield as Texas and Oregon, gave occasional lectures at the New School for Social Research (New York), formed a consultancy group, and served as President of the National Conference of Social Work. He died in New York City on 13th April, 1953, after an illness.

The breadth of his activities, both intellectual and organizational, mean that nowhere in his writings after the early statement in The Meaning of Adult Education, did Lindeman undertake a sustained elaboration of his ideas on adult education as a field of theory and practice. Indeed, many of his ideas concerning the field are to be found in

writings on apparently tangential issues, such as his
voluminous pronouncements on the workings of
democracy, his work for the birth control
organization Planned Parenthoood, and his analyses
of the pernicious and insidious influence of
propaganda in American life. Nonetheless, it is
possible to discern four recurring preoccupations
which engaged his attention as an adult educator
throughout his life; his attempt to articulate a
clear conceptualization of adult education, his
elaboration of appropriate curricula for adult
learning groups arising out of this conceptualization, his concern to develop methods of group
learning which he saw as fundamental to adult
education as properly conceived and practised, and
his belief that adult education was a force for
constructive social action. In addition he made some
telling comments on two important sub-themes in his
work; the influence of the capitalist system on
education, and the need to reconceptualize the whole
educational system in terms of a lifelong learning
enterprize. It is to these themes and preoccupations
that we now turn.

Conceptualization of Adult Education
In a recent essay on The Meaning of Adult Education,
Stewart (1984:1) identified as a major omission from
the book, a succinct definition of the concept of
adult education. The book identifies central
principles which are argued as endemic to adult
education, but does not articulate a crisp and clear
definition. This is surprising since in a paper
published the year previously entitled "What is Adult
Education?", Lindeman describes adult education as:

> a co-operative venture in non-authoritarian,
> informal learning the chief purpose of which is
> to discover the meaning of experience; a quest
> of the mind which digs down to the roots of the
> preconceptions which formulate our conduct; a
> technique of learning for adults which makes
> education coterminous with life, and hence
> elevates living itself to the level of an
> experiment (Lindeman, 1925:3)

In this paper he warned against the dangers of
faddism and linguistic debauchery which he felt were
confounding attempts to define adult education, and a
discussion of workers' education and public
libraries published in the next year (Lindeman,

1926b) afforded him the opportunity to differentiate adult education from other forms of education. Adult education was held to emphasize the primacy of personal experience, it had as its aim the interpersonal exchange and exploration of such experience, and it relied on discussion methods for this pursuit. The leader of the adult learning group was to be thought of as guide and stimulator, rather than as lawgiver - an early statement of a conceptualization of the educator's role which is now known as that of facilitator. This theme of adult education as the collaborative exploration and interpretation of experience was repeated in his writings and gave rise to the methodological imperative that "adult education must be confined to small groups and that lectures and mass teaching are automatically eliminated" (Lindeman, 1926a: 11). To Lindeman the current interest in adult education using distance teaching methods and educational broadcasting (as in the Open University in the United Kingdom), or through individual computer usage, would have been not only inexplicable, but a contradiction in terms. These activities would have been scorned as mass instruction or programmed instruction, rather than the collaborative articulation and interpretation of experience claimed by him as the quintessential adult educational activity.

In a later digression on conceptualizing adult education. Lindeman (1938) identified two opposing paradigms of thought within American adult education concerning what educators felt to be the proper realm of practice. The first of these, what he called the mechanistic school, viewed adult education as the extension of existing forms of education to the illiterate and underprivileged. To Lindeman this approach was naive, instrumental and essentially static. He contrasted it with what was called an organic conception of adult education. In the organic conception adult education was not seen as an extension of existing privilege to a new population, but rather as "a right, a normal expectancy" (1938:3). The idea that adult educators were bountiful philanthropists, bestowing their intellectual gifts on a disadvantaged but eternally grateful population, was repugnant and arrogant.

The single, best known statement of his ideas on the nature of adult education is contained in the four principles argued as endemic to the field in <u>The Meaning of Adult Education</u> (1926a). Education was, first and foremost, conceived as a lifelong process,

and to regard it as preparation for an unknown future
was to condemn teachers and students to intellectual
stasis. Secondly, adult education was held to be
unreservedly of a non-vocational character. He wrote
that "adult education more accurately defined begins
where vocational education leaves off" (5) and
condemned the fact that "the possibilities of
enriching the activities of labor itself grow less
for all workers who manipulate automatic machines"
(ibid.). In his view, for workers to experience "the
good life, the life interfused with meaning and with
joy ... opportunities for expressing more of the
total personality than is called forth by machines
will be needed" (ibid.). It was the task of adult
education to assist these workers to find meaning and
creative fulfillment in the areas of their lives
separate from the factory and to counter the
development of fractional personalities seen as the
inevitable consequence of a highly specialized
division of labor. This defiant rejection of adult
education having any involvement with vocational
training was characteristic of all his writings.
Indeed, in one of the last pieces he published he
reaffirmed his conviction that adult education "is
wholly lacking in coercive or compulsive elements"
and that it is "an act of free will" (1953:18). Such
unequivocal declarations concerning the centrality
of voluntary learner participation in adult
education have provided valuable sustenance for
current opponents of mandatory continuing education
in the United States (Rockhill, 1983).

The third principle of adult education - that we
emphasize situations, not subjects, in our teaching -
calls to mind the progressive educators' epithet that
'we teach children, not subjects'. Lindeman was a
personal friend and occasional intellectual
collaborator of John Dewey, and the emphasis on
situations not subjects evidently owes something to
Dewey's influence. Lindeman wrote that adult
education began at the point at which adults found
themselves needing to adjust to new situations, and
in this stress on the educational potential inherent
in adults' attempting to make sense of, and come to
terms with, changed realities at work, in the family
or in society at large, there are echoes of the ideas
of later theorists of adult learning. The idea pre-
dates Havighurst's (1952) notion of the developmental tasks of adulthood and the teachable moment
represented by adults having to adjust to changed
work, familial, social and economic conditions at
different periods in their lives. Knox's (1977) more

recent elaboration of change events as triggers for significant adult learning is also anticipated in this third principle of adult education as elaborated by Lindeman.

Finally, adult education was held to place primary emphasis on learners' experiences. In a passage evoking the ideas of educational praxis explored by Rogers (1961) and Freire (1970) among others, Lindeman asserted that "all genuine education will keep doing and thinking together" and that "experience is the adult learner's living textbook" (1926a:7). The importance of grounding curricula and methods in the experiences of adults is now something of a self-evident truism in adult education, enshrined as it is in the concept of andragogy (Knowles, 1984) and in Kolb's (1984) experiential theory of adult development. What remains distinctive about this, however, is Lindeman's constant attention to the connection between individual realization through experience, and the need for adults to be involved in social change movements. To him, a major learning need in adulthood was "to change the social order so that vital personalities will be creating a new environment in which their aspirations may be properly expressed" (1926a:9).

One aspect of Lindeman's conceptualization of adult education which has largely been ignored by commentators to date is the manner in which he outlined the beginnings of what is now called (in the work of later writers) a critical theory of adult education. In one of his earliest pieces he offered a critique of institutional education which pre-dates Freire's work on banking education (1970) by some forty years. Lindeman condemned the "merely additive process" of school education whereby the teacher "gets from his students what he has already imparted out of his academic repository" (1925:2). Adult education was the antithesis of this additive process representing as it did "a new technique for learning ... a process by which the adult learns to become aware of and to evaluate his experience" (1925:3). The adult learner was not viewed as "merely engaged in the pursuit of new knowledge; he is, in short, changing his habits, learning to live on behalf of new motivations" (1937:6).

In these passages adult education is charged with assisting adults to understand and interpret their experiences and to make explicit the preconceptions underlying their conduct. This idea has similarities to Freire's (1970) notion of dialogic education as the antithesis of the additive style, banking system. There is also a philosophical congruence (though not necessarily a direct causal link) between these ideas of Lindeman and Mezirow's (1981) critical theory of adult learning and education. To Mezirow a central task of adult education is that of "bringing psychocultural assumptions into critical consciousness to help a person understand how he or she has come into possession of conceptual categories, rules, tactics and criteria for judging implicit in habits of perception, thought and behavior" (1981:20).

Another point of similarity between Lindeman and Freire is the emphasis both placed on the futurist aspect of adult education. In <u>Pedagogy of the Oppressed</u> (1970) Freire constantly affirms the "revolutionary futurity" (p.72) of education, writing that "problem-posing theory and practice take man's historicity as their starting point" (p.71). A similar emphasis is evident in a paper Lindeman wrote toward the end of World War Two in which he declared that "adult education is always futuristic" (1944:116) and "a daring challenge to life that is to come" (ibid.). Adult educators were described as "heralds of the future" (1944:117), rather than as commentators on history, and the starting point for any analysis of the educational needs of adults was "not history but rather the contemporary situation" (1944:116). In adult learning groups members would analyse how present circumstances resulted from historical antecedents, would realize the culturally constructed nature of individual lives, and would thereby be encouraged to re-shape the future according to their own wishes and visions.

The final aspect of Lindeman's conceptualization of adult education to be discussed is, in many ways, the most unwarrantably neglected. The term 'andragogy' is probably the most common of adult educator's shibboleths. As a term summarizing a number of central beliefs concerning the unique character of adult learning and the implications for practice which flow from these, it is undeniably the most important concept in the field to many practitioners. Introduction of the term into adult education is generally credited to Malcolm Knowles who, in correspondence with Merriam-Webster dictionaries (Knowles, 1980: 253-254) could find no previous use of the term in the English language. Until recently (Brookfield, 1984) Lindeman's treatment of this concept sixty years ago has remained undetected.

In the 1920s Lindeman, together with Martha Anderson, undertook an interpretative translation of various articles describing the folk high school system in Germany. Under the title Education Through Experience (Anderson and Lindeman, 1927) the authors described the activities of the Academy of Labour in Frankfurt-am-Main. Early in their report is a section headed "Andragogy" in which Anderson and Lindeman declare that "Andragogy is the true method of adult learning" and that "life itself is the adult's school" (1927:2-3). Adult experience is located within the realm of action, so that "between the child and the adult lies the field of action. The adult enters history and becomes a link in the chain of guilt, entanglement, want and pain". In this same section the process of adult learning is described as "an effort toward self-mastery" (1927:3) and the realization of adulthood is signalled by a developing awareness of self and a readiness to make existential choices. Endemic to this process is the adult coming into conflict with previously untested conceptions and exploring oppositional viewpoints. In the emphasis on opposition, conflict and critical discussion as central to andragogy Lindeman formulates the concept in a way quite different to Knowles's later work. The language used by Lindeman in the description of adults entering history and becoming a link in a chain of guilt, entanglement, want and pain is imbued with a form of existential angst very different to Knowles's practice injunctions. For the student of Lindeman's work the lack of any further attention he granted to a concept which was to exercise such an influence on the minds of adult education theorists and practitioners in the 1970s and 1980s is one of the most frustrating aspects of his intellectual activities. We can only speculate on how he would have regarded Mezirow's (1981) charter for andragogy, emphasizing as it does the development in adults of habits of critical reflection, and the fostering of the willingness to change uncongenial aspects of their worlds.

Methods of Adult Education

Throughout Lindeman's writings on adult education there is a constant preoccupation with method, deriving partly, perhaps, from his own pragmatic orientation to changing the world rather than merely analyzing it. The stress on the discussion method as the educational method derived from, and uniquely

suited to, the effective facilitation of adult
learning was a theme he emphasised until the end of
his life. Not for him an acknowledgement of the
virtue of flexibility and eclecticism in choosing
appropriate methods; computer assisted instruction,
educational broadcasting and lectures would all have
been condemned as inherently anti-adult educational.
Although the stress on the importance of
discussion method was evident throughout his work, it
can be seen at its strongest in The Meaning of Adult
Education (1926a). He advised adult educators to
ignore questions of curriculum development and "to
devote their major concern to method and not to
content" (1926a:114). Such an oppositional dualism
of content and method would be rejected by analytic
philosophers of adult education such as Paterson
(1979) and Lawson (1979), both of whom argue that an
activity can only be considered educational if the
curriculum comprises knowledge deemed intrinsically
worthwhile. They would agree with Lindeman, however,
that educational activities must also be
characterized by morally acceptable pedagogic
procedures. The separation of content and method is
also criticized by Freire (1970) who regards a
collaborative analysis of individual and collective
experience to be essential to problem-posing
education and to the bringing of assumptions into
critical consciousness. Central to conscientization
is the nurturing of an awareness of power
discrepancies within society.
    The distinctive purpose of adult educational
method, according to Lindeman, was the inculcation in
learners of a set of analytical skills which could be
applied to understanding a range of different
situations. He wrote that "education is a method for
giving situations a setting, for analyzing complex
wholes into manageable, understandable parts"
(1926a:115). This idea of adults' developing a set of
analytical procedures applicable to a variety of
settings is, perhaps, a conceptual precursor of the
notion of mathematics, of learning how to learn, as
developed in adult education by R.M. Smith (1982). To
Smith the chief purpose of adult education is to help
learners to understand their idiosyncratic learning
styles and to develop skills of inquiry, analysis and
synthesis which can be adapted to different
intellectual pursuits.
    The medium through which these replicable,
analytic skills would be developed among adults was
the discussion group. Lindeman wrote enthusiastical-
ly of the use of discussion groups within the Danish

Folk High School and the Workers' Education Association, and he argued his case for the appropriateness of this method for adult learners in the following way:

> Small groups of aspiring adults who desire to keep their minds fresh and vigorous; who begin to learn by confronting pertinent situations; who dig down into the reservoirs of their experience before resorting to texts and secondary facts; who are led in the discussion by teachers who are also seekers after wisdom and not oracles: this constitutes the setting for adult education, the modern quest for life's meaning (1926a:7)

This theme of adult learning groups comprising small numbers of individuals involved in articulating, reflecting upon and analyzing their experience (and not relying on textbooks and secondary facts) has, if anything, even greater relevance in the 1980s than the 1920s. In the growth of the women's movement, and in a range of other consciousness-raising groups, we can see a direct realization of his ideas. The stress on teachers and learners using their experiences as educational material, rather than being constrained by pre-defined curricula, is at the heart of the encounter group movement and can be seen in the recognition by many colleges and universities of prior, experiential learning as being as meritorious and valid as institutionally sponsored learning. The most definitive statement regarding the inherent suitability of discussion to adult education was contained in his entry to the Encyclopedia of Social Sciences (1930) in which he declared that "if there is anything distinctive about method in adult education, it is derived from the growing use of discussion" and that "the discussion method has come to be the accepted learning process for large numbers of adult classes" (1930:465). At the end of World War Two he proposed the widespread use of discussion groups as a force for societal rejuvenation. In a paper (somewhat grandiosely) titled World Peace Through Adult Education (1945b) he wrote that "if we genuinely want understanding and a good peace, we must quickly bring into existence an adult education movement which springs from the 'grass roots' of American life" (1945b:23). This movement would be based on neighborhood discussion groups since such groups were held to be "essential for democratic life" and "the finest available medium for dealing with controversial issues" (ibid.). Such groups would combat propaganda, develop flexible modes of thought, and encourage the emergence of 'natural' leadership qualities in its members as a challenge to 'artificial' and 'arbitrary' leadership so characteristic of modern society.

In stressing the importance of discussion method Lindeman is reflecting the central importance accorded to this medium by adult educators throughout the world. In North American adult education it is the Junto groups, the Lyceums, the Farm Forum, and living room learning initiatives such as the Great Books program in the 1950s that come closest to constituting a distinctive adult education tradition. The Danish Folk High School relied on the use of discussion, and the culture circles used by Freire (1970) are a form of learning group as conceived by Lindeman. In Britain, Paterson (1970) has commented that advocacy of the discussion method is one of the chief articles in the catechism of liberal adult education, and it has certainly been the focus of the tutorial group movement in the extra-mural movement in that country. It is also, as Elsdon (1975) notes, the major training method used to prepare adult educators for their professional duties.

A Curriculum for Adult Education

In the previous section it was pointed out that Lindeman, in his early writings, was somewhat disparaging about what he saw as an unhealthy preoccupation of adult educators with questions of curriculum. On the whole, it is this element in his writings which has been emphasized by latter day interpreters such as Knowles (1980) whose andragogical tenets imply that questions of appropriate curricula are to be decided by learners' wishes and interests. In The Meaning of Adult Education (1926a), Lindeman expressed a disapproving surprise that "schoolmen now find their center of interest in curriculum-making" (p.11), an activity he regarded as "the process of transforming the school into a department-store bargain counter" (ibid.). To him the preoccupation with curriculum development sprung from the unfortunate centrality of subject teaching in American schools, a practice he attacked as "compatible with a shallow and perverted pragmatism and profitable to an industrial order which requires technicians, not educated men and women" (1926a:15). This repugnance for developing curricula grounded in, and suited to, the unique concerns of adulthood has, in general, typified the writings of adult educators since that time. Studies of participation, program development manuals and descriptive surveys of practice predominate within the literature of the field. Those seeking to maintain the a-curricular nature of adult education provision (saying, in effect, that it is up to educators to give learners what they say they want), frequently quote Lindeman in their defense. This is because his articulation of such a view is contained in his best known and most widely circulated work, The Meaning of Adult Education (1926a). As will be seen presently, his reversal of position on this to the extent that in the 1940s he was making very specific curriculum suggestions for adult education classes, is one of the most neglected aspects of his work.

One curricular mission which was emphasized in The Meaning of Adult Education, however, was his idea that adult educators should work toward making all forms of artistic endeavor more democratic in their creation and dissemination. His comments in the book on what he regarded as the sterility of highbrow culture are scornful and contemptuous. He condemned the kind of artistic snobbery which led many poorly educated people to believe that artistic appreciation "remains the inherited prerogative of a coterie of so-called cultured people" (1926a:66) and he was highly critical of universities trying to indoctrinate students with preconceived notions of correct criteria for judging 'good' music, painting or literature. We can only speculate on how his early exclusion from formal education was partly responsible for this attitude of contempt toward the cultural values and standards perpetuated in formal educational institutions.

Lindeman urged adult educators to reject formal ideas concerning what comprised 'worthwhile' art and he wrote that such a rejection would "aid greatly in the much-needed procedure of transforming a growing artistic snobbery into an indigenous folk-expression ... In short, adult education may justly be expected to do something toward democratizing art" (ibid.). Adult educators, in his view, were champions of popular culture and populist art forms. They were urged to oppose vigorously the academic sterility regarding the enjoyment of 'good' art, and thereby to give American art a new impetus. Central to this opposition was to be a rejection of criteria of good

Eduard Lindeman

taste and standards of excellence derived from
European cultural circles. Much as the Welsh and
Scots are wary of the cultural imperialism of the
English, or the Canadians of the United States,
Americans were urged to be wary of contributing to
the maintenance of a European cultural hegemony. Only
if ideas of discrimination and artistic appreciation
derived from European art were abandoned could the
United States develop an indigenous artistic
culture, grounded in, judged by, and reflective of
the American experience.

One aspect of tying adult education to the
emergence of an indigenous form of American folk art
was the need for adult educators to "teach people how
to make their thinking glow with the warmth of honest
feeling" (1926a:67). One result of too great a
respect for European cultural forms and artefacts was
a marked unreadiness to express honestly and
spontaneously feelings of warmth or approval toward
works of art, lest these be considered too lowbrow.
Americans had gained the habit of repressing their
instinctive reactions to art forms until they were
sure that these forms were culturally sound according
to the dictates of high culture. One task of adult
education was to "aid in delivering us from that
abject fear of expressing our quick and enthusiastic
enjoyments - the fear to which we have become
habituated under the discipline of professional
criticism" (1926a:70). Life itself could be
considered a work of art with its creative
constituents being the adding of a new dimension to
one's experience. His advocacy of a fusion of art and
life was expressed as follows:

> A well-organized and adequately expressed life
> deserves to be called beautiful no less than a
> well-conceived statue. Aesthetics suffers by
> reason of its artificial isolation, its
> exclusiveness. Beauty is not discovered solely
> by contemplation of beautiful objects; beauty
> is experiencing (1926a:55)

It was not until World War Two, nearly twenty years
after the publication of The Meaning of Adult
Education, that Lindeman's ideas on suitable
curricula for adult education classes were more fully
developed. At the end of the war he wrote several
pieces in which he proposed a curricular agenda for
the neighborhood discussion groups that he felt so
strongly were vital to the maintenance of democratic
societies in the post-war years. In "New Needs for

Adult Education" (1944) he stated that adult
education should be seen as a mode of social
adaptation which would assist adults "to learn how to
make important choices reflecting the issues they are
obliged to confront" (p.115). The liberal arts were
felt to be in need of a severe and critical review,
and much greater attention had to be paid to
education within labor unions, one of the most vital
and significant settings for adult learning. The
central curricular question which had to be discussed
concerned the form of economic arrangement which
Americans believed was best suited to a democratic
society. He suggested that a network of discussion
groups consider the merits of the free enterprise
system, socialistic ownership of the means of
production, and a form of mixed economy. Implicit in
his criticism of the kinds of discussions in which
people were forced to choose between free enterprise
capitalism and socialism, is his own preference for a
mixed economy in which the benefits of
individualistic enterprise were seen as married to an
expanded welfare state. He argued that adult
education and higher education were charged with
fostering a more pluralistic and tolerant conception
of economic affairs than had been the case up to that
time.

A further elaboration of his curricular ideas
was contained in a piece on the sociology of adult
education (Lindeman, 1945a). In addition to the need
to discuss the form of economic arrangement suitable
to democratic societies, he identified three
additional issues - "what is to be done about our
deep-seated habits of racial discrimination, how we
are to democratize our vast educational equipment,
how we are to play an appropriate role in world
affairs" (1945a:12). Discussion of these topics
would "furnish adult education with its program and
its mission" (1945a:13). If living room learning
groups across the country of ten to twenty Americans
were talking freely about these issues under the
guidance of a skilled leader, then "there would be no
cause to fear for the future of democracy" (ibid.).
Such an avowedly political curriculum for adult
education classes is very different to that currently
pertaining in American adult education where concern
for personal fitness, economic wellbeing and
recreational diversion is paramount, in non-credit
adult education at least. Debate on questions such as
the merits of free enterprise capitalism, socialism
and the mixed economy, or on how best to combat
racism, are rare indeed in public adult and

continuing education. The question of how best to democratize education is rarely raised in an era when public provision is being severely cut and attention is being refocused on the "back to basics" movement for the rote learning of literacy and mathematical skills.

Finally, the discussion of foreign policy and the role of the United States in world affairs, can hardly be said to be a central curricula concern of adult and continuing education programs. Initiatives along the lines of those envisaged by Lindeman, such as the recent experiment in developing a study circle movement in New York state to discuss questions of public policy (Osborne, 1981) are the exception rather than the rule.

Adult Education and Social Action

Throughout his writings, the social nature and purpose of adult education was a constant theme. In The Meaning of Adult Education (1926a) he urged that education orient itself as much to the social reality in which an adult lived, as much as to the individual person. Individuals were seen as caught inextricably within social milieu and forced to live collectively, so that "collectivism is the road to power, the predominant reality of modern life" (1926a:43). Adult education served as a catalyst to collective enterprise by revealing the nature of the social process, by replacing destructively warring interests with creative conflict, and by "making the collective life an educational experience" (ibid.). Distortions of reality could only result from viewing individual conduct as somehow separate from social behaviour. Moreover, such a view encouraged and justified a selfish pursuit of individual desires without regard to broader social concerns.

The replacing of warring interests by creative conflict was seen as most necessary in the arena of industrial relations. Through adult education workers and managers would become aware of the socially created nature of individual conduct and would cease to be as secretive and combative as was customary. Concealment and conflict would be replaced by open democracy - "the assumption that what we want is worth wanting, possesses sufficient integrity to stand comparison and is capable of making its way on merits and not through coercion" (1926a:102). Lindeman was scathing on the effects that unbridled capitalism would have on social relations and regarded nationalism and imperialism as "merely outward manifestations of this 'pseudo-power' which degrades us all" (1926a:26). He viewed "the pervading economic structure of our civilization" as being based on "a doubtful competitive ethic and avowedly designed to benefit the crafty, the strong and the truculent ... warfare is the rule of the game" (ibid.). Taken along with his comments on the debilitating dualism inherent in capitalism - "that my advantage must mean your disability; that efficacy for me can exist only through your disqualification" (1926a:28) - his condemnation of capitalism stands as the most vigorous statement on this theme by a mainstream American adult educator.

Of greatest concern to Lindeman was the insidious infusion of capitalist ethics into the educational system. He wrote:

> We may, for example, so far exaggerate the incentives and motives which are derived from capitalism and profit production as to cause the entire educational system to become a direct response to this system and to lead to its further emphasis ... If this system, both on its economic and educational sides, becomes too rigid and too oppressive and incapable of sincere self-criticism, nothing short of violent revolution will suffice to change its direction' (1926a:49)

This apocalyptic vision was speculation not prediction. It was based on an assessment of what might happen within American society if certain perceptible trends became ossified into institutional forms. Revolutions were, in fact, fundamentally anti-educational, signalling that the society concerned had suffered a collective loss of faith in the power of learning and the use of intelligence. In puzzling contrast to the force of this critique, however, were his ideas on industrial reform. He hoped for "a revolution of the mind" (1926a:27) which would develop "cleaner motives, sharper intellectual insights and finer wills" (ibid.) among workers. His belief was that through workers' education (the most vital sector of the adult education movement) workers would come to displace force by intelligence and thereby discover "better motives" (ibid.) for production. Trade unions would be turned into creating rather than fighting organizations.

As is evident from these comments, Lindeman stopped short of advocating a fundamental

135

restructuring of society in his prescriptions for reform. The worker-employer divide remained intact with reform occurring within the free enterprise, capitalist framework. Production was seen as becoming more participatory and collaborative, so that managers' "power over" workers was transposed into "power with" them. The contrast between the full-blooded critique of capitalism and the muted timidity of the reforms suggested above (a revolution in workers' minds to find finer meanings in, and better motives for, production) is puzzling. As Rockhill (1985:192) points out, however, the fusion of ideals of political democracy with free enterprise production is so strong in American culture, that socialist or even social democratic proposals for industrial reform are likely to be instantly condemned as examples of totalitarian communism. For making comments as mild as the above, Lindeman was publicly condemned at different times as an atheist and subversive communist.

In The Meaning of Adult Education (1926a:105) the following summation of the social role of adult education is given; "adult education will become an agency of progress if its short-term goal of self-improvement can be made compatible with a long-term, experimental but resolute policy of changing the social order". The form of this experimental policy was discussed in a number of works in the 1930s and 1940s, in which Lindeman wrote on the irreducibly social nature of adult education. He declared that "adult education is learning associated with social purposes" (1937:6) and that "the complete objective of adult education is to synchronize the democratic and the learning processes" (ibid.). The goals of adult education were "social in nature" (1938:5) and the distinctive feature of adult education was "the fact that its purpose is definitely social" (1945a:9).

This purpose was increasingly interpreted in an unequivocally political manner. Adult education was "the operating alternative for dominance, dictatorship, and violence" (1937:6) of the sort afflicting fascist dictatorships in Italy, Spain and Germany. He perceived democracy as under threat from forces of dictatorship and demagoguery and wrote that "adult education is the answer to blind prejudice and demagoguery" (1944:115). In commenting on the outbreak of World War Two he wrote that widespread political illiteracy among the peoples of western nations had made them susceptible to the diversionary strategems of skilled politicians. To combat this danger a nation's citizens must be politically sophisticated and used to participating in democratic groups. Since adult learning groups were of this nature they were a crucial training ground for democratic participation. For these reasons "the only reliable instrument for establishing confidence among nations is adult education" (1945b:23); hence, adult education was "integral to the democratic struggle" (1945a:10). A network of neighborhood discussion groups exploring issues such as those identified in the previous section, and characterized by shared authority and democratic collaboration, would be the most effective hedge a society could evolve against the danger of creeping totalitarianism.

In this repeated emphasis on adult education as a force to counter the threats of demagoguery and totalitarian dictatorship, Lindeman anticipates some of Freire's ideas. In his description of how education might combat the process of massification in Brazilian society, Freire wrote that "a critical education which could help to form critical attitudes" (Freire, 1973:32) would assist people to resist the diversions and myths peddled by the mass media. Only through participation in democratic learning groups (within unions, councils, associations, churches, schools and community groups) would people assimilate democratic habits. Freire wrote of the Brazilian people that "they could be helped to learn democracy through the exercise of democracy: for that knowledge, above all others, can only be assimilated experientially" (1973:36).

Almost three decades prior to these comments, Lindeman had declared that the participation of citizens in informed social action was the hallmark of a democratic society. Social action was, after all, essentially a forceful activity, hence it was important that the application of force and coercion occur only after the application of reason and intelligence. To make sure that social action was authentically democratic, it must be preceded by adult education. This meant that "adult education thus turns out to be the most reliable instrument for social actionists" (1945a:11). In his most unequivocal mood Lindeman wrote on the irreducible connection between social action and adult education as follows: "every social action group should at the same time be an adult education group, and I go even so far as to believe that all successful adult education groups sooner or later become social action groups" (1945a:12).

137

Summary
In recent years there has been something of a revival
of interest in Lindeman's ideas. A Delphi study among
professors of adult education in American
universities (Ilsley, 1982) found that <u>The Meaning of
Adult Education</u> (1926a) was chosen as the most
important book in the field, along with Malcolm
Knowles's (1980) program development manual. Despite
its being out of print for several years the book
commands a revered status in the minds of adult
education professors. Brookfield (1983) has examined
it as a visionary charter for contemporary adult
education and Stewart (1983:97) describes it as "the
best and most cogent synthesis of adult education as
a living activity that has been written to date". In
a re-review of the book Stewart points out that it is
"virtually the only volume written in the generative
period of adult education in the 1920s that is still
read by Americans today" (1984:1) and that "the
nation's entire structure of adult education
practice has largely been built upon Eduard
Lindeman's 1926 philosophical base" (ibid.).
Although Hesburgh <u>et al</u> (1978:38) point out that
American continuing education has developed in a
manner contrary to Lindeman's strictures concerning
the need for it to remain non-vocational, Jarvis
(1984:59) regards this claim as somewhat naive when
Lindeman's ideas are considered in their cultural and
historical context. Rockhill (1985:203-207) has also
re-examined Lindeman's ideas recently, this time for
their articulation of "the social reconstruction
stance in adult education" (Rockhill, 1985:202).

As Stewart (1984:1) points out, a characteristic feature of <u>The Meaning of Adult Education</u> (1926a)
is its rambling, lurching narrative, in which "ideas
popping up within the text, sometimes have only
tenuous connections to the announced subject
matter". This same comment might be applied to
Lindeman's intellectual effort as a whole,
characterized as it was by a diversity and
inchoateness to be expected of a renaissance liberal
progressive thinker in the early part of the century.
His adult educational writings are often to be found
in pieces which, at first glance, might appear to
have little to do with the field. In addition, his
writing style was one characterized by spontaneity,
so that articles and speeches would assume the format
of his thinking out loud to his audience.
Consequently many issues were raised and claims made
which were not fully developed or thought through.
This is perhaps a partial explanation of his enduring

influence; the questions he asked are ones perennial to the practice of adult education, yet his answers were often given in outline form only. Hence, contemporary readers can interpret his sometimes quasi-mystical language to conform to their own expectations, and can flesh out the outlines of his skeletal schemes for reform with their own substantive, concrete detail.

Six important themes have been identified in his work as regards the theory and practice of adult education. First, there is the conceptualization of adult education as a collaborative, informal, yet critical activity of a determinedly non-vocational character. Judging by current practice in the United States at least, this aspect of his thought has little contemporary relevance. Vocational education, in-service development, training in business and industry and continuing professional education are all seen by, for example, the American Association for Adult and Continuing Education, as legitimate areas of practice. In addition, those interested in the workplace as a setting for meaningful and critical adult learning (and not just mechanistic instruction in psychomotor competencies), would criticize the separation of work and non-work contexts for learning.

Second, the critical theory of adult learning in which the task of adult education is seen as prompting in adults an awareness of their historicity and of the culturally constructed nature of their environment, is reflected in recent contemporary critical theorists such as Freire and Mezirow. Assisting adults to reflect critically on their internalized values, beliefs and assumptions, is a thread common to all these thinkers. Freire and Mezirow did not, however, use Lindeman's work as a conceptual foundation for their theoretical edifices. There is no necessary causal connection between Lindeman's ideas and those of these other writers just because Lindeman's work was the first to appear.

Third, it was Lindeman (together with Martha Anderson) who introduced the concept of andragogy into the literature of American adult education. As with so much of his work, however, after introducing the idea he did not attempt to explore it very completely. It was not until the 1970s that Knowles took the idea as a conceptual anchor for a number of assumptions about adult learning and prescriptions for facilitating learning.

Fourth, Lindeman argued repeatedly and firmly

that, through practical necessity and moral imperative, adult education was a social effort. Adult educational goals were irreducibly social in nature and in its practice of democratic collaboration, adult education was a training ground for democratic participation. Through participation in adult learning groups Americans would cultivate a degree of political literacy which would serve as a shield against the propaganda and seductive appeal of simplistic solutions and convenient scapegoats offered by totalitarian demagogues.

Fifth, he wrote extensively on questions of method, emphasizing throughout how small group discussion was the distinctive and quintessential adult education format. Sixth, he outlined a curricular program for adult education which focused on social and political issues such as the form of economic arrangement most appropriate to an industrial democracy, how to combat racism, the international role of the United States, and how to democratize educational resources.

In a field characterized by a preoccupation with technique, it is heartening to record the contemporary influence of a writer who was neither a professional adult educator nor concerned chiefly with questions of technique. His ideas and the words used to express them continue to inspire successive generations of students and professors of adult education, to the point where The 1984 Adult Learning Review of Books (Collins, 1984:1) headed its reassessment of The Meaning of Adult Education with the phrase "possibly the greatest book of the century". Lindeman's ideas may have been scattered, and his articulation of them may have sometimes been brief, but their contemporary relevance and the force with which they are expressed continue to affect fundamentally how many adult educators practice their craft.

References
Anderson, M.L. and Lindeman, E.C. Education through Experience. New York; Workers' Education Bureau 1927
Brookfield, S.D. "Adult Education and the Democratic Imperative: The Vision of Eduard Lindeman as a Contemporary Charter for Adult Education", Studies in Adult Education, Vol. 15, pp.36-46, 1983
Brookfield, S.D. "The Contribution of Eduard Lindeman to the Development of Theory and Philosophy in Adult Education", Adult Education Quarterly, Vol. 34, No.4, pp. 185-196, 1984

Collins, M. (Ed.). The 1984 Adult Learning Review of Books. Manhattan Kansas; Learning Resources Network, 1984.

Elsdon, K.T. Training for Adult Education. Nottingham: Department of Adult Education, University of Nottingham, 1975.

Freire, P. Pedagogy of the Oppressed. New York; Continuum Books, 1970.

Freire, P. Education for Critical Consciousness. New York; Continuum Books, 1973.

Gessner, R. (Ed.). The Democratic Man. Boston; Beacon Press, 1956

Havighurst, R.J. Developmental Tasks and Education. New York; McKay, 1952.

Hesburgh, T.M., Miller, P.A. and Wharton, C.R. Patterns for Lifelong Learning. San Francisco; Jossey-Bass, 1978

Ilsley, P.J. The Relevance of the Future in Adult Education: A Phenomenological Analysis of Images of the Future. Unpublished doctoral dissertation, Northern Illinois University, DeKalb, Illinois, 1982

Jarvis, P. "Lindeman Revisited: Continuing Professional Education and 'The Meaning of Adult Education'". Paper presented to Standing Conference on University Teaching and Research in the Education of Adults, University of Bristol, July, 1984.

Knowles, M.S. The Modern Practice of Adult Education. New York: Cambridge Books, 1980

Knowles, M.S. Andragogy in Action. San Francisco: Jossey-Bass, 1984

Knox, A.B. Adult Development and Learning. San Francisco: Jossey-Bass, 1977

Kolb, D.A. Experiential Learning: Experience as the Source of Learning and Development. Englewood Cliffs, New Jersey; Prentice-Hall, 1984

Konopka, G. Eduard C. Lindeman and Social Work Philosophy. Minneapolis; University of Minnesota Press, 1958

Lawson, K.H. Philosophical Concepts and Values in Adult Education. Milton Keynes; Open University Press, 1979

Lindeman, E.C. What is Adult Education?, Unpublished manuscript, Columbia University, Butler Library Lindeman Archive, New York, 1925

Lindeman, E.C. The Meaning of Adult Education. New York; New Republic, 1926a

Lindeman, E.C. Workers' Education and the Public Libraries. New York; Workers' Education Bureau of America, 1926b

Lindeman, E.C. "Adult Education". In, Encyclopedia of the Social Sciences, Vol. 1. New York; Macmillan,

1930
Lindeman, E.C. "Introduction". In Brown, T.K. (Ed.). <u>Adult Education for Social Change</u>. Philadelphia; Swarthmore Seminar, 1937
Lindeman, E.C. <u>The Need of Prepared Leaders in Adult Education</u>. Unpublished manuscript. Columbia University, Butler Library Lindeman Archive, New York, 1938
Lindeman, E.C. "New Needs for Adult Education", Annals of the American Academy of Political and Social Science, Vol. 231, pp 115-122, 1944
Lindeman, E.C. "The Sociology of Adult Education", <u>Journal of Educational Sociology</u>, Vol. 19, pp 4-13, 1945a
Lindeman, E.C. "World Peace through Adult Education." <u>The Nation's Schools</u>, Vol. 35, p.23, 1945b
Lindeman, E.C. "Evaluating Your Program", <u>Adult Leadership</u>, Vol. 4, pp 13-20
Mezirow, J. "A Critical Theory of Adult Learning and Education", <u>Adult Education</u> Vol. 32, pp. 3-24, 1981
Osborne, K.Q. "Informal Adult Learning and Public Policy Isuses: The Study Circle Approach". In H.W. Stubblefield (Ed.), <u>Continuing Education for Community Leadership</u>. San Francisco: Jossey-Bass, 1981
Paterson, R.W.K. "The Concept of Discussion: A Philosophical Approach", <u>Studies in Adult Education</u>, Vol. 1, pp. 28-50, 1970
Paterson, R.W.K. <u>Values, Education and the Adult</u>. London: Routledge and Kegan Paul, 1979
Rielly, E.J. "Eduard Lindeman; Self-Directed Learner". In <u>Proceedings of the Adult Education Research Conference</u>, No. 25. North Carolina State University, 1984
Rockhill, K. "Mandatory Continuing Education for Professionals: Trends and Issues", <u>Adult Education</u> (USA), Vol. 33, pp. 106-116, 1983
Rockhill, K. "Ideological Solidification of Liberalism in University Adult Education: Confrontation Over Workers' Education in the U.S.A.". In, R. Rogers, C.R. <u>On becoming a person: a therapist's view of psychotherapy</u>. Boston, Massachusetts, Houghton Mifflin Co., 1961
Taylor, K. Rockhill and R. Fieldhouse, <u>University Adult Education in England and the U.S.A.</u>. London: Croom Helm, 1985
Smith, R.M. <u>Learning How to Learn: Applied Learning Theory for Adults</u>. New York: Cambridge Books, 1982
Stewart, D.W. "Eduard Lindeman and the Idea of Lifelong Learning in America". In <u>Lifelong Research Conference Proceedings</u>, No. 4, Department of

<u>Education</u> (E.C. Lindeman) in Collins, M. (Ed.).
op.cit., 1984

Part Four

RECENT THINKERS IN NORTH AMERICAN ADULT EDUCATION

Chapter Eight

CYRIL O. HOULE

William S. Griffith

> If a man does not keep pace with his companions,
> perhaps it is because he hears a different
> drummer. Let him step to the music which he
> hears, however measured or far away. (Thoreau,
> n.d:311)

Introduction
Cyril Orvin Houle is an adult educator who has never
been concerned with keeping pace with his colleagues.
Instead he has marched to a different drummer all his
professional life. The purpose of this chapter is to
review his career to date, identify some of the
influence he has exerted on adult education through
his writings, his students and colleagues, and his
associated activities. Finally, several of his
seminal ideas that have not yet been fully exploited
will be discussed, leading to a summary assessment of
the contributions of his scholarship to the field of
adult education.

Biographical Sketch
He was born in Sarasota, Florida, on March 26, 1913.
Upon graduation from Sarasota High School in 1929, he
was granted a State of Florida scholarship to the
University of Florida. Houle applied himself to his
academic work systematically and fruitfully,
receiving both his bachelor's and master's degrees in
education in 1934, three years after he had
matriculated. This remarkable pace of work
characterizes his career, impressing all who know him
for his amazing self-discipline and productivity.
    Following his graduation from the University of
Florida, he took several jobs, among which was that
of administering a statewide program for the Federal

147

Emergency Relief Administration for training out-of-work teachers to teach adults. Within a year he had committed himself to a career in adult education and sought an appropriate place to pursue doctoral study. Floyd W. Reeves, who was to become Houle's mentor at The University of Chicago, had been involved in the study of higher education there and had become deeply interested in the work of the Tennessee Valley Authority which was intended to employ education in the improvement of the resources, human and material, of the river region. On the basis of his experience in the innovative programming of that organization, Reeves modified the focus of his academic work at the University in 1935 and arranged to offer a graduate degree program in adult education. This was a pioneering move as only Columbia University had established such a department. Reeves's influence on Houle's perception of adult education has not been established, but it is interesting to note that for the last twelve years Houle spent at the University of Chicago, he was responsible for leading the graduate program in higher education, further strengthening the bond between it and adult education.

Houle was Reeves's first doctoral student and through their association Houle was involved in state and national projects. When Reeves undertook his study of adult education in the State of New York, he involved Houle. Out of that collaboration came the report, <u>Adult Education: The Regents' Inquiry into the Character and Cost of Public Education in the State of New York</u>, regarded by many as the first major study of a state system. Houle's dissertation was a part of that study. At the national level Houle served as a staff member of President Roosevelt's Advisory Committee on Education in Washington, D.C.

In 1939, a year before he had completed his dissertation, Houle was appointed an instructor in adult education at The University of Chicago, beginning a period of employment with the University that would last until 1979, the year of his retirement. In 1940 his Ph.D. was conferred for his dissertation entitled "The Coordination of Adult Education at the State Level." It may be noteworthy that his co-authorship of the Regents' Inquiry had occurred prior to Houle's having completed his dissertation, an experience that may have been instrumental in developing his self-image as a writer and scholar.

In 1942 Houle was named assistant professor; in 1945 he was promoted to associate professor, and in

1952 he became a full professor. From 1945 to 1952 he served as Dean of the University College, the adult education division of the University. His imagination in programming and his general administrative competence came to the attention of people on and off campus so that in 1947 he was named Outstanding Young Man in Chicago by the Chamber of Commerce, a rather remarkable accomplishment for a scholar. Relinquishing his administrative responsibilities for the University College in 1952, Houle focused his attention on research and teaching in adult education, an emphasis he retained until 1969, when he accepted the responsibility for chairing the higher education special field of study in the Department of Education.

During the time he was at the University of Chicago he also engaged in a number of significant activities at other locations in summers and during his terms out of residence. In 1940 he was a visiting instructor in education at the University of California, Berkeley. In 1950 he directed the UNESCO seminar on the Role of Libraries in Adult and Fundamental Education in Malmo, Sweden. In 1950-51 he was a Fulbright Fellow to the United Kingdom, basing his headquarters at Leeds and studying adult education throughout Great Britain. In 1958-59 he visited nine African countries and six in the Caribbean to study extension work at various universities. In the same year he made a visit to Denmark to study the folk high schools. During 1960 he was Knapp Visiting Professor at the University of Wisconsin, Milwaukee. The series of lectures he delivered there were subsequently published as The Inquiring Mind, probably the most influential book he has produced. The Director-General of UNESCO appointed him to the International Committee for the Advancement of Education in 1961. That summer he was a lecturer in education at the University of Washington. He was a visiting senior research specialist at Oxford University in 1968. President Lyndon Johnson appointed him to the National Advisory Council on Extension and Continuing Education in 1965, a position he held until 1969 and in which he helped to shape policy for the implementation of the Higher Education Act of 1965.

Having served as an advisor to the W.K. Kellogg Foundation for a number of years, and having been instrumental in the development of the Kellogg residential center for continuing education at the University of Chicago, he began serving the Foundation in a part time capacity as a Senior

Program Consultant in 1976 and continued in that role until his retirement from the University. Since becoming a professor emeritus in 1979 he has been employed solely by the foundation and maintains a residence in Battle Creek, Michigan, the home of the Foundation, in addition to his apartment in Chicago. He has also been a special advisor on adult and continuing education for the Jossey-Bass Publishers for over a decade.

Only a few of the most notable of his numerous honors and awards will be mentioned here. He was awarded the D.H.L. by Rutgers University, DePaul University, New York University, and Roosevelt University, and the LL.D. by the Florida State University and by Syracuse University. In addition, Syracuse University presented him with the William Pearson Tolley Medal for Distinguished Leadership in Adult Education. His contributions were recognized by his colleagues in the Association of University Evening Colleges in 1967 when they presented him with the Outstanding Achievement Award. In 1968 the National Association for Public School Adult Education honored his work by presenting him an Award of Merit. He was also named to the National Academy of Education, a recognition that has seldom been given to a scholar in adult education.

Influence on Adult Education

Assessing the influence of Cyril O. Houle on the field of adult education involves an examination of selected publications, a consideration of his impact on his former students, and a review of some of his many associated professional activities.

Through Writing - Selected Publications

Houle is a prolific writer with impeccable standards. This examination of selected publications, ordered chronologically, will indicate the breadth and depth of his contribution to the knowledge base of the field.

One of Houle's earliest contributions to the literature was made as a junior author of the Regents' Inquiry into the condition of adult education in the State of New York. Houle, whose own doctoral dissertation dealt with coordination, expressed a strong conviction of the need to rationalize the system of adult education provision. The report notes:

> ... adult education in New York is chiefly a
> group of disjointed and unrelated activities.
> For the most part, agencies at both the state
> and the local level pursue their ways serenely
> unconscious of other closely related programs
> in existence. When consciousness of these
> programs exists, it frequently results in
> bitter jealousy, and coordination is the
> exception rather than the rule. (Reeves,
> Fansler, and Houle, 1938:137-138.)

It is not certain how influential his
involvement in the examination of the panoply of
organizations providing adult education in New York
State was on Houle's perception of the need for a
broad perspective on the field. It is clear, however,
that from that point onwards he made a point of
emphasizing approaches that reflected an awareness
of the richness and diversity of the institutional
providers of adult education.

In 1947 Houle served as the leader of a team of
investigators examining the armed services and adult
education. From that inquiry Houle devised a typology
of adult education providing agencies. (Houle et al.,
1947:226). The first type consists of agencies
originally developed to provide adult education as
their major function. The second type includes
agencies originally developed for the education of
children and young people, but which have since taken
on the additional function of adult education. (This
category includes universities, colleges, and
secondary schools.) The third group is composed of
institutions originally established to serve the
whole community, such as libraries, museums, and
social settlements. The final type was intended to
serve non-educational purposes, and has taken on
adult education functions as a means of achieving its
primary functions more effectively. This type
includes churches, labor unions, prisons, cooperatives, hospitals and government departments. While
subsequent authors have made some modest
modifications of the classification of adult
education agencies, no superior classification has
been proposed.

In concluding the report Houle called attention
to the positive aspects of the educational work of
the armed services and its potential benefits to the
nation in the future. He said:

> The armed services blazed a tortuous trail
> toward a great truth, the truth that everybody

has a natural desire to learn and can profit
from that learning. If civilian society is
willing to accept this basic truth and begins to
realize its fullest promise, a great good can be
said to have come out of the war. Through the
very struggle for democracy, a new implement for
democracy will have been forged. (Houle et al.,
1947:252).

This assertion that all persons desire to learn
may not seem a revolutionary insight in 1986, but in
1947 it was commonly thought that there were large
numbers of people who had no desire to learn. Further
studies by Houle continue to support his assertion
that all adults desire to learn and that they all
engage in some kind of learning, whether or not
satisfactory means have been devised to measure their
learning.

In his work with UNESCO in directing the
international seminar on the role of libraries in
adult and fundamental education in 1951, Houle once
again held up the standard of learning for all and
the need for a supportive network of cooperating
agencies. He said:

If we work together both within the profession
of librarianship and as co-operators with other
agencies, perhaps we may hope to establish a
view which the modern world, with its nervous
pre-occupation with the immediate, has tended
to neglect. It is the idea that education should
be a lifelong process, so that the individual
develops his potentialities not merely while he
is a child but so long as he lives ... it is an
ideal which has never been realized by more than
a few, chiefly for the rich and the leisured ...
Adult education should become not the province
of the few but the democratic hope of the many.
(Houle, 1951:28).

The recurrent themes here are those of lifelong
learning and of the need to provide suitable
supporting structures to enable all adults to
participate. Houle enlarged the conception of the
participants to include adult education broadly
defined and called their attention to the need for
cooperative co-ordinated programming so that all
adults can be served.

In 1956 Houle and C.A. Nelson wrote The
University, the Citizen, and World Affairs, in which
they proposed a typology of adult citizens based on

the citizens' knowledge and concern about world
affairs (Houle and Nelson, 1956:34-35).

By applying this typology Houle and Nelson were
able to propose a set of principles by which each of
the categories of citizens would most appropriately
be served. It is typical of Houle's writing that
adults are invariably categorized in some manner
relevant to the educational objectives of the
programs being considered.

By 1959 Houle had formulated his basic approach
to the design of adult education. In a paper entitled
"Educational Engineering," which he had prepared for
the Commission of the Professors of Adult Education,
Houle outlined nine "Fundamental Programming
Situations" and ten "Basic Steps of Program
Development." He argued that "The competent educator
of adults must have a general theory of program in
which the various elements of the learning process
fit together into a coherent whole." (Houle, 1959).
He espoused the idea that adult educators might well
borrow a number of insights from other fields of
practice, but that unless they had something that was
particular to adult education and drawn from
reflection on adult education practice, there would
not be much basis for a claim of special competence.
Thirteen years later he presented a revised version
of the conception of fundamental programming
situations and basic steps of program development in
The Design of Education.

In 1960 Houle returned to the theme of
coordination in reporting on his consultation with
the Extra-Mural Department of the University College
of the West Indies:

> In every kind of society there must be many
> kinds of agencies to serve the diversified
> educational needs of adults. For the sake of
> economy and efficiency, these agencies need to
> work together, supplementing each others'
> efforts and preventing gaps and duplication of
> service. In an underdeveloped country it is
> particularly necessary that there be proper
> coordination, partly because of the scarcity of
> resources, and partly because of the need, as
> social services are developed, for each one to
> grow in the right way and not acquire the
> isolation shown by the large scale enterprises
> of more sophisticated societies. (Houle,
> 1960:25-26).

This persistent faith in coordination and

153

cooperation is a hallmark of Houle's thinking as expressed in the publications included in this biographical report.

Houle's investigations of phenomena others have examined consistently present new perceptions of the nature of the objects. His approach is exemplified by a statement taken from his 1960 publication, The Effective Board which was written as an outgrowth of his having conducted ten annual board members' training courses sponsored by the University College of the University of Chicago and the Welfare Council of Metropolitan Chicago. He noted, "... to become properly aware of the real nature of familiar objects and influences, it is necessary to bring them squarely into view, examining them with the same wonder and curiosity with which one would inspect the rare or the previously unknown" (Houle, 1960:166). This freshness of approach distinguishes Houle's observations from the bulk of the writing on adult education.

Houle's series of lectures at the University of Wisconsin, Milwaukee, as Knapp Visiting Professor, formed the material for his most influential book to date, The Inquiring Mind: A study of the adult who continues to learn. Based on interviews with little more than a score of adults who had been identified as continuing learners, Houle intuitively (without employing any procedures such as factor analysis) grouped the reports of these interviews into three categories to which he attached the term "orientations." Group one consisted of the goal-oriented - those who use education as a means of accomplishing fairly clear cut objectives. Group two was called the activity-oriented, for they seemed to take part in educational activities because of an attraction in the circumstances of learning rather than in the content or the announced purpose of the activity. Group three was labeled the learning-oriented because they seemed to seek knowledge for its own sake. (Houle, 1961:15-16).

The most direct influence of the presentation of the three orientations was the stimulation of a number of doctoral students in adult education at the University of Chicago to undertake research that would refine and advance the notions proposed in The Inquiring Mind. As this book and the subsequent related dissertations became known, investigators at other institutions began to mine the same intellectual vein, hoping to identify some particular insight that would produce a quantum leap in the knowledge base. A number of well known researchers applied quantitative methods and a variety of analytical techniques either to test or to refute Houle's categories. It is not surprising that the refined work involving large numbers of subjects produced refinements in the typology, but has not cast doubt on the soundness of the original conception. Houle's students have refined the typology to include eight major orientations, but it is fair to say that there have been no conceptual advances made in the approach to orientations since Houle proposed his framework twenty-six years ago.

The remarkable aspect of this study is the elegance of the interpretation of a modest amount of data. The slim, 87-page book is not prepossessing, but the freshness of approach which Houle brings to his investigations is the aspect that distinguishes it from ordinary adult education literature.

In 1964 Houle departed from his established pattern of writing and produced a publication designed to serve the adult student who was returning to study after a number of years away from formal education. This book, Continuing Your Education, is a compendium of sage, practical advice taken from years of working with adults of all sorts who had committed themselves to advancing their learning. He presents seven keys to effective learning, an approach that the readers would probably anticipate, and he also attempts to broaden the readers' vision beyond the narrow confines of their immediate learning tasks. He notes that

> The values of learning, while personally profitable, are not narrowly selfish. Both knowledge and the continuing growth of the mind are essential to society as well to the individual. Kingdoms and kingly eras were judged by the ability and wisdom of the king. In a democracy, the people themselves rule - and therefore democracies and democratic eras must be judged by the ability and the wisdom of the people. (Houle, 1964:171-172).

Houle's writing consistently reflects a respect for the individual learner and an appreciation of the responsibility of educators to work toward the improvement of their society.

In 1964 the Commission of the Professors of Adult Education produced a book, Adult Education: Outlines of an Emerging Field of University Study, which was intended to explain to those within the field and those who were trying to comprehend it from

outside just what constituted this new field. Houle
contributed a chapter, "The Emergence of Graduate
Study in Adult Education," in which he traced the
history of university study and university graduate
programs in adult education from 1917 to 1962. He
explained why adult education was introduced into
universities as a field of graduate study before any
undergraduate programs were developed in the field,
saying,

> It might seem appropriate that a field should
> first build its content and then be accepted as
> a discipline. The reason why this does not
> happen is because the university itself is the
> chief pioneer of knowledge. It develops fields
> after it admits them. (Houle, 1964:78).

In 1967 Houle, reflecting on the movement of
adult education from a craft to a profession,
characterized the professionals' approach to
practice as highly particular in each case. He stated
that:

> What the professional does is to face each new
> practical case with the awareness that it is
> unique ... Each new opportunity for service
> presents a problem different from any he has
> ever encountered before. What the professional
> knows is drawn from several bodies of subject
> matter, never just one. Medicine rests upon many
> disciplines, including anatomy, physiology,
> pathology and biochemistry. Law depends upon
> political science, economics, ethics and
> history. Adult education, like medicine and
> law, is an art based on many sciences. (Houle,
> 1967:15)

This capacity for viewing each new case as
unique is a hallmark of Houle's approach.
In 1971 Houle reflected on the promise
represented by the university residential centers
for continuing education and expressed disappointment that they were not achieving their grand goals.
After noting their potential to serve three
functions: (a) to be a major instrument for teaching
adults, (b) to provide a means for training leaders
of the adult education movement, and (c) to serve as
sites for research, he observed that:

> Some progress has been made in achieving ...
> goals: the training of educators of adults and

other advanced students; and the conduct of studies and research. As yet accomplishments in these two respects have been far less substantial than they should have been. Few centers have continuing budgets for these purposes and must sketchily improvise ways of taking care of them on a hit-or-miss basis, using the marginal time of staff members, the relatively unskilled and unpaid labor of graduate students undertaking projects and theses, and occasional evaluation funds provided in individual contracts for service. (Houle, 1971:81).

In attempting to show how the centers might be made more effective in carrying out all three of their functions, Houle called for "Vivid and dramatic examples of outstanding achievement." (1971:81). Drawing a parallel to university laboratory schools and hospitals, he expressed the hope that the desired stature of the centers could eventually be established through "brilliant leadership."

Thirteen years after presenting his conceptual scheme for program planning to the professors of adult education, Houle wrote The Design of Education, which he said was intended to present a system of educational design which may have relevance to education at any age of life - one which has grown specifically out of an analysis of the organized and purposeful learning activities of men and women. (Houle, 1972:2-3). In this book he made clear that he had rejected the notion that there should be a cleavage between the education of children and youth and the education of adults. He endorsed the idea that education is fundamentally the same wherever and whenever it occurs. His basic assumption is that the essentials of the educative process remain the same for all ages of life and the basic design of education is identical throughout life. Houle explains that "If pedagogy and andragogy are distinguishable, it is not because they are essentially different from one another but because they represent the working out of the same fundamental processes at different stages of life. (1972:222). In presenting his eleven categories of educational programs, he noted that the distinction among categories is in the source of authority and direction so far as planning and control are concerned and not in the apparent physical differences among them (1972:42). The framework for the analysis or the planning of programs consists of

157

a combination of decision points and components which must be kept in proper balance to achieve optimal program outcomes.

This concern for balance and for pattern is another lodestar for Houle's forays into various segments of the field. The artistry of adult education seems to lie in the educator's ability to recognize and to devise harmonious patterns and balanced configurations among the diverse elements in any program planning situation.

In 1973 Houle wrote <u>The External Degree</u>, widely recognized as the definitive work on external degrees. Houle traced the development of the extension degree, the adult degree, and the assessment degree, pointing out how they evolved as institutions became increasingly aware of the special learning needs of adults. He refers to the assessment degree as the "third generation external degree" in that it focuses on the actual learning of the student, rather than on the student's completing a number of formal requirements (1973:14-15). He saw the desirable outcomes of the increasing acceptance of the external degree approaches as enabling the institutions to reach new clientele, enabling students to begin studies who otherwise would not have had an opportunity, increasing the vitality of internal degree programs through the introduction of new content and methods, and finally, stimulating the instructors by providing them with experienced adults whose knowledge of the world is superior to even the brightest of the young students of traditional university age (1973:170-171).

Possibly because of his appreciation of balance, Houle did not join the parade of adult educators who turned their attention to literacy programs in the second half of this century. Instead he conducted complementary inquiries, examining the educational pursuits of the most highly educated members of society. In 1980 he wrote <u>Continuing Learning in the Professions</u>, in which he drew upon his studies of seventeen professions, seeking to demonstrate that the needs, the general objectives, the specific goals, and the methods used all have a marked resemblance (1980:15-16). His analysis revealed three modes of continuing learning in the professions: (a) inquiry - the process of creating some new synthesis, idea, technique, policy, or strategy of action, (b) instruction - the process of disseminating established skills, knowledge, or sensitiveness, and (c) performance - the process of internalizing an idea or using a process habitually, so that it becomes a fundamental part of the way in which a learner thinks about and undertakes his or her work (1980:31-32). Sensing so many commonalities among the professions, Houle concluded that much could be gained through inter-professional cooperative and coordinated planning for continuing education.

In Houle's most recent book, <u>Patterns of Learning: New Perspectives on Life-Span Education</u>, he brings to bear all of the previous considerations of what it means to engage in learning at different stages of life and for a panoply of motivations. He introduces the idea that at any one time an adult is likely to be engaged in several different kinds of learning. He sought a pattern that can be discerned only when these learning activities are seen as interwoven life experiences. He uses a "sequential patterns of learning approach," otherwise known as life-span education, to examine the meaning of education and learning in the lives of a number of individuals. From his analysis he was able to identify five major patterns (1984:172-178). Houle concludes that "patterns of learning in the lives of individuals are emerging as still pictures reporting a cluster of activities at a moment in time. As yet, however, the way by which such patterns change during the course of life has not been generally studied nor widely speculated" (1984:231).

The persistent search for balance, for perspective, and for harmony among the elements characterizes Houle's approach to the study of each aspect of adult education. Never content to take the narrow view, he is committed to the notion that perspective is of central importance in establishing the meaning of all of the phenomena he investigates. Along with this commitment comes an appreciation for the practical aspects of adult education. This appreciation is shown by comments such as "The effect of a method depends not so much on its inherent efficacy as on the intent and the talents of its user" (1984:209). Further, his persistent concern for the improvement of practice is reflected in his reminder that "To be fully successful, therefore, the professional educator of adults must be deeply conversant with the goals and methods of learning, gaining such knowledge from study in university graduate departments, from other organized training efforts, from self-directed programs of study, or from the contemplative examination of his or her own experience" (1984:219).

In his overview of continuing professional

education which he presented to the 20th annual
conference of the Society for Research into Higher
Education, Houle asserted that:

> The valid but limited view that the purpose of
> continuing education is "to keep up to date on
> the new research" has been supplemented by an
> increased awareness that the appropriate goals
> broaden out to include all the needs for the
> growth of a profession, beginning with an
> awareness of its appropriate mission and
> continuing through a mastery of both its
> knowledge base and its methods of treatment, its
> internal structuring, its code of ethics, its
> relationships with allied professions, and its
> responsibilities to both its clients and its
> society (1984:193)

This enlarging of the scope of the problem under
consideration is characteristic of Houle's approach
to the examination of most phenomena as he seeks to
establish a broad perspective in which to view the
elements of interest.

One of Houle's many current interests is the
study of those who participate least in adult
education. At the 1983 European conference on
Motivation for Adult Education Houle presented a
paper on structural features and policies promoting
or inhibiting adult learning (1985:64-73). In that
paper he makes the point that for each learning
venture adults have some immediate reason for seeking
learning and that this purpose arises from either a
sense of desire or from a sense of deprivation.
Considering all adults, from the least to the most
actively involved in learning, Houle classified them
into six categories with sub-categories in some
cases. These six classifications of orientations are
as follows: (1) the oblivious person, (2) the
uninvolved person, (3) the resistant person, (4) the
focused participant, (5) the eclectic participant,
and (6) the comprehensive learner (1985:67-70). He
further subdivided the third and the fourth
categories, suggesting that if adult educators are to
be successful in assisting learning within the far
broader span of lifelong education, it will become
increasingly important that they study and
understand the learning patterns and sequences of
individuals (1985:72).

From this limited report on books and recent
articles he has written, Houle's impressive
contributions to the literature of academic adult

education is readily apparent. Scores of monographs, chapters in edited collections, and individual journal articles have not been included. Nevertheless, the reader should have no doubt that they, too, reflect the same freshness, perspective, and creative insights as have been noted in the limited literature mentioned in this chapter.

At this point it is appropriate to turn to a consideration of the influence Houle has exerted through his work with graduate students in the forty years he was at the University of Chicago.

Through Students and Colleagues at Chicago

At least 130 individuals earned their doctorates in adult and higher education at the University of Chicago while Houle was a member of the faculty of the Department of Education. Among the more prolific writers who have gone through the program are Allen Tough, Professor of Adult Education at the Ontario Institute for Studies in Education, who began his studies of self-planned learning under the tutelage of Cyril Houle. Probably the most widely known graduate of the program is Malcolm Knowles, Emeritus Professor of Adult Education at the North Carolina State University. Chicago alumni are conspicious throughout North America, with a small number making their contributions on other continents. For the most part the graduates of the program appear to be performing in administrative roles, ranging from conference managers to chief executive officers of colleges, yet they are also disproportionately represented in the Commission of the Professors of Adult Education. Testimony from a graduate and from a former colleague at Chicago will demonstrate their assessment of Cyril Houle's influence on their lives and on the adult education field.

When asked what influence Houle had had on him, Malcolm Knowles wrote first about the contribution "Cy" had made to Malcolm's self-concept as an author, and then went on in glowing terms to describe the positive effects on his self-esteem during the course of his doctoral program. But Houle's most profound contribution, in Malcolm's opinion, is "The inculcation of a deep commitment to excellence. Houle has served as a role model for all of us in the field of adult education ... and the improvement in the quality of our literature is at least in part a reflection of his influence" (Knowles, 1985).

George Aker, who was Assistant Professor of Adult Education at the University of Chicago in 1962-

Cyril O. Houle

63 and who is now Professor of Adult Education at
Florida State University, commented that "the
writings of Cy Houle contain the most profound,
insightful, coherent, rational, and intelligible
descriptions that exist about the field of adult
education. Houle's genius in extracting meaning from
his observations of practice have produced
knowledge, theories, hypotheses, and typologies
that, while underutilized by practitioners and
scholars alike, provide the best frameworks that we
have for advancing the field" (Aker:1985).

The addition of countless other statements by
other scholars and administrators whose lives have
been changed and enriched and whose appreciation of
the field has been shaped by their association with
Houle would not alter the prevailing tone of respect
and appreciation, so no further testimonials will be
reported. It is useful, nevertheless, to consider
briefly some of the associated activities and actions
that are significant in any consideration of the
influence of Cyril Houle.

Through Associated Activities
In addition to performing his central responsibilities for conducting research, for teaching and
advising graduate students, and for administering
the office of Secretary of the Department of
Education at the University for a period Houle
managed to establish, support, or work on behalf of a
prodigious number of related organizations and
programs, only a few of which will be mentioned here
for the purpose of demonstrating the variety of his
interests. As a member of the Chicago Literary Club,
he sought to broaden his own appreciation of the
world of letters and in turn to help others
appreciate his field. To increase his understanding
of the situations of poor people living in the inner
city, he lived and worked part-time for a year at
Hull House, Chicago's best known settlement house.
In collaboration with Robert M. Hutchins, who was
President of the University, and Mortimer Adler, he
developed the series of readings and discussion
techniques that became the heart of the Great Books
Program. The experience of selecting the readings,
coupled with his disciplined yet insatiable reading,
helped to develop him into probably the most
liberally educated American adult educator (Blakely,
1981:12).

To encourage the professional growth of adult
educators in the Chicago area, he established the

162

Northern Illinois Round Table of Adult Education, an
informal organization that met monthly to facilitate
communication and cooperation among the administrators of adult education. With the support of the
Carnegie Corporation, he mounted and conducted a
series of summer workshops for administrators of
university adult education, drawing upon creative
and effective administrators and scholars for his co-
leaders and providing adult education administrators
who had been given their positions without having had
any academic preparation in their new field, a taste
of adult education as a field of study. As would be
expected, Houle supported the Adult Education
Council of Chicago, the Adult Education Association
of Illinois, and the Adult Education Association of
the United States persistently, ever prepared with
wise counsel and practical advice when it was sought.

The extent of his work in voluntary
organizations and on behalf of international,
national, regional, state and local causes will
probably never be known, for he is reticent to
identify or to discuss these, possibly because of a
concern that his motivation for involvement would be
misunderstood. His entry in Who's Who is extremely
modest, overlooking what lesser scholars would
regard as significant accomplishments.

In 1947 Cyril Houle married Bettie Eckhardt
Totten, who is also a serious lifelong learner,
having also earned her Ph.D. degree from the
University of Chicago. They have one son, David, who
agrees with Bettie that Cy Houle is the best water
skiing instructor they've ever known.

That he should also excel in the teaching of
physical skills may come as a surprise to those who
consider him to be almost purely a cerebral creature,
but it would not be surprising to anyone who has come
to understand his commitment to excellence in
whatever he undertakes.

Seminal Ideas Not Yet Fully Exploited

If one were to judge the extent of popular acceptance
of Houle's ideas on the basis of the number of his
publications, his honorary degrees, his appointments
to international and national positions, and the
awards he has been given by practicing adult
educators and adult education researchers, it would
be reasonable to conclude that his ideas are eagerly
seized upon and readily become part of the commonly
accepted body of knowledge about the field. The
situation is not so clear.

163

Much of the best selling literature on program
planning in adult education tends to deal with a
restricted range of program forms and situations,
possibly because authors find it easier to write
prescriptions for behavior for highly specific
settings and purposes. In The Design of Education
Houle described in precise detail eleven different
kinds of program planning situations, each with its
own particular constraints on the planning process.
Such a perspective is of great value to a person
seeking to analyze a variety of instances of program
planning. It is not highly useful to a harried
program planner, rushing to complete a menu of course
offerings in time to meet a printer's deadlines. The
Design of Education will never become popular as a
how to do it sort of manual. Instead its most
appropriate audience seems to be the reflective
student of adult education who is prepared to spend
the time required to analyze his own practices from a
new perspective and to seek to develop future
programs that reflect an optimal balance and harmony
among their elements.

Houle's monumental work, Continuing Learning in
the Professions, demonstrated his capacity to
perceive commonalities as well as differences among
the continuing education practices of the members of
seventeen professions. Although this work was given
the prestigious Imogene Okes Award by the Commission
on Research of the Adult Education Association of the
United States, his insightful discussion of the modes
of inquiry, instruction, and performance is still
known to only a small group of scholars who are
seriously interested in the conceptualization of
means for facilitating continuing learning. Little
has been done to utilize this conception of modes of
continuing professional learning, so exploitation of
the implications of a coordinated approach, building
upon all three modes, is still some time in the
future.

The study of adult education participation has
been a persistent concern of Houle for decades and
his approaches to studying it have developed as his
conceptualization of the process has evolved.
Beginning with a unidimensional approach which
counted the number of episodes of different kinds of
learning activities, he soon concluded that to make
sense of the phenomenon it would be necessary to move
beyond the refinement of methods of quantification.
In The Inquiring Mind he advanced the notion of
orientations to learning and proposed three
categories as a tentative classification. As has been

164

noted earlier, graduate students and other researchers expended a great deal of energy refining these initial three orientations to eight through quantitative analytical approaches, but they made no appreciable change in his conceptual approach. Then, in 1984, with the publication of <u>Patterns of Learning</u>, Houle shared his latest approach to the study of participation. Although he identified five major patterns, he observed that he had measured a dynamic process by the use of still photographs so that he was not able to examine fully the pattern of activities at various points across the life span. And even though his studies of six notable individuals, some living and others dead, allowed him to reach some conclusions regarding the use of various methods, he did not have access to information that would enable him to reach defensible conclusions about the succession of patterns of learning across the life span. That task lies ahead, and there is as yet scant evidence that it will be undertaken by other researchers.

Even though Houle's ideas have received appreciable recognition by scholars, their influence on the practice of adult education appears to be less than they deserve. Blakely, in attempting to explain why <u>The Design of Education</u> and <u>Continuing Learning in the Professions</u> have not had their anticipated impact, said:

> Perhaps the field of adult education has not yet reached a stage of high enough common awareness to use a design that is at the same time simple and comprehensive. Certainly continuing education in the several professions is not yet sufficiently advanced to accept a scheme based on commonalities. I foresee that both of these books will become increasingly influential as adult education matures into a more self-recognized and self-analytical field, and as continuing education in the several professions, after working through their pecularities, approaches a point where it can recognize its commonalities (Blakely, 1985:14).

It seems reasonable to predict that although Houle's work is among the best known in the world of educational scholarship, its fullest impact on the practice of adult education lies somewhere in the future.

Summary Assessment

Cyril O. Houle has been widely regarded as a leading scholar in adult education for at least the last 35 years. A prolific writer, yet one with the highest of standards, he continues to produce significant books and articles that reflect fresh insights into complex phenomena. His eminence in his chosen field both now and in the future is assured by the quality of his contributions to the literature and to his inculcation of standards of excellence in the hundreds of graduate students he has guided and taught. The fact that the American Association for Adult and Continuing Education established an award, The Cyril O. Houle World Award for Literature in Adult Education, is clear testimony indicating the esteem in which he and his writing are held.

As an individual, he has impressed many of his students and associates with his air of self-restraint, seeming always to be wary of offering unsolicited advice or counsel. Although a highly articulate person, he is a quiet man, observing and reflecting on those observations. Though admirably self-disciplined himself, he is never harsh in judging the performance of those who are less gifted or unorganized. His compassionate sensitivity and concern for students, colleagues, and other associates often is unsuspected by those who perceive only an austere scholar.

Dedicated to a philosophy that values cooperation, coordination, individual excellence, and balance in all aspects of life, Cyril Houle has done more than any other scholar to establish adult education as a legitimate field of university study and professional practice.

Bibliography

Aker, G.F. (May 16, 1985), Personal letter to W.S. Griffith. (In the personal files of W.S. Griffith).

Blakely, R.J. (1981). "Cyril O. Houle." (Unpublished manuscript in the personal files of W.S. Griffith.)

Houle, C.O., Burr, E.W., Hamilton, T.H., and Yale, J.R. (1947). The Armed Services and Adult Education, Washington, D.C. American Council on Education.

Houle, C.O. (1951). Libraries in Adult and Fundamental Education.: The report of the Malmo seminar. Paris. UNESCO.

Houle, C.O. and Nelson, C.A. (1956) The University, the Citizen, and World Affairs. Washington, D.C. American Council on Education.

Houle, C.O. (1959). "Educational Engineering." A

working paper prepared for the annual seminar of the Professors of Adult Education meeting at Madison, Wisconsin, March 19-21, 1959. (Unpublished manuscript in the personal files of W.S. Griffith.)

Houle, C.O. (1960). Adult Education in the British West Indies. Notes and Essays on Education for Adults, No. 31. Chicago: Centre for the Study of Liberal Education for Adults.

Houle, C.O. (1960). The Effective Board. New York, Association Press.

Houle, C.O. (1961). The Inquiring Mind: A study of the adult who continues to learn. Madison, Wisconsin, University of Wisconsin Press.

Houle, C.O. (1964). Continuing Your Education. New York, Macgraw-Hill.

Houle, C.O. (1964). "The Emergence of Graduate Study in Adult Education." Adult Education: Outlines of an Emerging Field of University Study. Edited by G. Jensen, A.A. Liveright, and W. Hallenbeck. Chicago. Adult Education Association of the U.S.A.

Houle, C.O., Blackwell, G.W., Kallen, H.W., and Whipple, J.B. (1967). The Continuing Task: reflections on purpose in higher continuing education. Notes and Essays on Education for Adults No. 54. Brookline, Massachusetts. Centre for the Study of Liberal Education for Adults at Boston University.

Houle, C.O. (1971). Residential Continuing Education. Notes and Essays on Education for Adults, N. 70. Syracuse, New York. Syracuse University Publications in Continuing Education.

Houle, C.O. (1972). The Design of Education. San Francisco, Jossey-Bass.

Houle, C.O. (1973). The External Degree. San Francisco, Jossey-Bass.

Houle, C.O. (1980). Continuing Learning in the Professions. San Francisco, Jossey-Bass.

Houle, C.O. (1984). Patterns of Learning: New Perspectives on Life-Span Education. San Francisco, Jossey-Bass.

Houle, C.O. (1984:191-196). "Overview of Continuing Professional Education. Education for the Professions: Papers presented to the 20th annual conference of the Society for Research into Higher Education 1984. The University, Guildford, Surrey. The Society for Research into Higher Education and NFER-Nelson.

Houle, C.O. (1985:64-73). "Structural Features and Policies Promoting or Inhibiting Adult Learning." Motivation for Adult Education. Working papers presented to the European Conference on Motivation for Adult Education organised by the German

Commission for UNESCO and the UNESCO-Institute for Education, Hamburg, 28 February - 4 March, 1983. Edited by J.H. Knoll. Bonn. German Commission for UNESCO.

Knowles, M.S. (May 1, 1985). Personal letter to W.S. Griffith. In the personal files of W.S. Griffith.

Reeves, F.W., Fansler, T. and Houle, C.O. (1938). Adult Education. The Regents' Inquiry. New York, Mc-Graw-Hill.

Thoreau, H.D. (n.d.:311). Walden. New York, Peter Pauper Press.

Chapter Nine

MALCOLM S. KNOWLES

Peter Jarvis

Introduction

Malcolm Knowles is, for many people, the creator of
the concept of andragogy and it is true that much of
his work, both in theory and practice, has focused
upon the concept. But Knowles was around the adult
education scene long before the term became
fashionable although the term itself was coined long
before Knowles actually learned it. This chapter
will, naturally, focus upon the idea of andragogy as
Knowles has conceived it, but it also seeks to
examine the development of his thought and will,
therefore, include some reference to his career but
only in relation to the way that it influenced his
thinking.

Knowles was born in 1913 and intended to enter
the United States Foreign Service after he graduated
in 1935, but since there were no vacancies that year
he took a temporary job as director of related
training for the National Youth Administration based
in Massachusetts while he awaited for a vacancy to
occur. The focus of this work was with unemployed
young adults. But like many who entered the field of
adult education he had no training for the work that
he was to do and neither did he have an occupational
identity. It was 1937 before he discovered that he
was an adult educator! In those early years he was
also unable to discover a manual to guide him in his
work. However, he was very fortunate in another way,
since the person to whom he was responsible and who
became his mentor was Eduard Lindeman. Knowles says
that it was the many hours that he spent with
Lindeman and also Lindeman's influential book The
Meaning of Adult Education (1926) that helped to
guide his thinking. Yet it is interesting to note
that it was not Lindeman who taught Knowles the term
'andragogy'; Lindeman used the word in 1927 but, it

169

was not until forty years later that the Yugoslav adult educator, Dusan Savićević, introduced Knowles to the word and its meaning, since the term has had much more currency in the Eastern European countries than it has had until recently in the West. In addition to Lindeman, the local director of adult education in Boston, Dorothy Hewitt, was an influence on Knowles; he says that the book that she co-authored with Kirtley Mather, Adult Education: A Dynamic for Democracy is one that he still reads on occasions.

Hence, like many adult educators, Knowles learned a great deal about his work on the job, a form of experiential learning that appears less popular these days, even though learning in the work-place is becoming a more popular idea! By 1940 Knowles, having long rejected the idea of entering the foreign service, was appointed director of adult education at the Huntington Avenue Y.M.C.A. in Boston. He claims that it was during this time he began to read adult education literature and became aware how adult educators generally regarded adults' learning processes to be different to those children. After navy service, Knowles was appointed director of adult education at the Central Y.M.C.A. in Chicago and, like many Americans, he enrolled in the local university graduate programme – his subject, needless to say, was adult education. It was here that he was to meet and be influenced by another of America's leading adult educators, Professor C.O. Houle. Knowles says that it was both Houle's intellectual rigour and his ability to practise adult education principles in the traditional setting of a university that impressed him. It was also during this period that Knowles became acquainted with the work of Carl Rogers, who was already teaching that learners could and should be self-directed. The culmination of these influences was such that Knowles embarked upon a task for his thesis at the university that was to occupy the remainder of his academic life – that of constructing a comprehensive theory of adult education. This led to the publication of his first book in 1950, Informal Adult Education.

In 1951, Knowles became the executive director of the newly formed Adult Education Association of the United States of America. There he remained for nine years, a period in which he was able to influence the growth and direction of the organization. The history of the organization in this period is well documented in his own writings (Knowles: 1962; 177 ed:190-248) but he does point out

170

in the Preface to the later edition how his
involvement as executive director made his
interpretation a little subjective. The book in which
Knowles records the growth and development of The
Adult Education Association of the United States of
America was published in 1962, just after he had
actually finished his term of office in the
association. This book, The Adult Education Movement
in the United States, records the first major attempt
to draw the early threads of adult education together
in a historical sequence. As such, it provides an
overview of the development of adult education, but
on no account can it be claimed to be a detailed
historical study. Indeed, Knowles (1977:x-xi) states
that while he was seeking to locate adult education
within a wider perspective there were many gaps in
the historical data that he was able to employ. While
Knowles was able to undertake some archival research
for this study, mainly in the archives of the Adult
Education Association, much of the remaining data
were gathered through questionnaire research and
wide reading of already published material. However,
for more than twenty years this overview was the only
major source book of the historical development of
adult education in the United States, and it was not
until the 1980s that there was a growth in academic
interest in this field of study.

Even in this book Knowles (1977:249-280) was
arguing that adult education is a separate field of
study. In seeking to describe this field he suggested
that adult education is: expansive and flexible;
taking the shape of a multi-dimensional social
system; institutional; a field that has its own
subject matter; geographical; orientated to specific
personnel - both leaders and consumers; highly
interactive with the social system; in the process of
developing a distinctive curriculum and methodology;
becoming delineated as both a field of study and
practice. Throughout Knowles's writings there is a
propensity to list characteristics in this manner, as
will become clear as this chapter proceeds, and this
approach is open to the criticism that it provides no
conceptual basis by which to assess the validity of
the characteristics listed. It thus becomes possible
to add or to subtract any characteristic from the
list as any scholar desires without reference to the
conceptual basis of the phenomenon being described.
It might be claimed that observation of what is
happening is sufficient, but observers do have a
tendency to see events differently and also to
interpret them differently, so that this is not

sufficient grounds for omitting the theoretical underpinning of either the phenomenon or the interpretation. At the same time it is most significant that Knowles should have been seeking to delineate the parameters of the field of study in this way - this is a topic which receives considerable attention in the final chapter of this book.

In a similar manner, Knowles indicated in the Handbook of Adult Education (1960) and in the historical overview (Knowles 1977:252-253) that the subject matter of adult education was beginning to appear as programmes developed in the following areas: academic education; education for ageing; community development; creative arts; economic education; fundamental and literacy education; health education; home and family life education; human relations and leadership training; inter-group education; liberal adult education; public affairs education; adult recreation education; science education; occupational education. While it is undoubtedly true that the provision of adult education relates to the division of labour in society, this list appears to confuse the process of education (the first in the list and may be the second) with the provision of education for adults (the remainder). In addition to this list of characteristics, Knowles (1977:257-260) specified some generic principles that appeared to him to guide the development of the field: these institutions emerge in response to specific needs; that development is episodic rather than consistent; institutional forms of adult education survive when they become attached to agencies established for other purposes; adult education programmes must appear as secondary within those agencies; adult education programmes differentiate into administration, finance, curriculum and methodology; adult education emerges in different sub-structures of society without general reference to the general adult education movement.

Thus, without the benefit of an extended knowledge of philosophy or the insights of the sociology of movements and organizations, Knowles tried to illustrate the direction that the adult education movement was taking. His concern for adult education was profound and his understanding of many of its manifestations extremely insightful. He saw that the movement was, in a sense, peripheral to the dominant institutions in society and yet important to it. He recognised that the very disparate nature of

the movement prevented its being adequately co-
ordinated from a centralised position. His position
has subsequently been described as a free-market
needs model of adult education provision (Jarvis
1985:184-186). It is a position that he has
maintained (Knowles 1980a:12-40) even after adult
education became much more established and scholars
were calling for a more centrally co-ordinated
approach to adult education provision (Griffith
1980:78-114). However, implicit within this position
of Knowles is perhaps one of the central planks of
his own philosophy; that adult education must be free
to respond to need, wherever it is discovered. Need,
however, is a contentious concept in adult education,
as a multitude of publications reveal. While it is
not the place to explore those here, it is important
to understand Knowles's own approach to the subject.
In a later work, he (1980b:88) argued that:

> An educational need ... is something people
> ought to learn for their own good, for the good
> of the organization, or for the good of society.
> It is the gap between their present level of
> competencies and a higher level required for
> effective performance as defined by themselves,
> their organization, or society.

Two points, at least arise from the above quotation
that require further discussion: what he means by
need and the concept of goodness. In a sense, he was
arguing that need is the difference between 'want' or
'expectation' or 'demand' and 'performance'. But
what if the expectations are conflicting? What if the
demands are unrealistic? What if they are
unachieveable? If there is no agreement about the
former concepts, then the assertion of need becomes
meaningless. There are, additionally, problems of
deciding who has the right to define need within the
organization or society at large. This, then, leads
directly into the second problem in this quotation;
the concept of good is not self-evident and,
therefore, it must be asked whom Knowles considers
the decision makers to be in his formulation of
needs. Therefore, Knowles does not really do justice
to the self-evidence of his own understanding of the
service ethic of adult education in this analysis.

However, embedded in this historical study lie
the seeds of what was to become a crucial issue for
him. He (1977:273-276) claimed that rapid social
change created a whole new set of assumptions about
education and these he proceeded to specify:

173

The purpose of education for the young must shift from focusing primarily on the transmission of knowledge to the development of the capacity to learn;

The curriculum of education for the young must shift from a subject mastery basis to a learning skill basis of organization;

The role of the teacher must be re-defined from one who primarily transmits knowledge to one who primarily helps students to inquire;

A new set of criteria must be applied to determine the readiness of youth to leave full-time schooling.

Here, at the start of the 1960s Knowles' ideas were developing in a specific way which, when combined with his earlier observation that adults learned differently to children, would lead to his new theoretical understanding of adult education. By the time that this book was published Knowles had left the Adult Education Association and had begun his academic career at Boston University. He himself (1984:5) claims that it was during 'this period that a theoretical framework regarding adult learning evolved.' It was also during this period that the Yugoslav adult educator Dusan Savićević, attended one of his summer schools and introduced him to a concept that he was subsequently to make famous - andragogy.

Andragogy
The term 'andragogy' was originally formulated by a German teacher, Alexander Kapp, in 1833 who coined the phrase to describe the educational theory of Plato. A few years later the philosopher, Johan Friedrich Herbart, was the first to dispute the validity of the term and so the word fell into disuse for nearly a century. It was revived in 1921 when the German social scientist, Eugen Rosenstock, used it in a report to the Academy of Labour in Frankfurt and Lindeman employed it in the U.S.A. in 1927. Thereafter it appears to have gained some currency in Eastern European countries, but Knowles clearly knew little of its history when he first employed the term. Indeed, with characteristic honesty, he later admitted to misspelling it when he wrote his first article about it, entitled 'Androgogy Not Pedagogy'

in <u>Adult Leadership</u> in 1968 (Knowles; 1978:49).
However, it was in this address, first given in 1967,
that he claimed that adult education had been
'hamstrung by the concepts and methods of the
traditional education of children'. (Knowles,
1968:350-351).

The title of that article indicated the theme of
Knowles's next major publication <u>The Modern Practice
of Adult Education: Andragogy versus Pedagogy</u> which
appeared in 1970. Here he brought together the fruits
of his years in adult education and the book has
become seminal to the field. It set out to be a
complete practical guide for the adult educator and
as such it covered all the ground that he considered
should be examined by adult educators. In this book
he suggested that there are two opposing fields of
education, andragogy and pedagogy, the former he
defined as 'the art and science of helping adults
learn' and the latter as 'the art and science of
teaching children' (Knowles, 1980b:43). These two
forms of education he thought were opposed to each
other and he depicted this in the following manner
(see Table 9.1).

This rather crude distinction was to set off a
debate in adult education circles that was continuing
well into the 1980s, the same debate, in fact, that
it started in the nineteenth century when the term
was originally used, and one that has apparently been
conducted in the Eastern European countries if the
discussion by Skalka and Livecka (1977:79-85)
adequately reflects the state of the art in those
countries. However, before examining that debate in
the West, it is necessary to recall that in 1973
another book appeared from Knowles, <u>The Adult
Learner: A Neglected Species</u>. This book was also to
prove an important one, covering some of the same
ground as the first one, but seeking to locate
andragogy more specifically in the area of the theory
of adult learning, although it did not really expand
the andragogy-pedagogy debate. It did, however,
raise important questions about the accepted
theories of learning, although it did not seek to
engage them in academic debate. This book is easy to
read and seeks to illustrate 'an andragogical theory
of adult learning' (Knowles, 1978:51) rather than
seeking to produce a new theory of learning.
Reference will be made later to the significance of
this.

It must also be noted here that within a very
short space of four years Knowles produced two
seminal books in the field of adult education which

Table 9.1: A Comparison of the Assumptions of Pedagogy and Andragogy

Regarding:	Pedagogy	Andragogy
Concept of the learner	The role of the learner is, by definition, a dependent one. The teacher is expected by society to take full responsibility for determining what is to be learned, when it is to be learned, how it is to be learned, and if it has to be learned.	It is a normal aspect of the process of maturation for a person to move from dependency toward increasing self-directedness, but at different rates for different people and in different dimensions of life. Teachers have a responsibility to encourage and nurture this movement. Adults have a deep psychological need to be generally self-directing, although they may be dependent in particular temporary situations.
Role of learners' experience	The experience learners bring to a learning situation is of little worth. It may be used as a starting point, but the experience from which learners will gain the most is that of the teacher, the textbook writer, the audiovisual aid producer, and other experts. Accordingly, the primary techniques in education are transmittal techniques – lecture, assigned reading, AV presentations.	As people grow and develop they accumulate an increasing reservoir of experience that becomes an increasingly rich resource for learning – for themselves and for others. Further-more, people attach more meaning to learnings they gain from experience than those they acquire passively. Accordingly, the primary techniques in education are experiential techniques – laboratory experiments discussion, problem-solving cases, simulation exercises, field experience, and the like.

Table 9.1: continued

Regarding:	Pedagogy	Andragogy
Readiness to learn	People who are ready to learn what-ever society (especially the school) says they ought to learn, provided the pressures on them (like fear of failure) are great enough. Most people of the same age are ready to learn the same things. Therefore, learning should be organized into a fairly standardized curriculum, with a uniform step-by-step progression for all learners.	People become ready to learn something when they experience a need to learn it in order to cope more satisfyingly with real-life tasks or problems. The educator has a responsibility to create conditions and provide tools and procedures for helping learners discover their "needs to know". And learning programs should be organized around life-application categories and sequenced according to the learners' readiness to learn.
Orientation to learning	Learners see education as a process of acquiring subject-matter content, most of which they understand will be useful only at a later time in life. Accordingly, the curriculum should be organized into subject-matter units (e.g. courses) which follow the logic of the subject (e.g. from ancient to modern history, from simple to complex mathematics or science). People are subject-centred in their orientation to learning.	Learners see education as a process of developing increased competence to achieve their full potential in life. They want to be able to apply whatever knowledge and skill they gain today to living more effectively tomorrow. Accordingly, learning experiences should be organized around competency-development categories. People are performance-centred in their orientation to learning.

177

were to be the focus of much debate in the following years. They constitute the culmination of his thinking about the practice of adult education and they are also the foundation of the on-going debate in the field that can only enhance the knowledge base of adult education as an area of study.

The Andragogy-Pedagogy Debate

From the outset Knowles's theory was not accepted uncritically by scholars in the field. Houle (1972:221), for instance, was gently critical of the distinction between the two terms, but the main debate did not begin until a few years later. This started when McKenzie (1977) sought to provide Knowles's rather pragmatic formulation about adult learning with a more solid philosophical foundation by claiming that andragogy had an existential basis. He pointed out that since adults are existentially different to children, andragogy and pedagogy must be logically different. However, Elias (1979:254) responded to this by claiming that this distinction is not necessarily significant since men and women are existentially different but that nobody claimed that 'the art and science of teaching women differs from the art and science of teaching men'. Feminists now would probably make this claim! This, however, was not the substance of McKenzie's response; he accepted Elias's point but claimed that this existential difference was insignificant in relation to the lifespan but that the lifespan difference between children and adults was significant to the position under discussion. While there may be some element of truth in McKenzie's position, this may lay in the utilisation of experience by the learner rather than age per se. McKenzie proceeded to try to show that andragogy should not be equated with progressivism, since the latter a is more complete philosophical system and that this is something that andragogy has never claimed to be. Indeed, this is true but this is because andragogy had never been sufficiently elaborated in philosophical terms. Neither did McKenzie recognise that children might have the same propensity as adults to learn and a similar orientation to problem solving; rather he concentrated upon the differences in learning between children and adults, as he understood them, but these were perhaps more directed to the nature of the learner than to the learning processes.

In 1979, Knowles chose to re-enter the debate and now he recognised that andragogy and pedagogy are not two discrete processes based upon age; he (1979:53) claimed that 'some pedagogical assumptions are realistic for adults and some andragogical assumptions are realistic for children in some situations'. In 1980, a revised edition of <u>The Modern Practice of Adult Education</u> appeared and this time it was sub-titled 'From Pedagogy to Andragogy'.

By 1984 and the publication of another book which he edited, <u>Andragogy in Action</u>, Knowles had shifted his position about the distinction between andragogy and pedagogy, so that the child-adult dichotomy was less significant. He (1984:13-18) now claimed that pedagogy is a content model and andragogy a process model in the design and operation of educational programme. This is in the realms of curriculum theory (Jarvis, 1985:45-55) despite the fact that he once claimed, in a personal communication, that adult education has no curriculum. The tenor of his work still seems to suggest that he still regards andragogy as being related to adult learning and pedagogy to child learning, probably since this is how the distinction appears to him in the practice of education. However, the latest book contains examples of process orientated education, rather than adult education, and this he now regards as andragogical, a point to which further reference will be made below.

Thus it may be seen that the crude distinction drawn between adult learning and child learning cannot be sustained and this is the crux of the position advocated by Knudson (1979:261) when he suggested that the variety of terms that were beginning to appear, e.g., andragogy, pedagogy, gerogogy (Label 1978:261) should be replaced by a single concept, humanagogy, which is:

> a theory of learning that takes into account the differences between people of various ages as well as their similarities. It is a <u>human</u> (his italics) theory of learning and not a theory of 'child learning', 'adult learning' or 'elderly learning'. It is a theory of learning that combines pedagogy, andragogy and gerogogy and takes into account every aspect of presently accepted psychological theory.

While Courtenay and Stevenson (1983:10-11) would clearly agree with Knudson and 'gogymania' has to be avoided, they would still like to retain a 'tenuous distinction betwen andragogy and pedagogy'. Perhaps Knudson's position is the logical outcome of the debate, but humanagogy is a clumsy word which has not gained a great deal of currency since it was first introduced and, in any case, what makes humanagogy any different a concept from that of human learning? Knudson's term is probably unnecessary, even though his emphasis on human learning is very important, it was an emphasis that Knowles himself made when he wrote The Adult Learner. However, Knowles has also changed his position since then and, indeed, he (1984:12) has added a fifth assumption about andragogy - that the motivation to learn is internal - which he does not equate with adult learning. Obviously the concept itself is still very fluid and so it is necessary to re-examine it now.

The Concept of Andragogy Revisited

At the outset, it is necessary to enquire what 'andragogy' means to Knowles. In the 1984 publication Andragogy in Action the definition has not changed although the emphasis and the formulation have. There is a certain confusion between it and self-directed learning, although they are certainly not synonymous concepts. It is also now more concerned with the process model of programme design than with 'helping adults learn', which is an element within the wider curriculum analysis of adult education. He (1984:14-18) suggests that it has seven elements: climate setting (physical, psychological and human); involving learners in mutual planning; involving learners in diagnosing their own needs for learning; involving learners in formulating their own learning objectives; involving learners in designing their own learning plans; helping learners carry out their plans; involving learners in evaluating their own learning. In many ways this is a formulation of the romantic curriculum which was popular in school education in the 1960s and can be traced back to Dewey (Jarvis 1985:45-55). Indeed, this is what some scholars have claimed for andragogy for a number of years: Day and Baskett (1982:143-155), for instance, claimed that it was an ideological formulation; Boyer (1984:17-20) likened it to Rogers' student-centred learning, which is not surprising when it is recalled that Knowles admits to having been influenced by Rogers' work many years earlier; Yonge (1985:160-167) suggested that the difference between andragogy and pedagogy lies in the manner by which the learner is accompanied by the teacher through the learning process, since the child is not yet an adult the child is accompanied through the learning process by a teacher with whom there is a relationship of trust, understanding and authority but when the child becomes an adult the nature of the relationship changes and becomes an adult one. Many of these later formulations seem to be pointing in the same direction, but it remains a position without a thorough-going theoretical underpinning. Hartree (1984:203-210) showed that andragogy lacks an epistemology and a coherent discussion of the different dimensions of learning. She (1984:9) suggests that:

> Whilst in a sense he (Knowles) has done an important service in popularising the idea of andragogy, it is unfortunate that he has done so in a form which, because it is intellectually dubious, is likely to lead to rejection by the very people it is most important to convince.

Hartree wrote before Knowles's 1984 publication occurred but much of what she claimed remains a valid criticism of his work. Indeed, Tennant (1986) has even more recently attacked the concept, claiming that in this latest work Knowles implicitly admonishes educators for structuring the content of the course while praising them for structuring the process, which is rather a logical inconsistency. Additionally, he points to the fact that there is no distinction made between the need for and the ability of adults to be self-directing. However, Knowles (1984:7) suggests that there is now 'a substantial enough body of knowledge about adult learners and their learning to warrant attempts to organize it into a systematic framework of assumptions, principles, and strategies', and this is what andragogy tries to do. But it is evident from this quotation that Knowles has not really broken away from the idea that andragogy is about adult teaching and learning in some way, since he is still relating it quite specifically to adults here. Perhaps this signifies the sense in which Knowles has been committed to the cause of adult education and has sought to make it a distinctive discipline. Cross (1981:227) appears rather dubious that andragogy can ever perform the function of providing an overarching theory of failure to locate his work within a wider curriculum theory, especially as the 1984 publication seems to include examples of andragogy from educators who adopt a broadly similar position to his own. Indeed, all that the volume actually demonstrates is that there are many people utilising a humanistic, egalitarian approach to education rather than demonstrating the validity of his own formulation.

Throughout this discussion it is clear that the failure to produce a rigorous and well argued exposition of his position has resulted in some of the present confusion about the concept. Even so, it would be possible to claim that Knowles has been trying to let the theory evolve as a result of observing practice and because adult education itself is a very young field of study it would be quite inappropriate to utilise research from other disciplines, especially child education, in the first instance. It would, however, be difficult to sustain this because he has consistently contrasted the education of children to the education of adults. Hence, such reference to the established research could legitimately have been expected.

Since Knowles had noted a difference between adult and child learning so early in his own career, he had perhaps taken it for granted, rather than trying to demonstrate it. But the correlation that he made then between types of learning and age, which has remained with him in part ever since may be spurious, since it may relate to other factors, such as hierarchical traditions, adult authority, etc. In these instances recognition of the significance of the social setting in which education occurs would have added another important dimension to his thinking and might have, perhaps, led to a slightly different formulation in the first instance. Even so, the formulations of the concept of andragogy has been crucial to the development of theory about the education of adults. The debate has led to a broadening of the theory of the field of study and, even, to a reconceptualization of the concept of andragogy itself (Nottingham Andragogy Group 1983). However, before any assessment is made of the work of Malcolm Knowles it is important to recognise that he has written more widely than in just this area and so it is necessary to examine some of this other work.

Other Aspects of his Work
One element of Knowles's work which has not yet been mentioned is that of contract learning; he developed this approach to teaching in a small book published in 1975, <u>Self-Directed Learning</u> in which he expanded the idea of the self-directed learners discussing their learning needs with the teacher and then entering into a contract with the teacher to have

achieved their learning objectives by a specified date. While Knowles clearly saw this as part of the practice of andragogy, it was not so clearly spelt out in that earlier publication but by 1984 it was much more explicit. Here he (1984:18-20) suggests that this is one way to help students to structure their own learning, which may be seen as a partial response to Tennant's criticism, cited above. It is clearly one way in which the learners may be encouraged to structure their own learning, to work at their own pace and in their own time. It is certainly an approach that may be very useful in individualized teaching and learning situations (Jarvis 1986), but this is perhaps also one of the weaknesses implicit in much of Knowles's work, as Tennant (1986) claims. Learning per se is certainly individualistic, but there is a danger in omitting the social context within which it occurs, and the influence that that environment exerts upon the learning process. However, the question still remains as to the precise relationship between contract learning and andragogy.

Apart from this small study, Knowles has co-authored a book with his wife on group dynamics Introduction to Group Dynamics (1959), which also reflects his own approach to teaching through the use of groups. While this is in accord with much of Knowles' other writing and practice, no further discussion will occur about it here since he was not the sole author.

Acting as a consultant to a project on Faith Development in the Adult Life Cycle, Knowles recognized that one of the reasons why there was a poverty of research related to the interface between the adult life cycle and faith development is because the latter concept has not been operationally defined. He (in Stokes 1982:73) then went on to write:

> If we could discover what the developmental tasks of faith development are at various life stages are, we would have some clear guidelines for designing adult educational experiences that would facilitate the developmental process.

However if both the structure of the process and the end product are already determined then this raises major questions about the nature of this process, whether it is education at all, or merely an indoctrinational technique. This position reflects a similar one to that which he produced in another context, where he suggested that needs refers to meeting the organizational, or the societal, good as well as the individual one. Indeed, Knowles changed this position little from the time when he (1957:237) claimed that while these are all valid sources of objectives, their differences are often magnified, which really demonstrates an underlying belief in the functional interdependence of society without working out the implications of holding such a position. An indoctrinational position is probably far from the position that Knowles would want to adopt, or to be argued from his writings, but that it can be logically deduced from what he has written demonstrates his failure to work out systematically the implications of his position.

Conclusions
It may be seen from the above discussion that a frequent criticism of Knowles's writing is that he has not sought to develop his ideas fully and that he tends to be descriptive rather than analytical or critical. This is clearly a valid criticism and a simple example of this may be seen from the fact that andragogy is still defined in the 1984 publication in terms of helping adults learn although he has changed his stance twice since the time when he actually did define the concept in this manner. Even allowing for the change in position, a question must be raised about whether andragogy is the art and science of helping adults learn or whether it is his own ideological exposition? In other words, is it a psychological position based on research or is it a philosophy of adult education based on his own humanistic ideals? A similar example might be the fact that Knowles has consistently claimed that adulthood is in some way related to autonomy and self-direction. This may be true, but Riesman's (1950) classical study The Lonely Crowd showed that there were some adults within his study who were 'other directed' as well as those who were 'inner' or 'tradition' directed. The latter may be construed as self-directed but the former cannot be seen in this manner. Hence it is either necessary to argue that those who are other directed are not adults or that his approach to adulthood is ideological. If it is ideological and every adult should be self-directed, then Knowles has to face the question that Hobbes discussed as long ago as 1651 in Leviathan. In any case his conception is clearly individualistic and as

such needs to respond to the types of criticisms raised of individualism by Keddie (1980). However, the frequent exposition of his position has led to profound debates within the field of study of adult education which have resulted in an enriched academic understanding of the process of the education of adults. When a debate has convinced him that elements of his position were untenable, then with characteristic openness and honesty he has responded by changing his position, although never changing his value system. This openness and humanity characterise both his writing and his person. Knowles's writing has also resulted in many people from different areas of work becoming much more aware of this humanistic approach to adult teaching and learning than they would have done had he not proclaimed his message so forcefully and so widely.

Malcolm Knowles's formulation of andragogy was the first major attempt in the West to construct a comprehensive theory of adult education and this has been one of the constant concerns that he has held throughout his career. While it will have become apparent that it is not as comprehensive a theory as he would have perhaps anticipated, he has provided a foundation upon which such a theory might eventually be erected.

As a teacher, writer and leader in the field, Knowles has been an innovator, responding to the needs of the field as he perceived them and, as such, he has been a key figure in the growth of the theory and practice of adult education throughout the Western world this century. Yet above all, it would perhaps be fair to say that both his theory and his practice have embodied his own value system and that this is contained within his formulations of andragogy.

References

Anderson, M.L. and Lindeman, E.C. 1927 <u>Education Through Experience</u> New York, Workers Education Bureau

Boyer, D.L. 1984 Malcolm Knowles and Carl Rogers: A Comparison of Andragogy and Student-Centred Learning in <u>Lifelong Learning: an Omnibus of Practice and Research</u> Vol 7 No. 4 Washington

Courtenay B. and Stevenson P., 1983 Avoiding the Threat of Gogymania in <u>Lifelong Learning: the Adult Years</u> Vol 6 No. 7 Washington

Cross, K.P. 1981 <u>Adults as Learners</u> San Francisco, Jossey Bass

Day C and Baskett H.K. 1982 Discrepancies between Intention and Practice: Re-examining some Basic Assumptions about Adult and Continuing Professional Education in <u>International Journal of Lifelong Education</u> Vol 1 No. 2

Elias, J.L. 1979 Andragogy Revisited in <u>Adult Education</u> Vol 29 Washington

Griffith, W.S. 1980 Co-ordination of Personnel, Programs and Services, in Peters, J.M. et al <u>op cit</u>

Hartree A 1984 Malcolm Knowles' Theory of Andragogy: A Critique in <u>International Journal of Lifelong Education</u> Vol 3 No. 2

Hewitt, D. and Mather, K.F. 1937 <u>Adult Education: A Dynamic for Democracy</u>, New York, Appleton-Century-Crofts

Hobbes, T. 1651 - 1968 (ed) <u>Leviathan</u> Harmondsworth, Pelican

Houle, C.O. 1972 <u>The Design of Education</u> San Francisco Jossey Bass

Jarvis, P. 1985 <u>The Sociology of Adult and Continuing Education</u> London, Croom Helm

Jarvis, P. Contract Learning in <u>Journal of District Nursing</u>, (Nov.) pp. 13-14

Keddie N. 1980 Adult Education: An Ideology of Individualism in Thompson J. (ed) <u>op.cit.</u>

Knowles, M.S. 1950 <u>Informal Adult Education</u> New York, Association Press

Knowles, M.S. 1957 Philosophical Issues that Confront Adult Educators in <u>Adult Education</u> Vol 7 No. 4

Knowles, M.S. (ed.) 1960 <u>Handbook of Adult Education in the U.S.A.</u> Adult Education Association of the U.S.A.

Knowles, M.S. 1968 Androgogy Not Pedagogy in <u>Adult Leadership</u> No. 16

Knowles, M.S´ 1970 <u>The Modern Practice of Adult Education: Andragogy versus Pedagogy</u> New York, Association Press

Knowles, M.S. 1973 <u>The Adult Learner: A Neglected Species</u> Houston, Gulf Publishing Co.

Knowles, M.S. 1975 <u>Self Directed Learning</u> Chicago, Follett Publishing Co.

Knowles, M.S. 1977 <u>A History of the Adult Education Movement in the U.S.A.</u>, New York, Krieger (first published 1962)

Knowles, M.S. 1978 (2nd ed) <u>The Adult Learner a Neglected Species</u>, Houston, Gulf Publishing Co.

Knowles, M.S. 1979 Andragogy Revisited II <u>Adult Education</u> Vol 30 Washington

Knowles, M.S. 1980a The Growth and Development of Adult Education in Peters J.M. et al <u>op cit</u>

Knowles, M.S. 1980b (2nd ed) <u>The Modern Practice of Adult Education: From Pedgagogy to Andragogy</u> Chicago, Association Press

Knowles, M.S., 1982 Faith Development in the Adult Life Cycle: an Adult Educator's Reflections in Stokes, K. (ed) <u>op cit</u>

Knowles, M.S. and Knowles, H. 1959 <u>Introduction to Group Dynamics</u> Chicago, Association Press

Knowles, M.S. et al 1984 <u>Andragogy in Action: Applying Modern Principles of Adult Education</u> San Francisco, Jossey Bass

Knudson, R.S. 1979 Andragogy Revisited: Humanagogy Anyone? in <u>Adult Education</u> Vol 29 Washington

Label, J. 1978 Beyond Andragogy to Gerogogy in <u>Lifelong Learning: the Adult Years</u> No. 1 Washington

Lindeman, E.C. 1926 <u>The Meaning of Adult Education</u> New York, New Republic.

McKenzie, L. 1977 The Issue of Andragogy in <u>Adult Education</u> Vol 27 Washington

McKenzie, I. 1979 Andragogy Revisited: Response to Elias in <u>Adult Education</u> Vol 29 Washington

Nottingham Andragogy Group 1983 <u>Towards a Developmental Theory of Andragogy</u> University of Nottingham, Dept of Adult Education

Peters, J. <u>et al</u>. 1980 <u>Building an Effective Adult Education Enterprise</u> San Francisco, Jossey Bass

Riesman, D. 1950 <u>The Lonely Crowd</u> New Haven, Yale University Press

Skalka, J. and Livecka, E. 1977 <u>Adult Education in the Czechoslovak Socialist Republic</u> Prague, European Centre for Leisure and Education.

Stokes, K. 1982 <u>Faith Development in the Adult Life Cycle</u> New York, W.H. Sadlier.

Tennant, M. 1986 An Evaluation of Knowles' Theory of Adult Learning in <u>International Journal of Lifelong Education</u> Vol 5 No. 2

Thompson, J. 1980 <u>Adult Education for a Change</u> London Hutchinson

Yonge, G.D. 1985 Andragogy and Pedagogy: Two Ways of Accompaniment in <u>Adult Education Quarterly</u> Vol 35 No 3 Washington

Chapter Ten

ROBY KIDD - INTELLECTUAL VOYAGEUR

Alan M. Thomas

> Human beings seem to seek after learning;
> learning seems to be the condition of a healthy
> organism. The main task is to provide the
> climate and the atmosphere and stimulus and
> self-discipline in which learning is promoted.
> (Kidd unpublished memoirs, a, p.8)

> Our first problem is to survive. It is not a
> question of the survival of the fittest; either
> we survive together or we perish together.
> Survival requires that the countries of the
> world must learn to live together in peace.
> Learn is the operative word. Mutual respect,
> understanding, sympathy, are qualities that are
> destroyed by ignorance, and fostered by
> knowledge. In the field of international
> understanding, adult education in today's
> divided world takes on a new importance.
> Provided that man learns to survive, he has in
> front of him opportunities for social
> development and personal well-being such as
> have never been open to him before. Declaration:
> Second UNESCO World Conference on Adult
> Education, from Kidd (1974a, p.35.)

In many respects the two preceding statements
represent the continuing polarities, the Scylla and
Charybdis, of the life and thought of J. Robbins
Kidd. Both life and thought have to be considered in
any appreciation of him. To treat them separately
would be to risk failing to grasp the essence of the
man, the essence of the "adult education movement"
with which he was so intimately associated, and the
character of the relationship between the two.

I have believed for many years that no one

188

learns anything without involvement. I am convinced that when someone has learned something well he ought to express that learning in action. From personal experience I know that learning of depth and power occurs when one takes part in significant action, and reflects, studies, analyzes and observes one's own behaviour and that of others engaged in action. I even see that temporary withdrawal from action, to seek quiet and contemplate, the contribution of Asian scholars in particular, is part of the total process of engagement, not disengagement. (Unpublished Memoirs, b.)

The maintenance of a coherent life of thought and action dominated Kidd's writing and speaking - those two activities were never widely separated - revolving constantly on such themes as learning; learning in action; learning with others in pursuit of collective goals; the demands of rational behaviour; and the ability to rise beyond one's own cultural and national limitations. More than anyone else among his contemporaries, Kidd reflected upon, articulated, and tried to embody the wonderful and inscrutable relationship between individual learning and the world in which that learning manifests itself. For Kidd, it seems, thinking and learning were virtually indistinguishable, and reciprocal action inescapable. For him, that relationship was compellingly implicit in the practice and advocacy of adult education. Practitioners throughout the world, in the years between 1954 and 1982 came to see him as the embodiment of those convictions.

J. Robbins Kidd was born in the small town of Wapella in the Canadian province of Saskatchewan in 1915. Early in his life, following the death of his father, the family moved to Vancouver, British Columbia, where he completed his formal schooling. If the Canadian prairies left their characteristic stamp upon him, even at so early an age, it was not particularly noticeable in his later years, though he remained an enthusiastic admirer of the adult education programs of the Wheat Pools, those most characteristic of all prairie institutions. However, his informal and perhaps non-formal education was very much more the product of adolescent periods spent in Gibson's Landing, a small coastal settlement north of the city of Vancouver. Like all sea coasts, British Columbia has attracted wanderers from all parts of the world. "However my old grandfather had built a tall, gaunt, shingled house on a hill at

Gibson's Landing, to which seaside village had come the poor and the lost and adventurers from everywhere, including some Finnish communists fleeing from the persecution of Marshall Mannerheim, social democrats from many countries of Europe. It was here in the bush and the fishing boats and the road gangs that I learned economics and Canadian history, this was my real college." (Kidd, 1975a, p.228) Kidd's speeches and writings throughout his lifetime were sprinkled with references to his years in Gibson's Landing.

He joined the staff of the Young Men's Christian Association of Canada (YMCA) in 1935 where he was responsible for Adult and Boys' Work. In 1943 he moved to the Ottawa "Y" where he was involved in adult education and in 1947 he left to take a position with the Canadian Association for Adult Education (CAAE).

Having moved to Montreal, in the service of the YMCA, he completed his BA at Sir George Williams University (1939), his MA at McGill University (1943), both in that city, and his Ed.D. at Teachers' College, Columbia University in New York City (1947). In an address to the first international conference of university evening students in Montreal in 1960, he said, "... let me confess that I was never an evening student. But let me hastily tell you that I have some claim to be here; every part of my undergraduate and graduate work was taken while I was fully employed. That should qualify me in spirit if not in fact." (Kidd, 1969, p.189.) Long before there was much official interest in the unconventional student, except perhaps at Sir George Williams University, the YMCA university expressly designed for them, Kidd demonstrated personally that an individual could do what he later argued ought to be possible for everyone with the appropriate qualifications and determination.

In the same address, true to his relentless advocacy for adult education, even among those who were both prime participants and beneficiaries, he went on to say: "The fact is that in almost every single list where the results of evening students are compared with those of regular college students, the older student has a better performance." (ibid: p.191)

It is not entirely clear just under what circumstances and why Kidd developed his interest in and commitment to the education of adults. Possibly it arose in part from his work with the YMCA programs for boys and men, an experience denied to most formal educators, which allowed him to witness the precious continuity in the lives of individuals who were, by means of various programs, engaged in learning of equal significance to anything they experienced in school. In Ottawa he had been involved in the creation of Carlton College, a new post-secondary institution designed largely to provide university education for fully employed civil servants. In addition, counselling for the New York YMCA had brought him into regular contact with relatively uneducated veterans who were trying to continue the transformation of their lives that military service had begun. Certainly the "Y" left its stamp on him as it has, indelibly, on the many Canadians who have passed through its employment. Receptiveness, interest, compassion, and a consuming curiosity about other individuals are among those characteristics. But perhaps more than anything else, the "Y" reinforced his natural optimism about the world and all of its people, an optimism, that despite considerable test, dominated all of his work.

He was not unaware of the effects of the ethos of the "Y" on him, especially when he found himself among the somewhat more sophisticated participants in the work of the Canadian Association for Adult Education in the late nineteen-forties.

> The fact that I was a YMCA secretary did not endear me to many ... When I joined the CAAE staff, some of the board members exercised tolerance for the rather breezy salutations that I had learned in dealing with boys' gang personnel in Montreal as well as the informality of my dress. But it was an association in which differences were accepted and the tolerance eventually turned to a kind of affection which I may not have deserved, but which warmed me. Neither then nor since have I been able to describe an adult educationist as belonging to a particular type. (Kidd, Unpublished Memoirs, a, p.29)

Whatever his preparation, once Kidd found himself in the company of dedicated adult educators, voluntary and professional, there was no turning back.

Kidd became the director of the CAAE in 1951. The post allowed him, indeed insisted on engagement with national Canada. A glance at the geography of the country and a slight acquaintance with its pre-war society will explain why until then, national experience had been largely the preserve of commercial representatives and politicians. His early responsibility for the Joint Planning Commission, a device of the Canadian Association for Adult Education for developing cooperative relationships between voluntary organizations and government agencies active in adult education of all kinds, introduced him to the complex subtleties of the management of education in Canada where the Federal Government, denied an official role by the constitution, must accomplish its inescapable educational objectives by a combination of stealth and diplomacy. Similary his work with Farm Radio Forum and Citizens' Forum, the two national public affairs programs operated by the CAAE, in cooperation with the Canadian Broadcasting Corporation, provided experience in the precarious area of adult education centred on contentious political issues involving wide public concern.

Travelling across Canada several times a year in the following decade, Kidd quickly came to see the tangled multiplicity of voluntary organizations and the tiers of frequently overlapping government jurisdictions, as a community open to development, to development on the most humane and rewarding of all imaginable bases, the potential of adult learning. He learned to exert the type of persuasive, non-threatening, supportive leadership that such a small, threadbare, voluntary vehicle as the CAAE demanded, and exercised those skills with great success everywhere in Canada, with the exception of the Province of Quebec. Perhaps it was no more than the problems of the historical moment, characterized by the growing, restless nationalism in that province, but Kidd was never able to establish the rapport and mutual trust with French-speaking, adult educators in Quebec that he maintained so successfully in English-speaking Canada and with adult educators throughout the rest of the world.

Working with all types of public and private organizations, large and small, with respect to any problem or opportunity where adult learning might be involved, Kidd developed the special skills and attitudes appropriate for working on the margins of established interests and organizations. In particular he developed an ability to see large organizations not as impersonal, mostly impenetrable systems, but in terms of particular individuals within those organizations, individuals who could be talked with, who could be both understood and persuaded, and above all who could have an effect on the organizations themselves.

In the late nineteen-forties Kidd undertook the establishment of national awards for achievement in film and radio. He knew that these achievements were already being much admired outside of Canada, and he also understood the powerful educational value of public recognition no matter how modest the actual prize. At the same time he demonstrated what became a life-long interest in and enthusiasm for film and broadcasting as vehicles for artistic accomplishment of the first rank, and as educational instruments of immense potential.

Kidd participated substantially in the first two national conferences on education held in Canada in the late nineteen-fifties and early nineteen-sixties; was the first president of Canadian Library Week; and managed to be nearly everywhere in the country where the interests of adult learners needed nurture or protection.

These were not easy years, either financially for the CAAE - it was almost always on the verge of bankruptcy - or for the growth of programmatic or financial support of adult education by the dominant educational institutions. Writing in 1950, Kidd said: "Even where adult education is well established it has not won a very important place for itself. It may have become the 'third' partner along with the public school and the university, but if so it is most certainly a very green and junior partner." (Kidd, 1950, p.12)

Characteristically, he did not lay all the blame for this state of adult education at the door of the institutions of formal education or of the formal educators. In addition he cited the failure of nerve and determination among Canadian adult educators themselves. "We are quite likely to make the claim that adult education is needed to save our society and in the next breath ask for a budget for an entire province that would scarcely run a single public school." (ibid:p.12) In the same article there is a flash of the enthusiasm, generosity, and tempered optimism that informed all of his life.

Adult education in Canada could certainly not be considered very radical or very reactionary, or even very daring. But it is based on a respect for reason and belief, and particularly a respect for people ... And what does it mean on balance? A history that is brief but full and rich. A list of remarkable accomplishments already, with present and future opportunities and responsibilities that overmatch anything

that came before ... Will it be enough? Not that
there is any doubt that genuine achievement will
come. These are certain. But such efforts may
still not equal what could and should be done.
Will we muster the vision needed and the
resources? (ibid:p.23)

In 1961, after fourteen years at the CAAE, he left to
become the Secretary-General of the Humanities and
the Social Sciences Research Councils of Canada. But
he did not leave his commitment to and participation
in adult education.

From the earliest days at the CAAE, Kidd became
increasingly involved in international adult
education. "I began to look after the study-
observation experiences of foreign educationists in
1947, and went first in 1954 into the Caribbean for
field work." (Kidd, 1974b, p.8.) While his
involvement in retrospect, seems little more than
casual, Kidd observed later that for him it had a
certain inevitability.

I was as ready as any lover for an offer of
marriage, as any actor for a bit part, or any
sailboat addict receiving an invitation to
leave his office when the sun is high and the
wind is fresh ... one of the strongest reasons
was that I had not been to war. International
development seemed to offer some of the
possibilities for service, and some of the
adventures I had missed. (Kidd, Unpublished
Memoirs, d, p.35)

Opportunities and self-incurred international
obligations followed relentlessly. In 1953 he was
invited by UNESCO to become a member of a committee.
In 1959 he was elected the first president of the
Adult Education Section of the World Conference of
the Organizations of the Teaching Profession. In 1961
he became president of the Advisory Committee to
UNESCO on Adult Education, a post he was to hold for
five years. In 1965 he conductd a study of university
extension for the State of Alaska. In 1965 he left
his position with the Canadian Research Councils to
spend a year developing a major project in adult
education for the Indian State of Rajasthan, a
project supported by the Canadian International
Development Agency, the University of British
Columbia, and the Government of India. In 1969 he was
appointed a member of the UNESCO jury for the
awarding of world prizes for achievement in the

development of adult literacy, a position he retained for the rest of his life.

But there can be little doubt that his election as President of the second UNESCO World Conference on Adult Education in the city of Montreal in 1960 both symbolized and established irreversibly his personal and intellectual presence on the world stage. The conference convinced Kidd that world cooperation was not only a necessity, it was a possibility, and that adult education was not only a means but an end in that context. "Considerable doubt and pessimism were expressed about the Montreal conference even before the delegates began to arrive. The time was 1960, the period of the deepest freeze in the cold war; the U-2 incident had just occurred and President Eisenhower's planned trip to Moscow had been abruptly cancelled. Moreover the Montreal conference was the very first international conference in which Communist countries were represented in force." (Kidd, 1974a, p.13) ... and "Understanding requires a will for it. The delegates at Montreal came for a serious purpose and were an exceptional group of men and women who were bent on talking and working together and were not easily deterred." (ibid:p.14).

Kidd's fundamental belief in the final efficacy of individuals talking reasonably with each other in circumstances that permitted, indeed encouraged such exchange, even at a global level, seemed to him to have been confirmed.

Following his year in India, in 1966 Kidd joined the newly created Ontario Institute for Studies in Education (OISE) as the first chairman of the Department of Adult Education. The Institute was one of the many research and development agencies in education founded throughout the world during the educationally opulent nineteen-sixties, but unlike most of the others, incorporated graduate instruction among its functions. That inclusion probably saved it from the loss of support experienced by so many others a decade later, and the combination of the three activities, research, teaching, and field development, allowed Kidd to continue the major tasks of his life with only a slightly different emphasis. During his years at the CAAE (see Selman, G., 1982). Kidd worked strenuously for the increase in opportunities for the systematic preparation of practitioners of adult education. Almost every summer Kidd had taught often the first course in adult education at universities throughout Canada. His teaching style never lost the casual somewhat hurried quality so characteristic of

university summer school. With little asssistance
and ferocious acquisitiveness he had assembled the
best library on adult education in Canada. Within the
limits of money and space characteristic of a small
voluntary organization, the latter was no mean
accomplishment. The department quickly became one of
the strongest in Canada and a beacon for
practitioners throughout the world. While concentrating on building up the faculty, Kidd was also able
to turn the natural extension of his international
work, the development of comparative studies in adult
education.

Nevertheless, his "trigger-finger" continued to
itch and in 1972, with modest support from the
Canadian International Development Agency he
launched the International Council for Adult
Education (ICAE). Despite criticism from some
national adult education bodies that the support of
the Council would undermine UNESCO, Kidd persisted,
and by the time of his death the Council had become a
non-governmental organization for adult education of
major influence. The need for such a non-governmental
organization in international adult education, as a
counter-point to the influence of governments which
was growing steadily through UNESCO itself, was a
consistent thread in Kidd's beliefs. Just as he had
extended his "community-development" skills from the
volatile organizational turmoil represented by
Canada to the international stage, so he extended
ideas and practices that arose from his Canadian
experience. Kidd was intensely aware of the
ambivalence with which most governments regard
"learning" however democratic they profess to be. The
Council represented an alternative world vehicle for
the nourishment and protection of the principles of
life-long learning.

In the late nineteen-seventies Kidd was invited
to edit the adult education section of the new
International Encyclopedia of Education to be
produced by Pergamon Press. In many respects the
planning of that section represented the apotheosis
of his life and work. A glance at the range of
categories which he believed necessary for the
understanding of the scope and importance of adult
education, in contrast to coverage in earlier
educational lexicons, indicates something of the
breadth and depth of his experience and his
imagination. Kidd died in 1982 before that work could
be completed but the section remains as a monument to
his life and work.

Intellectual Forebearers

It is not an easy task to identify Kidd's intellectual ancestors and models. Friends, colleagues and above all his audiences throughout the world, grew accustomed to the frequency and variety of the references with which he populated his spoken and written words. He read widely and had an unerring eye for the statement in any text of any historical period that could be used to justify and expand a commitment to adult education. His imagination seemed to be a sponge for examples, anecdotes, and statements about learning in any context.

Nevertheless, some ideas and images repeat themselves with sufficient frequency to reveal a pattern of example and influence. He was particularly impressed by examples of men and women who, in terms of educational achievement, had literally dragged themselves up by their bootstraps. He refers repeatedly to Louis de Wolfe, a Canadian educator who rose to the top of his profession with little early schooling; to Eduard Lindeman, with whom he worked in New York during his years of graduate study, and who seemed to epitomize the self-made scholar with a limited regard for intellectual and academic shibboleths; and to other individuals with similar energy, curiosity, and determination. Perhaps the seeds of Kidd's fascination were supplied by the example of his father, of whom, in one of his rare references to him, he said, "He never went beyond grade four. Still he served his town as mayor for many years, took an active part in provincial and national politics, started the first insurance business and the first garage and automobile agency in that part of the West." (Kidd, 1966, p17) While often discouraged by what he saw in partisan politics he was an admirer of many of the political leaders he met during his lifetime. Of Julius Nyerere, President of Tanzania, and President of the ICAE, he said, "He seems to hunger for and need direct physical and intellectual contact with people." (Unpublished Memoirs, e, p.11) Kidd might have been describing himself.

He was at Teachers' College Columbia University during the last years of the influence of John Dewey and his colleagues and disciples. Men like Kilpatrick, Child, Countz, and others of the optimistic, liberal, developmental school of education were still in the ascendancy. It was an intellectual atmosphere that Kidd was to find when he joined the staff of the CAAE, and he often refers to Edward (Ned) Corbett, the original director, as his mentor. But the roots of such attitudes and the corresponding ideas are to be found earlier in Kidd's western adolescence and his experience with the YMCA. While there is little trace of formal Christianity, or of any other formal doctrine to be found in his work, he had been deeply influenced by what came to be known as Christian humanism. It represented a belief in human value in both thought and action that characterized the pioneer socialists of the Canadian West. The ideas and example of the Canadian pastor-politician, J.M. Woodsworth, founder of the first socialist party, and many of his associates, influenced Kidd profoundly and were easily translated to the education of adults and his work at the CAAE. In commenting on the relationship of the social gospel and adult education he said:

> It took effort but it wasn't impossible to bring together in the Joint Planning Commission organizations of churches, social agencies, universities, school boards and libraries, business and professional organizations, corporations, trade unions and cooperatives, and cultural societies, because there were some common bonds. One strand that united most, though not all, was an acceptance of much of the social gospel - albeit often stated in secular terms. (Kidd, 1956, p.258).

It seems to have been the combination of thought and action in company with the belief in the self-perfectibility of human beings and society represented in that doctrine that fused so gracefully in Kidd. In <u>While Time Is Burning</u>, a major recapitulation of his thought, he said: "I believe that guidance may come best from the doers, rather than the critics or theorists, although some of the best doers and critic-theorists turn out to be the same people." (Kidd, 1974b, p.30)

Obviously the roots stretch farther back to the enlightenment and its liberal thinkers. There was not much of Rousseau in Kidd's thought since he did not believe that institutions inevitably corrupted individuals, despite his frequent impatience with them. Like Locke he believed that democracy was the preferred form of government simply because it worked, and because it represented both end and means for learning. Perhaps his closest counterparts are to be found in men like Fourier and Owen, who believed that given the right environment, human beings could move towards perfection, and who set out to demonstrate that their beliefs were true.

Ideas

> There is a perpendicular dimension of learning
> continuing through the entire life-span and
> consonant with all of the divisions of
> education. There is a horizontal dimension of
> learning penetrating into every form of
> intellectual and spiritual activity known to
> man ... There is a depth dimension to learning
> responding to immediate and simple needs, on,
> up, and in the most sublime search for the truth
> that makes us free (Kidd 1966, p.72)

> Learning is the key to the effective response to
> change. As we shall see, continuous learning as
> a concept can be both a compass and a gyroscope,
> both guide and stabilizer. (J.R. Kidd
> ibid:p.25)

The fascination for the meaning of learning, both
individually and in a social context is the
foundation of Kidd's thought. The more visible
commitment to the education of adults occasionally
obscured his preoccupation, though a brief contact
with that vocation indicates the inseparability of
both pursuits. Kidd entered the world of adult
education at a time when the world, industrial and
otherwise, was relapsing into an even more
encompassing belief in the education of the young as
the principal key to every sort of development than
had been the case previously. That relapse was
occurring despite the fact that a dependence upon the
learning capacities of millions of adults had been
the primary factor in the prosecution of a global
war. In arguing for the commitment of greater
resources to the education of adults, it became
immediately necessary to dispel a number of myths and
prejudices about the learning capacities and will of
adults, but also to develop much more precise
understanding of actually how adult learning was best
accomplished.

Kidd had begun his interest at least as early as
his undergraduate years with his thesis on Henry
Marshall Tory, the founder of "frontier"
universities in Canada. In his graduate studies at
Columbia University he had been impressed by the work
of Thorndyke and Lorge, and deeply influenced by the
life and achievements of Eduard Lindeman.

One of the greatest needs, at the mid-century, was for a book or series of texts that would bring together the scattered information and make some coherence of what was known as well as identify problems for further study ... While I was an admirer of Irving Lorge, I pointed out that his remarkable findings, while important, constituted only part of the story, and that something much more comprehensive was needed ... My recommendations were for a statement that would capture what was relevant from philosophy and all the social sciences, would analyze many fields of practice, for example, mass communications, training in industry, and the armed forces, adoption of new farm practices, learning a second language. For several years I made attempts, none successful, to interest some of our colleagues to undertake the work, but nothing happened. So, with considerable temerity, I decided to bring out a book myself ... a practitioner's book, written by a practitioner, with just as much theory as I thought I understood (Unpublished Memoirs, a, p.9)

The result of that temerity was How Adults Learn. (Kidd, 1959). Despite his belief that it was not a text book, by the time of the revision in 1973, it had become a standard text in the field and had been translated into more than ten languages.

The book established the canons for the approach to adult education, and while as Kidd himself insisted, it was not based on his own research, it was one of, if not the earliest collection and interpretation of available data to be found in one place. However, it went beyond simply being a collection and representation, since it bore the stamp of Kidd's original approach to adult learning and adult education. Two themes predominate. First, as our opening quotation indicates, Kidd had concluded that learning, not just for adults but for all humans, comes closest to being what earlier social psychologists had termed a "drive"; a wholly natural impulse of the living organism. Individuals do not need to be "motivated" to learn, that is persuaded, seduced, bullied, or tricked, but only into learning certain things that other individuals or collectivities believe will be good for them. The impulse to learn, to change oneself, is a wholly natural one, and is only absent by force of unyielding circumstance, which can be cumulative in its effects. "Men and women are all different. Each has two kinds of limitation, that imposed by his nature and development and that which he imposes on himself. Usually, if not always, the self-imposed restriction, the shackles each man fixes on himself, are the more binding." (Kidd, Unpublished Memoirs, a, p.9). These arguments in the early 1960s were in considerable contrast to the views about resistance to learning that had arisen from the understandable, if unfortunate, identification of learning with the schooling of children.

The second principal theme is the assertion that since adults learn throughout their entire life, any understanding of the nature of learning must be drawn from the fields of enquiry that deal with all of life, not just that section of psychology and educational theory focused on children and youth. Kidd established the need and the right to draw information from all the exercise of human imagination and study in order to truly understand learning and adult education. This conviction not only involved the inclusion of history, philosophy, all of the social sciences, and many natural sciences, it also involved the arts. While his direct experience had been in the utilization of what were occasionally called the "democratic arts" - film, radio, theater - he was, throughout his life, a keen observer of paint, music, and the crafts. He could easily have written the phrase from the Harvard Report he was so tireless in repeating, "Precisely because they wear the warmth and colour of the senses, the arts are probably the strongest and deepest of all educative forces."

His arguments, based on the range of his investigation of various literatures, became, in turn his convictions. Not only could adults learn, but they did, and it was of enormous importance for everyone, and especially adult educators to accept, in fact welcome, the fact that adults were quite capable of learning independently of their teachers.

A third theme, that appeared throughout the book, and that was to preoccupy Kidd increasingly throughout his life, particularly the years of activity in international development, was that of the inescapable social context of adult learning. Since learning always extends far beyond the limits of education, even the most generous definition of adult education, its manifestations will always be felt in all of the social, political and economic affairs of mankind. For Kidd, there was a continuing fascination in examining social events for evidence of who had or who had not learned something of significance in the situation. Colleagues who travelled with him frequently experienced an absorbing analysis of the newspaper from the learning perspective.

Kidd himself acknowledged repeatedly, how astonishing it was that these canons of adult learning, almost all stemming from the renewed belief in the autonomy of the learner, became accepted so quickly, in theory, if not always in practice.

Learning is a voluntary act. Kidd's belief about the intimate connection between learning and other actions made him particularly sensitive to that fact. In addition, he believed that the most effective learning arose from the voluntary association of individuals. "Ideas may come from almost anywhere but shared purposes and the commitment that leads to action seems only to be created in face-to-face meetings." (Kidd, Unpublished Memoirs, d, p.19).

From the commitment to the voluntary, he developed, particularly in the special political atmosphere of Canada, a belief in the efficacy of sensibly designed and administered voluntary organizations. He was not a blind enthusiast, for he knew that voluntary organizations could be corrupt, and willful, and obstructive, but he did develop an abiding conviction of the value of some independence from government. In commenting on the relationship of voluntary activity and government in Canada, in one of his first publications, Kidd observed that, "... nothing in that experience has caused us to cower before our own government ... The availability of public funds for these (voluntary) purposes, has brought to adult education a wide variety of film and radio programs that would and could not have been provided in any other way." (Kidd 1950, p.22) It was this same belief that led him to the creation of the International Council for Adult Education in 1972; a voluntary, non-governmental organization that could perform the same role with respect to advocacy, experimentation, and coordination on a world scale. Basically Kidd believed that organized voluntary behaviour allowed for an opportunity for human learning that was denied to government, and that every society, and the world, needed both.

The commitment to face-to-face environments, and to voluntary activity, placed for Kidd considerable emphasis on the "community" and on community control.

It is the growing realization that the setting

> for adult education is the community itself.
> While there is nothing novel about such an idea,
> it never had such widespread acceptance before.
> ... in increasing measure then, those working in
> adult education will have to have knowledge,
> skill, and insight about the forces affecting
> community life and the organizations which can
> be the most meaningful. (ibid:pp.14-15)

Written at the beginning of his career, and in the
"community enthusiasms" of the immediate post-war
years, Kidd was increasingly obliged to work in
"national" and "international" settings where the
notion of "a Community" became increasingly
esoteric. Nevertheless, he retained throughout his
working life a remarkable ability to create under
many different circumstances, some of the most
powerful characteristics of community life, whether
it was in the direction of international conferences,
the creation of academic departments, or the
stimulation of small meetings. All were perceived as
essential but not necessarily automatically,
successful vehicles for learning.

Adult Education

In the light of Kidd's public and life-long
association with adult education, it is surprising to
discover in his thought and writing that the term is
used only as frequently as the two other terms that
dominate his thinking - continuous learning and lifelong education. He was uncomfortable with the term,
"continuing education" since he believed, correctly
in the context of his time, that it was inextricably
associated with education undertaken only after the
formal period, and therefore too restricting for his
purposes. In addition, he seems to have been uneasy
with the lengthy definition of adult education
arrived at by his colleagues at UNESCO in 1976. For
him it was too clumsy, and he appears to have
preferred the simpler ones he used in the works of
encyclopedic character which he edited or
contributed to. The definition to which he returned
repeatedly was "Any activity with an educational
purpose, planned and arranged for those who have
passed adolescence and are not engaged in full-time
study." (Kidd, 1961a, p.3.) While this definition
possessed an admirable simplicity for audiences
uninterested in the complicated categories of UNESCO
and others, it did eliminate full-time adult
students, a group that has been growing in numbers

and significance over the past decade.

However, to discover Kidd's complete idea of adult education, it is necesary to go beyond definitions and examine the interpretive comments that can be found throughout his work. First of all, he extended the education of adults, beyond the preoccupations of the post-war period when so much development took place, much of it under his leadership. Writing in the Encyclopedia Canadiana in 1975 he pointed out, "Adult Education activities in Canada are usually dated from the time of the first national survey that was completed in 1934. Actually there is a much longer history than this. In Champlain's first settlement at St. Croix in 1604, the men kept up their spirits through the first long terrible winter by organizing "L'Ordre de Bon Temps", a society for debates, good talk, music, drama, and dance." (Kidd, 1975b, p.51). One could be forgiven for concluding that 'L'Ordre' was closer to a "service club" than an agency of adult education, nevertheless, the point about its occurrence must earlier in the history of Canada than generally thought, and about the range of activities it included, is not be be overlooked.

Second, Kidd repeatedly extended the area of adult education activities beyond the narrow precincts of formal education.

> First comes the realization that adult education is not walled in by the classroom or the institution. It occurs all over the community and not always in groups. There is also a recognition that adult educators have and should collaborate with many others, teachers, librarians, recreation specialists, broadcasters, union and management, civic government, artists and other groups. (Kidd, Unpublished Memoirs, b, p.32)

Noticeably absent are politicians. Nevertheless it is clear that Kidd believed that the practice of adult education should be as catholic in its everyday character as should be research on which the practice is based.

Third, he extended its significance in social and political terms. "The organization of adult education has been fueled by faiths, by revolution, by immigration, by inventions and renaissances, by nationalist ardour, by international organizations, and now by the demands of high technology." (Kidd and Titmus, 1985, Vol. 1, p.94.) In this light it is characteristic of Kidd, as the original editor of the adult education section of the Encyclopedia to include so wide a range of categories as are represented, especially such sections as "Music and Adult Education; and Adult Education and the Plastic Arts".

For Kidd, the objectives of adult education included the entire spectrum of human objectives, individual and collective. His early commitment to the liberal education of adults, reinforced by his association in the 1950s with the American "Fund for Adult Education", and its programs in liberal adult education, perhaps prevented him from narrowing his concepts and interests as adult education became more specialized and to a degree competitive. Despite his long association with the literacy work of UNESCO, and his obvious personal commitment to universal literacy, he never allowed himself to adopt a single focus. In 1950 he wrote, "However, it is now recognized that such professional men as engineers, and doctors need a program of adult education to give them an understanding of their responsibilites as citizens, as much as any other occupational groups". (Kidd, 1950, p.21.) Then years later, he said to a group of European adult educators:

> No nation is so well developed (not even in North America or Western Europe) that it can neglect fundamental education for children or for undereducated adults ... on the other hand, no notion is so backward, so quiescent, so deprived, that it does not require the nurture of all of the most able people it can muster, that it does not depend for its survival upon many forms of adult and higher education. (Kidd, 1969, p.253.)

Kidd believed that adult education was a world movement whose time had come. But it had to be based upon constructive theory, proper and increased training of its practitioners, and the development of an appropriate, and to a degree distinct, collection of institutions. For the first objective, his summary of the three international conferences, Elsinore (1949), Montreal (1960), and Tokyo (1972), provides a perspective.

> At Elsinore, so soon after the termination of World War II, the delegates agonized over man's condition, and wondered if adult education had any answer or could speak to the problems of man

and human bestiality. At Montreal, the
conference and international adult education
were threatened alike by the cold war and power
politics, yet not only survived but triumphed.
In Tokyo the prevailing note was that adult
education is an established part of the learning
system - a system that goes far deeper and far
beyond conventional schooling. (Kidd, 1974a,
p.3.)

But it was to the Montreal conference that Kidd
turned again and again for stimulation and
inspiration. It had been a crucial personal event for
him, the first major test of the application of his
beliefs about learning and "community" on the
international stage. Most of his deepest convictions
were represented in the final recommendations of that
conference.

1. The conference urges governments to regard
    adult education not as an addition, but as
    an integral part of their national systems
    of education.
2. Economic development programs, both
    bilateral, multilateral, and through the
    United Nations and specialized agencies,
    should include adult education, in order
    to prepare the minds of people to receive
    the benefits and participate actively in
    improving their own conditions.
3. Recognizing that the nature of government
    participation in adult education will vary
    according to the different stages of
    development and educational traditions in
    countries, this conference nevertheless
    affirms that it is the duty of governments
    to create the conditions, both financial
    and administrative, in which satisfactory
    adult education can be carried on.
4. The conference urges governments to
    encourage the development of voluntary
    organizations since without the freedom,
    the creative resources, and experimental
    approach that should characterize such
    bodies, an essential element in education
    is lacking.
5. The conference urges all Member States to
    make provisions for the necessary
    resources - for example, payment of
    salaries and expenses for travel and
    subsistence - to enable adults in all

occupational groups, to participate in vocational, civic, social and cultural adult education. (Kidd, 1974a, p.17)

It would be difficult to find a more concise summary of Kidd's beliefs, and to find them stated collectively in so fragile and potentially explosive a setting seems little short of miraculous.

Governments were not the only institutions that Kidd addressed. Next in line were the formal educational agencies whose interest in and support for adult education in Canada and elsewhere had been either limited or entirely lacking. In Canada he addressed the universities in 1956 (Kidd, 1956) and the local Boards of Education in 1961 (Kidd, 1961b). In each case he pointed to the existence of a history of support by some of the agencies addressed, to the need among the adult population of Canada, and to the reforming impact that a concept of continuing education would or could have upon the practices of those agencies. Kidd took seriously the statement in the 1976 UNESCO statement that one of the functions of adult education was to reform the existing systems of education in the interests of equity and justice. Speaking of the universities he said, "If we really accept the view that there is a lifetime for learning then it might be possible to teach all vocational courses within a broad humane tradition, helping each student to understand that there are opportunities for further learning and growth open to him later." (Kidd, 1956, p.98).

Ten years later in his study of a program of continuing education for the University of Alaska, he described a "concept of higher education reaching and permeating every kind of intellectual need; of a university extension system that was planned in relation to the total ecology of the region; of an educational program that reached out to people where they lived, and one that was planned for all of life." (Kidd, Unpublished Memoirs, d. p.46.)

However, despite the characteristic optimism, an attitude he frequently criticized in himself, and then surrendered to, he was constantly ambivalent about the imagination or the will of the dominant institutions. He seemed to believe that adult education in the context of those institutions offered a second chance both for the populations concerned and the institutions themselves. But occasionally the optimism faltered. "But continuous learning does not depend upon the university. It will come, in any case. It is coming. Without the intellectual leadership of the university, however, growth may be slower, and the vision clouded." (Kidd, 1956, p.116.)

His optimism is less as well, when he became deeply embroiled in education and development, despite his successes in persuading a variety of formal agencies to support his work. In his major statement to the International Development Research Center in 1974, he said:

> It has been difficult to obtain a rational consideration of the role of education in development because of the romantics who favoured any and all forms of education regardless of costs; pessimists have felt that the educational processes were too slow and uncertain of results; and those who consider themselves economic realists, and who deny that education or training is relevant to development. (Kidd, 1974b)

But a greater recognition is found in: "And it is now clear that at least during the present century, these objectives could not be attained by many simply by adding further units of conventional school, not even if the total, or a major share of the gross national product were to be used solely for this purpose." (J.R. Kidd, ibid: p.8)

In addition there seemed to be a growing, perhaps it was primarily personal, discomfort with the increased participation of the very governments for whose attention and commitment he had so long and aggressively worked. Of the UNESCO World Conference in Tokyo he wrote:

> Since 1960 UNESCO had become much more an organization of governments and much less the domain of the individual scholar or academic society. Governments selected and instructed the delegates, yet some of the most colourful or best known personalities or prophetic voices in adult education were not even present or heard. (Kidd, 1974a, p.26)

For Kidd, a circle had been completed, with mixed and even disconcerting results. The achievement with respect to the inclusion of some forms of adult education in the regular educational systems and providing agencies of most of the world's countries had been rapid and even breathtaking. But that seemed now not to be the solution to the primary problems of the world that he and others had hoped for.

Despite his achievements with the International Council for Adult Education; the academic Department of Adult Education at OISE in which he had been able to strengthen the scientific basis and the training for adult education; his development of the field of comparative studies, which he hoped would primarily be of help to practitioners in developing countries, the goal seemed to have receded just a little to a farther horizon.

Occasionally he raised the question of why, despite the achievements, the growth in stature of adult education seemed so slow. For the most part he blamed the lack of vision among adult educators, himself included, for the failure. He was not above the occasional scolding.

> ... the lack in ourselves is more serious, more debilitating. It is not so much how we are regarded by others but our self-regard that is at fault. Some of us do not seem to value our own calling. The economists and educational planners know we are essential and wonder why we seem so diffident and unsure ... We are the future. Yet some of us seem jaded; we hark back to older "better" days, the days of Comenius, or Froebel, or Grundtvig, or Mansbridge. We talk and act as if opportunity or excitement was found only in the developing countries. One hears such talk even in Europe where such fantastic economic and social changes are occurring daily; where miracles are common place ... In what other time did men soberly plan to make education the central motif of life? (Kidd, 1969, p.241)

In While Time is Burning, Kidd reintroduced a concept that he had first articulated in How Adults Learn, that of the learning system and the learning force. Of the learning system he said:

> that there exist a totality of planned learning activities for people of all ages including (a) programs organized in institutions such as schools, colleges, universities, libraries and museums, (b) educational activities offered by organizations such as corporations, whose primary objective is something other than education, (c) many non-formal experiences through the electronic media, travel, etc. which are planned to have an educational result.

> These activities are so disparate that many
> people have failed to consider them a part of a
> system ... The learning force is the totality of
> individuals who are engaged seriously, albeit
> recurrently or intermittently, in systematic
> learning ... Unless such a system and such a
> force is postulated it is not possible to
> undertake an analysis of systematic learning.
> (Kidd, 1974b, p.35)

In the same context Kidd argued that much more
could be accomplished in development, but only if "a
coherence, a wholeness, a genuine learning system in
which all parts are valued and have their place"
(ibid: p.30) was utilized as a basic principle. In
this context Kidd seems to have been re-asserting the
value of learning over education, though the ideas
were not developed a great deal further. What
characterized a great deal of his thought in its
development, was a long reluctance to accept that
separation. In many cases he used the terms education
and learning as though they were interchangeable, and
much of his view of the nature of learning was drawn
from examination of essentially educational
environments. He was deeply affected by the work of
Allen Tough (see Tough, 1971) and argued that: "A
program of motivation that maximized improvement of
performance in self-directed learning may turn out to
be the most productive education for development as
measured in relation to resource investment and could
result in a radical readjustment of traditional
inputs to education." (Kidd, 1974b, p.37)

In one of his last writings Kidd summarized the
"paradigm shift" that he believed had taken place
with respect to the understanding of "learning" in
the past several decades. He reviewed the various
context in which the term was being used, "the
learning society", "life-long learning", self-
directed learning", "learning at a distance", etc.,
indicating some discomfort with the terms
"andragogy" and enthusiastic support for "mathetics".

The importance of the concept of mathetics is
that it is a way of linking together most of the
fields from which a data bank about learning is
developing. The concept stresses interrelation-
ships at a time when increasing specialization
has tended to impede knowledge. It also
recognizes that important research about
learning may not only be discovered in special

applied fields, such as library science, but
that it may integrate contributions from the
"regular" fields of scholarship in almost every
discipline. (Kidd, 1983, pp.525-542.)

But in a section entitled "Learning as a Human, Not
Just a Cultural Phenomenon", he indicates that he has
still not broken entirely from the idea of learning
as an individual phenomenon, with education as its
collective or cultural counterpart.

Perhaps his claim for the need for coherence
reflected the difficulty he was having in finding
coherence in his own thought. Just as he had
represented and reflected so consistently the
development of adult education in his own life, he
was reflecting the declining enthusiasm for
education of any kind in the world, and the rising
skepticism about the universal value of the formal
providing agencies. The center showed signs of not
holding.

It would be impossible to imagine, and to
evaluate, the past forty years in adult education in
the world without taking account of Roby Kidd. He
emerged from a small "l" liberal tradition in his own
country, and remained faithful to it on the broader
stage. He appears to embrace no formal ideology,
except that associated with learning, perhaps
because he believed that any world-view that did not
allow for the unsettling factor of unpredictable
individual change resulting from unanticipated
learning, was simply inadequate. He did believe in
the perfectability of human beings though he knew
what traps and accidents lay in the path of any one.
He was a westerner who learned how to work in the
East, if he did not, like most of us, fully
understand it. He was a male of his generation, with
the result that his writing abounds with the male
pronoun, yet he believed that much of his work in
adult education was devoted to the liberation of
women, as has turned out to be the case. He really
tried to model his life on his beliefs at every
stage, and if they, the beliefs, were sometimes at
odds and contradictory, he usually acknowledged that
fact with both grace and humour.

There was a certain innocence about Roby Kidd
but it was not naivete. He knew very well what the
stakes and the dangers were, if not before the
Montreal conference, then certainly afterwards.

The man who is offered only a minimum of
learning, skills enough for drudgery but not for

development, may turn on us and destroy us. It
is the scarcely literate, the partially
educated who are the pawns and dupes of the
political adventurers, half skilled people,
scarred with failure and eaten by envy of those
who have had greater opportunities. Dangers
lurk for all of us when we refuse anyone the
chance to develop towards his full capacity.
(Kidd, Unpublished Memoirs, f, p.13.)

Dangers were also to be found in the limits,
sometimes self-imposed, of the remedy to which Kidd
had devoted his life. Kidd saw those limits without
the time or opportunity of going beyond them.

Nevertheless human and financial resources are
limited so there are finite and practical
boundaries to purpose and curriculum even if
there are no theoretical ones. The self-
directed learner is more free, but even he or
she is for the most part restricted by the
availability of library and other learning
resources. The participant in organized
education experiences can only study what the
providers offer. There is a compromise between
what the providers wish and what the learners
will accept which is largely determined by the
priorities of the former, which in turn are set
by the social, cultural, political and economic
factors in society as a whole. (Kidd and Titmus,
1985, Vol. 1, p.99.)

The commitment to learning really only in the context
of education, led Kidd, in the circumstances of the
early nineteen-eighties, to some dismay about the
future.
Nevertheless he continued to believe that hope
was to be found in the minds, imaginations and hearts
of individuals, who were willing and capable of
learning beyond their existing limitations.
Confrontation and collective ideologies were not his
style. Persuasion, argument and demonstration were
the markers of the path he preferred. In commenting
upon his major published work, How Adults Learn, he
said:

I have wished sometimes that I had written with
greater lucidity and thought that I might have
chosen other examples and illustrations, but I
would not alter the tone or the conclusions,
except to accentuate the chief conclusion, that

> people of all kinds, in all places, and of all
> ages, have a marvellous capacity to learn, and
> grow, and enlarge. (Kidd, Unpublished Memoirs,
> a, p.4.)

The comment on the book might well serve as a comment
on his life.

Kidd emerged first as a national figure and then
on the international stage on the crest of the
contemporary interest in the education of adults. He
rode the wave with style and compassion, giving it a
shape and substance that will inform the decades
during which adult learning is once again
incorporated into the everyday affairs of human kind.

Acknowledgement

The author wishes to acknowledge the permission given
him by the Kidd family to draw from personal papers.

References

Allen, R. (ed) 1975 The Social Gospel in Canada
Ottawa National Museum of Man. Mercury Series

Kidd, J.R. 1950 Present Trends and Developments in
Kidd (ed) 1950 op cit

Kidd, J.R. (ed) 1950 Adult Education in Canada
Toronto Canadian Association for Adult Education

Kidd, J.R. 1956 Adult Education in Canadian
University Toronto. Canadian Association for Adult
Education.

Kidd, J.R. 1959 How Adults Learn New York.
Association Press.

Kidd, J.R. 1961a Continuing Education Toronto
Canadian Conference on Education Publications.

Kidd, J.R. 1961b 18 to 80: Continuing Education in
Metropolitan Toronto Toronto. Board of Education

Kidd, J.R. 1966 The Implications of Continuous
Learning Toronto. W.J. Gage

Kidd, J.R. 1969 Education for Perspective Toronto.
Peter Martin Associates.

Kidd, J.R. 1974a A Tale of Three Cities - Elsinore,
Montreal and Tokyo Syracuse. Syracuse University

Kidd, J.R. 1974b While Time is Burning Ottawa
International Development Research Centre

Kidd, J.R. 1975a The Social Gospel and Adult
Education in Allen R (ed) op cit

Kidd, J.R. 1975b Adult Education in Encyclopedia
Canadiana

Kidd, J.R. 1983 Learning and Libraries: Competencies
for Full Participation in Library Trends (pp 525-542)

Spring.

Kidd, J.R. (unpublished memoirs, a.) <u>The High Road to Learning</u> Toronto. The Kidd Family

Kidd, J.R. (unpublished memoirs, b.) <u>Open Roads</u> Toronto. The Kidd Family

Kidd, J.R. (unpublished memoirs, c.) <u>Roadblocks and Detours</u>. Toronto. The Kidd Family.

Kidd, J.R. (unpublished memoirs, d.) <u>The Road Leading Forth</u> Toronto. The Kidd Family.

Kidd, J.R. (unpublished memoirs, e.) <u>Untitled manuscript</u>. Toronto. The Kidd Family.

Kidd, J.R. (unpublished memoirs, f) <u>The Road to the Indies</u>. Toronto. The Kidd Family.

Kidd, J.R. and Titmus C. 1985 An Overview of Adult Education in <u>International Encyclopedia of Education</u>. (Vol. 1)

Selman, G. 1982 <u>Roby Kidd and the CAAE (1951-1961)</u> Vancouver. Occasional Papers in Continuing Education, University of British Columbia

Tough, A. 1971 <u>Adult Learning Projects</u> Toronto Ontario Institute for Studies in Education Press.

<u>Encyclopedia Canadian</u> 1975 Toronto Grolier Society of Canada

<u>International Encyclopedia of Education</u>. 1985 Toronto Pergamon Press

Part Five

THEORISTS OF ADULT EDUCATION AND SOCIAL CHANGE

Chapter Eleven

MOSES COADY AND ANTIGONISH

John M. Crane

Nearly twenty years after his death, in a way that
was both symbolic and yet very real, Moses Coady's
presence could be felt at the 1978 International
Symposium on Human Development Through Social Change
held to commemorate the fiftieth anniversary of the
Antigonish Movement. Several hundred educators,
economists, politicians, labour leaders, development
workers and students from around the world gathered
at St. Francis Xavier, a small, Roman Catholic
university in the small Canadian town of Antigonish,
Nova Scotia, to attend the symposium. Photographs
taken at the event often show, looming over their
heads, the larger-than-life Karsh portrait of the
larger-than-life Monsignor Moses Coady, Ph.D., D.D.,
priest, philosopher, educator and social reformer,
first Director of the University's Extension
Department and the man who led the Antigonish
Movement through its first quarter century, its
formative and most dynamic years. Ranging from such
world leaders as Sir Shridath S. Ramphal, Secretary-
General of the Commonwealth, to earnest students from
across the Third World, the participants came
together because they shared a concern for human
development in that Third World and an appreciation
for the increasing contribution made by the
Antigonish Movement through its philosophy and its
training centre for adult education and social
action, the Coady International Institute.
    Hailed as "the most outstanding education
contribution Canada has made to the world" (Milner
1979:7), the Antigonish Movement has been described
by Alexander Laidlaw (1961:58), an early Associate
Director of the Extension Department and devoted
supporter of Dr. Coady, as "a blending of adult
education, Christian ethics and a program of social
justice, directed through a university extension

217

department." As Barbara Ward, the Baroness Jackson of Lodsworth, noted economist and author and renowned as a leading spokesman for Third World development, asserted in the tape recording that introduced her paper (1979:80), the emphasis that the Antigonish Movement has always put "upon people and upon what people can do to help themselves and to help each other ..." has been a fundamental insight only now beginning to be appreciated by the great institutions like the World Bank and the influential government supported programs. So hypnotic has been the appeal of the high-science, high technology, big growth, "trickle-down" theory of development and modernization, Ward argued (1979:80), that only now are donors realizing that under that system "much of the work is just wasted or leads, in fact, to social disruption and dislocation." They "are all suddenly beginning to realize that if you don't get to the community itself, that if you don't help men and women to take responsibilty, to get the leadership that they can give, ... you cannot get basic development. It will escape you." (Ward 1979:80).

Six years later Wasserstrom (1985:2) would confirm that the Foundation he reported on did not simply focus "upon transferring money to community groups of one sort or another, but rather upon the more delicate and challenging task of empowerment, of helping poor people to create viable organizations of their own ... Social change necessarily requires the extension of effective citizenship."

Did Coady and the Antigonish Movement really espouse such convictions fifty or sixty years ago, convictions that are now becoming what Ward (1979:80) characterizes as "the conventional wisdom of the new economic thinking ..."? Certainly Msgr. Joseph Gremillion, the man who presented Barbara Ward's paper to the Symposium and was at the time the Co-ordinator of the Interreligious Peace Colloquium in Washington, D.C., and a Fellow in Theology at Notre Dame University, held that belief. In 1928, according to Gremillion (1979:84), "the Antigonish Movement began creating, applying, and spreading concepts and methods for human development which have received attention and acceptance by the "development elite" only during our own decade." "Echo(es) and counterpart(s)" of some of the characteristics of Coady's philosophy and the "trademarks" of the Antigonish Movement are turning up now under new names "amidst other climes and contexts" claims Gremillion (1979:84-85) who then lists, among others, such modern approaches as: conscientization,

Ujamaa, farmer-fisherman-worker self-determination, leader formation, subsidiarity, solidarity, promocion humana and "small is beautiful".

The problem of exaggerated praise and extravagant overstatement by enthusiastic admirers is not a new embarrassment for the Antigonish Movement.

In 1938, as Laidlaw (1961:92) quotes, the October 18 edition of The Extension Bulletin editorialized:

> **Exaggerations**
> Exaggerations concerning the Movement ... do no good to the cause ... It is not necessary to exaggerate the material achievements of the work - which are considerable. The idea of the Movement, however, the restoration of effective ownership to the people and making clearer their way to participation in the heritage of our age, is one the need of which cannot be exaggerated. But no one should underestimate the difficulties in the way. Wishful thinking is the pitfall of the enthusiast.

Coady and the Antigonish Movement

Coady's Role

No one appears to claim that Coady founded the Antigonish Movement. That responsibility, as Douglas Campbell of the University of Toronto's Sociology Department records in The Canadian Encyclopedia (1985:1829), is justly attributed to Father Jimmy Tompkins. (see also Boyle 1953:209; Laidlaw 1961:57-58; Faris 1971:18; MacEachen 1979:12). Nor is Coady mentioned among the earliest pioneers in adult education at St. Francis Xavier. Laidlaw (1961:61-62) writes that Dr. Hugh MacPherson, whom M. Coady (1939:6) himself calls "the "father of cooperation" as far as St. F.X. is concerned", was engaged in agricultural extension services at the University, organizing a fertilizer co-operative as early as 1912, and a letter exists in which Coady declares that "the person most responsible for the creation of the St. Francis Xavier Extension is, of course, Father Michael Gillis ..." (quoted in Laidlaw 1961:67). Nor is Coady seen blazing a solo path. Those who recall the events in the Antigonish Movement's history always remember a team at work. Corbett (1953:65) claims, that "the three men largely responsible for the spectacular success of the St.

Francis Xavier Movement are Dr. James Tompkins, Dr.
M.M. Coady, and A.B. MacDonald. ..." King Gordon
(1979:164), formerly international relations profes-
sor at the University of Alberta and later with the
International Development Research Centre in Ottawa,
expands the team, the "remarkable team" beyond
Tompkins, Coady and A.B. MacDonald to include Sister
Mary Michael, Sister Anslem, Kay Thompson and Alex S.
McIntyre. J.R. Kidd (1960:12) also makes a point of
mentioning the work of some of the women on the
Antigonish team when he writes of "the talents and
incredible devotion of those like Miss T. Sears, Mrs.
K. (Thompson) Desjardins, (and) Sister Mary Michael
... But larger or smaller, more or fewer, Antigonish
was always seen as a team." The enthusiastic
contemporary, R.J. MacSween, reduces the team to the
essential two but, "What a team they were! Dr. Coady,
learned, dynamic, impressive, yet humble, zealous
and kind; A.B., charming, jovial and good natured,
but at the same time ambitious, practical, and with a
rare genius for organization." (MacSween 1953:93)
But even as part of the team, Coady is not remembered
as "the person mainly responsible for getting things
done - he usually left that to others." - usually
A.B. MacDonald! (Laidlaw 1971:75) Lotz 1977:109), in
stressing that point, claims that Coady "never
organized a co-operative in his life" and then goes
on to contrast that with MacDonald and others like
him who "helped to set up study clubs, showed people
how to organize meetings, co-operatives and credit
unions, taught them how to read and write, checked
the books, and did the thousand and one small,
mundane things that are the basis of good
organization."

What then was Coady's role in the "educational
adventure" known as the Antigonish Movement?
Alexander Laidlaw, who knew Coady and the other
leaders at the Extension Department as a result of
his own devoted service within the Movement, asks and
then answers that very question. In Laidlaw's
judgement (1971:14) Coady was the keystone. He held
the diverse parts of the Movement together and he
integrated the various contributions and resources.
"For about thirty years", writes Laidlaw (1971:75),
Coady was the "chief guide and mentor of the work
..., and he was its ablest interpreter right up to
the time of his death."

In lesser hands, under less spirited and
courageous leadership than his, the Antigonish
movement could easily have been a milk-and-

water affair with nothing to stir men's hearts
and imagination; but with him as a sort of
father figure who, by the way, took considerable
pride in his guerilla role in a war for social
and economic change, Antigonish came to mean
something stirring and dynamic, something that
struck at the roots of things while others were
hacking away at the branches. (Laidlaw 1971:75)

Coady, it appears, was a charismatic leader.
(MacDonald 1979:157: Lotz 1977:107).

The Man

Sooner or later, all who knew Coady, all who speak or
write of him, emphasize his physical stature and in
doing so seem to be trying to convey the impact this
man had on others. E.A. Corbett (1953:63) calls him
"... a giant of a man, six feet four with the
shoulders, chest and limbs of a wrestler." Although
Lotz (1977:107) shrinks Coady by an inch, he too
describes " a big man, standing 6'3", strong, rugged,
well-educated, a simple and eloquent speaker who got
along well with everyone, a happy-go-lucky person who
could laugh at himself." Joseph Hernon, in
extravagant apostrophizing of both the man and his
work, calls him the "Giant of Margaree." "Coady was
big." says Hernon (1960:68,69). "He thought big and
talked big ... He was a new and disturbing figure,
both on the maritime scene and in the ranks of the
Catholic Church."
   But there is something more to this picture. As
MacPherson (1979:169) gently hints, the Antigonish
Movement thrived on publicity and "At the heart of
this publicity was Moses Coady, a saintly though
forceful figure whose physical presence and
searching intellect dominated most meetings he
attended." "In the Maritimes," declares Hernon
(1960:69) in another extravagant metaphor, Coady
"became the Pied Piper because he was big, he exuded
confidence and toughness, he was a learned man who
commanded respect (sic) ..." But even Hernon who,
after all, was penning an appreciation of Coady only
a few months after the great leader's death, even
Hernon realized there was something unsatisfactory
about the picture he drew. "Scanning early records,"
writes Hernon (1960:69-70), "could give a picture of
Coady as a shouting, arm-waving radical, given to
exaggeration and shot with overtones of conceit.
Coady consciously created much of that image himself.
The times called for it. At heart he was truly a

humble giant ..."
    Others have also remarked on Coady's speaking style. Often several describe nearly identical scenes. Corbett (1953:63) relates how Coady "began haltingly, as though he was not quite sure how he was going to develop his subject. His great hands pawed awkwardly at a few notes; his brow was furrowed and anxious." Hernon (1960:69) describes Coady as he "stood and flexed his great hands and seemed to grope for words. The first two minutes often left the audience wondering if the man could talk at all." But soon he seemed to find his theme; the words would come easily. "Then he used the huge hands daintily and with great effect to emphasize a fact, expose an injustice, ridicule an absurdity or drive home a point." (Laidlaw 1971:15). And he was a talker far more than he ever was a writer. Although he left one book, Masters of Their Own Destiny, which is still in print and has been translated into seven languages, as well as what Laidlaw (1971:9) describes as a "mountainous" output of written speeches and short articles, "only rarely ... did he write with the same vigor and imagery as he achieved in everyday conversation and impromptu speeches."
    Although characterized as a deep thinker and intelligent and certainly widely read, Coady's restless, importunate, even dogmatic nature meant that scholarship held no appeal for him. Nor did he write for scholars. Coady's offerings, says Laidlaw (1971:94-95), are presented "bluntly and unrefined ... with the florid appeal of the idealist rather than the cold analysis of the social scientist." Indeed, Coady could become "impatient with the jargon and the "sociologese" of the theorist" (Laidlaw 1971:57); his own writing was "simple, brusque and straight-forward, but often eloquent." (Laidlaw 1971:94)

Coady's Background

Moses Coady was born on January 3, 1882, in the lovely Margaree Valley, in Nova Scotia's Cape Breton Island. He came of hard-working, modestly successful farming folk who nurtured in their children both the strong religious faith of their Irish Catholicism and what Corbett (1953:64) calls the "innate regard for education which has always characterized the Nova Scotia people." Along with these values, Coady absorbed the rich, earthy idioms of his people's speech, a heritage that served him well in the work of his adult years. Often when in need of a telling

phrase or a vivid image, Coady was able to reach back
to his origins and find an apt metaphor that carried
his point or sharpened his message.

A big, strong, youth, it was only natural that
the farm and its demands made many calls upon his
time and his energies. Nevertheless young Coady
pursued his education and immersed himself in reading
and study at home.

It was at this time that the most significant of
the influences that were to shape his life can begin
to be traced. In a pattern that was to persist for
many years, Moses Coady put first one step and then
another upon the path already trod by his cousin -
his double first cousin - Jimmie Tompkins. Tompkins,
in turn had been inspired by their uncle, another
Moses Coady, who had left the Valley to pursue his
studies and to become a priest and had then returned
to his people.

Older than his cousin Moses by 11 years and 4
months, Jimmie Tompkins was in many ways his
antithesis. Small, even skinny, often in doubtful
health, Tompkins even lacked the physical magnetism
that made it easy for Coady to command the attention
of others. But they shared the same ancestry and the
same background and they shared their zeal. First the
one and then, ten to a dozen years later, the other
left the Valley to complete high school, to take
teacher's training, to teach and then to continue
further education, enrolling at St. Francis Xavier
University. Each, in turn, was selected to go to Rome
to the Urban College of the Propaganda; each was
ordained priest, Tompkins in 1902, Coady some eight
years later, and each returned to join the faculty of
St. Francis Xavier University.

In countless ways that path that Coady followed
had been smoothed by Tompkins' earlier passage.
George Boyle (1953:28), Tompkins's biographer,
describes how a steady stream of letters, pamphlets,
books and cards poured from Tompkins in Rome
"directed to those whom he had picked out to
influence." "One of the targets for this shower of
ideas," Boyle (1953:28) continues, "was ... young
Moses Michael Coady." Corbett (1953:65) agreed. He
wrote that "Dr. Tompkins, from the very beginning,
was always prodding people, opening up their minds
and pushing them to a realization of the abilities
and problems of society. One of the persons he thus
influenced early in life was M.M. Coady ..." The
flavour of this smoothing of the way, this pushing
forward of his proteges, can be discerned in a
selection from a 1931 letter to Archbishop McNeil

223

which Boyle (1953:170) quotes where Tompkins writes
that "... Dr. Coady is fast becoming one of the most
influential men in Eastern Canada. Discerning people
are beginning to call him one of the great Canadians
..."

Was Tompkins as generous of heart as this and
similar reports would make him appear? Perhaps there
was both a measure of genuine selflessness as well as
an innate gift for spotting talent, particularly
talent that could produce the results he sought.
Boyle (1953:19) records how, as early as the rugged,
lonely, difficult days of Tompkins' first school
teaching, "his discernment widened and deepened. He
was conscious of an insight regarding individual
pupils which was sometimes as tenuous as an
intuition, and frequently turned out so right as to
be uncanny. He was quick to discover the personal
circumstances and mental capacities of his students,
and wherever he noted a trace of talent, this he
nourished with lavish praise." And Joseph Hernon
(1960:67) recognized that in the later years Tompkins
"worked best in his glebe house with a small group in
whom he had cannily spotted the potential for
leadership." Then Hernon goes on:

> There is no question that Tompkins visualized
> Coady as the heart and voice of any real
> movement that might emerge from his thinking ...
> And Tompkins kindled the flames of learning and
> social thought in the brash young giant. He
> counselled him through youth and during his
> studies in Rome. He saw in Coady the commanding
> personality he could never have and he set about
> to groom him for the future he envisioned.

The Middle Years

"All in all," says Laidlaw (1961:14), "there was
nothing remarkable in (Coady's) career before middle
age." He had returned from Rome with his two
doctorates and began teaching philosophy at St.
Francis Xavier. He did some post-graduate work in
education in Washington, D.C., and even served as a
high school principal for a few years. Nevertheless,
some special talent for leadership occasionally
showed itself. It was during those years, for
instance, that he is credited with being "chiefly
responsible for reviving the Nova Scotia Teachers'
Union ... when it was in danger of extinction."
(Laidlaw 1961:55). And, too, although Dr. Tompkins,
Father Gillis, Father MacDonald and others were the

originators, Coady was being "prodded" into more and more participation in such adult education activities as the People's Schools of 1921 and 1922 and the later Rural Conferences.

These early, pioneering ventures reflected an intuition that adult education, to be successful, must be linked with the most concrete reality in people's lives. In Nova Scotia that reality was material poverty. Later, under Coady's inspiration, it came to be understood that relieving the peoples' economic hardships was only the first step in an adult education program. Addressing the needs of the intellectually starved, the level at which more fortunate institutions could begin, remember that "Livingstone described adult education in England as having sprung from "the desire to combat intellectual poverty"" (Laidlaw 1961:59), would have lesser emphasis for St. Francis Xavier. And even that was not the ultimate goal, for true adult education was seen by Coady as embracing the political, the social, the cultural and the spiritual as well as the intellectual and the economic.

Father Tompkins and his early, pioneering associates were keenly aware of another certainty of adult education: the lack of a continuing organization could nullify the good work of their ventures. As Boyle (1953:84) writes, "Adult education was not new. Specific projects had been carried on. But the tendency was that after a time they deteriorated and disintegrated. They were sporadic. They did not have the organism of continuation. Father Tompkins wanted to create that." Unfortunately, in what seemed at the time a crushing and humiliating blow, Father Tompkins was not to be left to continue his work at St. Francis Xavier. A prolonged and, perhaps, intemperate conflict with the hierarchy over a quite unrelated question - the federation of Maritime universities - saw Tompkins "banished to Canso ..." (Campbell 1985:182) (see also Lotz 1977:105) His dream of the creation of the Extension Department was not to be easily realized. And in fateful confirmation of their fears, the pioneers of adult education at St. Francis Xavier saw Tompkins' People's School - that Nova Scotia reflection of the great Gruntvig's inspiration - leave Antigonish, shifting to Glace Bay, only to be discontinued some two years later.

They redoubled their efforts. Father Coady and the others within St. Francis Xavier persisted; Father Gillis and, now, Father Tompkins and others worked from outside. Numerous influences were

focused on the reluctant University. The efforts of
the diocesan clergy, the Alumni Association,
interested government officials, and strong-willed
Protestant friends whose support had begun as early
as the People's Schools were finally successful
although it had taken six years to get the Board of
Governor's resolution. And even then, it was another
two years, the summer of 1930, before a budget was
approved and the great work of the St. Francis Xavier
University Extension Department began in earnest.

Coady, who had been named to head the Extension
Department, had, at at the same time, become deeply
involved in another of Father Tompkins' projects.
Outraged by the poverty, squalor, and despair,
malnutrition, ignorance and apathy that he had found
among the fishermen of his parish, Father Tompkins
had tried to improve their condition. However,
despite his best efforts, despite his pushing and
prodding, despite a few small improvements, he had
been quite unable to bring about any major change in
his people's lot. But on the evening of July 1, 1927,
the sixtieth anniversary of Canada's Confederation,
while the rest of the nation was celebrating the
jubilee, Father Tompkins organized a mass meeting.
"By calling in the press and asking "But What Have We
To Celebrate?", the fishermen ... created a uproar
that resulted in that most Canadian of responses to
urgent social problems - a Royal Commission of
Enquiry." (Crane 1983:154)

Dr. Coady's efforts on the fishermen's behalf
resulted in an invitation to him to present a
submission. "Clearly and forcefully he advocated,
first, the organization of the shore fishermen so
that they might be able to assist in formulating
policies for the industry; second, the promotion of
scientific and technical education; third, the
teaching to the fishermen of the methods of producer
and consumer co-operation." (Boyle 1953:142) These
recommendations were included in the Commission's
final report and in 1929 Coady was asked by the
Federal Government to undertake the organizing of the
fishermen along the eight thousand mile coastline of
the Maritimes and the Magdalen Islands. Boyle
(1953:142) records that Father Tompkins had pressed
the Government for Coady's appointment. He
continues:

> The choice of this man was fortunate ... Dr.
> Coady, a big man physically, was a gripping
> speaker at meetings. While he had the same
> outlook as Father Tompkins and the other

Antigonish men whose fund of thought had made the People's School, he had the platform presence ... that Father Tompkins lacked. He exuded courage and optimism, grand scale. Master of the humorously graphic and folksy phrase, when he spoke to the fishermen he could invoke the plain and apt illustration that made him famous. He showed the people their lost opportunities, their disunity, their obligations to themselves. Co-operation was the message. He shocked, jolted, and prodded the villages into an awakening. (Boyle 1953:142)

Within a year the fishermen, having first gained confidence and experience with small, tentative ventures, had their own packing plants, their own adult education programs and their own United Maritime Fishermen underway.

The Good Years

Coady and the Movement never looked back. Their history becomes so inextricably bound together over the next twenty-five years and the philosophy of the man appears as the philosophy of the Movement and the accomplishments of the Movement are often taken to be the accomplishments of the man.

A dynamo of adult education activity, Coady was often giving over 150 speeches a year in person or over the radio. At first in the Maritime provinces, then throughout Canada, and ultimately across the United States as well, Coady spoke and taught and prodded, exploding his "intellectual dynamite" (Coady 1939:30). He stressed his ideas on so many occasions, in so many places, on so many levels, and in so many ways that the sheer volume of the material he produced renders it difficult to extract a concise and definitive expression of his principles, theories, and philosophy.

One approach, however, exemplified by A.A. MacDonald's report to the 1978 Symposium, may be to analyse the Antigonish Movement and, therefore, Coady's contribution, in terms of sociological phenomena. Possessing "all the characteristics of a reform social movement as identified in the sociological literature," according to MacDonald (1978:157), the Antigonish Movement "was a deliberate collective effort for social change – an effort which followed a commonly recognized and predictable social pattern."

The first circumstance of the pattern required

227

"(1) the existence of social strain which results in
mental stress and feelings of relative deprivation."
(MacDonald 1979:157) Certainly that social strain
and those feelings of deprivation existed in Maritime
Canada. Visibly less prosperous than many other parts
of Canada, convinced that "the economic set-up within
Confederation was at fault" (Coady 1943:2),
comparisons, always invidious, were made. As Coady
explains, it wasn't the great economic crash of the
1930s that initiated the Movement. The Extension
Department had been established before then, in 1928,
"one of the peak years of the so-called prosperity
era, ... the good times of the "twenties"" (Coady
1943:1), precisely because the farmers and fishermen
of the area had been missing out on those good times.
"For decades before this (they) had endured their
great depression." (Coady 1943:1). Furthermore,
Coady (1943:3) argued from his Maritime perspective,
"... the old order was simply not ... a good order.
It was unkind to the great masses of the people even
in the best of times. The kind of life it gave ...
was not good. It was insecure. It engendered a social
atmosphere which impeded Christian living for our
people." The perceived inequity of the economic was
then deemed to explain any real or imagined
educational, social, cultural or spiritual
backwardness.

The next step, MacDonald (1979:157) writes,
requires "(2) the development of a philosophical or
ideological belief which categorically defines the
causes of the strain and infallibly prescribes the
solution for the problem." For Coady, education was
the answer. The "education of the past", his term for
conventional schooling, defined the cause of the
problem and "adult education", lifelong learning,
identified the solution. While praising the belief in
the Western democracies that education is the
instrument of human progress, Coady often condemned
the "education of the past", as embodying an elitist
philosophy that effectively stripped the ordinary
people of their brightest and best, thus depriving
them of the energy, brains and leadership that would
let them improve their own lot in society. But, even
sadder than "robbing our rural and industrial
population of their natural leaders" (Coady 1943:20)
is an additional phenomenon. Once "the highly
energetic and ambitious escape to the most desirable
jobs in the nation ...", (Coady 1943:17) once the
"escape mechanism" has been activated "by which the
lowly can rise from their class and join the elite"
(Coady 1943:17-18), "their interests are ...

different from what they would be back home. They
have new masters and if they are to succeed they have
to promote the interests of the class which they
serve. They thus turn against their own flesh and
blood and in many cases are the most bitter enemies
of any movement calculated to give the people a
chance to rise to a better life." (Coady, 1943:20).

Over thirty years later, another challenging
educator would make many of the same observations
about his own people. (Freire 1972:22). And Paulo
Freire, just as Coady had done those many years
before him, turned to adult education for the
solution that would break the cycle.

In part because of his natural impatience but
also in part because he could not abandon the poor of
his generation to a life without hope of improvement.
Coady never pursued the idea of reforming the
conventional school system. He chose, instead, to
work directly and immediately with the adults in
economic need. "Children do not run society." Coady
(1945:10) argued. "Clearly the techniques by which we
can improve the social order and hold an educated
generation of our youth must be achieved by the adult
population." And yet, it is a measure of the man that
in time his vision broadened. He came to believe in
lifelong education, in "continuous adult learning."
He argued (1943:16) that it was "necessary for
education to be coterminus with active human life."
While admitting that Antigonish was not at the stage
in its development where it could undertake the whole
task, Coady (1943:16) believed that "any program of
adult education should be for all the people, even
the so-called educated classes."

Over the years Coady and his fellows synthesized
into an ideological statement a selection of
"theological, philosophical and behavioural science
concepts concerning man and the society in which he
lives" (MacDonald 1979:157) - a philosophy upon which
the Antigonish Movement was built. According to
Laidlaw (1961:97-98) the essence of this philosophy
was contained in six basic principles given in
several publications of the St. Francis Xavier
Extension Department.

1. The first of these is the <u>primacy of the
    individual</u>. This principle is based on both
    religious and democratic teaching: religion
    emphasizes the dignity of man, created in the
    image and likeness of God; democracy stresses
    the value of the individual and the development
    of individual capacities as the aim of social

organization.

2. ... <u>social reform must come through education</u>.
Social progress in a democracy must come through
the action of the citizens; it can only come if
there is an improvement in the quality of the
people themselves. That improvement, in turn,
can only come through education.

3. ... <u>education must begin with the economic.</u>
(Since) the people are most keenly interested in
and concerned with economic needs, ... it is
good technique to suit the educational effort to
the most intimate interests of the individual or
group ...

4. ... <u>education must be through group action</u> ...
man is a social being. Not only is man commonly
organized in groups, but his problems are
usually group problems. Any effective adult
education program must, therefore, fit into
this basic group organization of society.

5. ... <u>effective social reform involves fundamental changes in social and economic institutions</u>
... real reform will necessitate strong
measures ... which may prove unpopular in
certain quarters.

6. ... <u>the ultimate objective of the movement is a
full and abundant life for everyone in the
community</u>. Economic co-operation is the first
step, but only the first, towards a society
which will permit every individual to develop to
the utmost limit of his capacities.

According to MacDonald (1979:157) the next
characteristic identified in the sociological
literature as illustrative of a reform social
movement is "(3) the activity of charismatic leaders
who espouse the belief and instigate a core
following." That leadership and that core following
are classically illustrated in Moses Coady and the
team that made up the Antigonish Movement.

The fourth requirement, "(4) physical and
social proximity of leaders and potential
followers;" (MacDonald 1979:157) is clearly
fulfilled as well. As Lotz (1977:112) exults "Father
Jimmy, Moses Coady and the other leaders were born
and raised locally, ... They were known, trusted,
loved and respected ... None of the workers was a
fuzzy do-gooder, parachuted in to help the local
people. They had status, prestige and a base at the
university's Extension Department."

Fifth, writes MacDonald (1979:157) is "(5) the
organization of efforts to implement the prescribed

solutions;" From their hard-won base within the University, those in the Movement strove to achieve their objective of a better life for "the people of the Maritime Provinces ... a better economic status, more culture, ... greater spirituality; ... equality of opportunity to achieve the realization of all their possibilities through voluntary action in a democratic society." (Coady 1943:66)

Financially unable to implement their plans with "lectures and professors and put(ting) the people back to school ... through actual teaching (or) by correspondence courses" (Coady 1943:66), they found what Coady later judged to be a better technique.

> The technique was discovered by facing the actual situation and planning a way by which the people of eastern Canada could be mobilized to think, to study, and to get enlightenment. We found the discussion circle. This did not involve any teachers. It was in line with our whole co-operative idea. We would make education part of the self-help movement. The people would come together by themselves and discuss their problems. The first logical step in this process was for someone to round up the people, so to speak. This involved the mass meeting. (Coady 1943:66)

He continues, in that 1943 radio broadcast, to describe the Movement's adult education techniques as they evolved. In brief, it was the task of the speaker at the mass meeting to inspire, through his personality and the dynamics of his message, the organization of the community into small groups which they called study clubs or discussion circles. These, as Laidlaw (1961:116) writes, were "the key educational technique in the Antigonish Movement ... the method of Socrates brought up to date ..." They discussed real, everyday problems in order to solve them. Realistic action was to be the goal of the talk. Every month or so all the little groups came together into one large community group to share each other's triumphs or problems, to hear inspirational speakers, and for social, cultural or recreational activities. The Extension Department acted as a resource, providing the literature and the specialized information as the study clubs determined what they needed to know.

In time, Antigonish came to offer leadership schools, specialized training courses on the organizing and administering of co-operatives and credit unions, community refresher courses, industrial study classes, weekend institutes for labour leaders, credit union and co-operative directors and leaders of the ladies guilds. They began a journal; originally the Extension Bulletin, it later became The Maritime Co-operator. They branched into radio, at first locally but later with contributions to the national broadcasting system and in 1955 a start was made in the use of television.

According to MacDonald's reading (1979:157) of the sociological literature, the sixth point says that a social reform movement requires "(6) the existence of societal conditions, e.g. laws, social control, etc. which permit the effort to be exerted;" Again, the Antigonish Movement conforms to the pattern. Indeed, in many ways the Movement was born and developed in a very positive and favourable environment. Not only had individuals within the government service contributed their support as far back as Tompkin's People's School and, later, to the establishment of the Extension Department itself, but in some instances the provincial Department of Agriculture and Antigonish worked together so closely that they appear to be sharing extension personnel and responsibilities. Similary, Coady's selection by the Federal government for the task of organizing the fishermen and, provincially, the role he played in obtaining credit union legislation both indicate the degree to which the authorities respected and supported Antigonish. In the latter instance, Boyle (1953:157) bluntly states that "... Dr. Coady took measures to have a Credit Union Act passed by the Nova Scotia Legislature" while Laidlaw (1961:85) quotes a report that says that "... Dr. Coady, with the sponsorship of Premier Harrington, had it put through the 1932 session of the Legislature."

This respect and support for Antigonish continues to present times. As Allan MacEachen, then Deputy Prime Minister of Canada, said at the 1978 Symposium, "Through the Canadian International Development Agency, the Government of Canada is actively supporting the work done by ... the Antigonish Movement."

And beyond governments, the support was real and significant. As early as 1938, Pope Pius XI was indicating his approval and, of course, Coady was eventually honoured by his church with the rank of Monsignor. Even in the material realm, early and continuing support came from, among others, such diverse bodies as the Carnegie Corporation of New York, now the Carnegie Foundation, and the Scottish Catholic Society.

In still another sense, societal conditions favoured the Antigonish approach. In both the Protestant and the Roman Catholic communities of rural Maritime Canada in the 20s and 30s of this century, the habit of looking to the clergy for leadership was still an almost automatic reaction. If Antigonish could win the influential local leader to the Movement, their parishoners could be expected to follow.

The last of the characteristics of a reform social movement identified by MacDonald (1979:157), "(7) the routinization of the organizational effort with increasing emphasis on organizational maintenance and decreasing emphasis on philosophical goals", seems to be applicable as well. Perhaps the clearest evidence of this stage is the almost inevitable diminishing of concern and emphasis on educating the people to think and to reason and to learn to solve their own problems in favour of efforts dedicated to helping the people overcome their immediate economic concerns.

It is much easier to proclaim your organization's success by pointing to such quantifiable changes as the number of credit unions formed, the new membership numbers in producer or consumer co-operatives, the amount of money saved or loaned over a period of time, or even the number of students registering in a certain course or program, than it is to identify the changes in the quality of a man's thinking and living.

It was, perhaps, an understanding of this instinct for institutional self-aggrandizement that inspired Coady's most memorable exhortation:

> We have no desire to remain at the beginning, to create a nation of mere shopkeepers, whose thoughts run only to groceries and to dividends. We want our men to look into the sun and into the depths of the sea. We want them to explore the hearts of flowers and the hearts of fellow-men. We want them to live, to love, to play and pray with all their being. We want them to be men, whole men, eager to explore all the avenues of life and to attain perfection in all their faculties. We want for them the capacity to enjoy all that a generous God and creative men have placed at their disposal. We desire above

all that they will discover and develop their
own capacities for creation. It is good to
appreciate; it is godlike to create. Life for
them shall not be in terms of merchandising but
in terms of all that is good and beautiful, be
it economic, political, social, cultural, or
spiritual. They are the heirs of all the ages
and of all the riches yet concealed (Coady
1939:163).

Coady - A Man Before His Time

In addition to the problem presented by the sheer
volume of Coady's work, there is another aspect that
makes it difficult to present his thoughts to the
satisfaction of today's reader. He was a man ahead of
his time. His ideas in so many fields were so
advanced that many find it difficult now to credit
him with the positions he advocated then. Today's
temporal chauvinist finds it easier to spurn the
evidence than to believe that over fifty years ago
someone could have been put into into practice the
social and educational reforms they affirmed in the
last two decades.

But consider a few examples. In an area and at a
time when religious divisions were deep, wide, and
strongly held, Coady and the Antigonish, in daring to
be different, anticipated the ecumenism of Vatican II
by a generation. While the participation of
Protestants is not always apparent even in today's
descriptions of St. Francis Xavier and the Movement,
it should be noted that their contributions were
significant. As Laidlaw (1961:75) confirms, "from
the outset Protestants were selected for its staff if
they were the right ones for the job."

In environmentalism, another area that elements
of our contemporary society have taken for their own,
Coady anticipated today's views. Laidlaw (1961:12)
writes that Coady "as a Jeremiah about the waste and
destruction of natural resources to a generation that
wasted and destroyed with abandon. He warned of
"poisoning our earth and our waters" at a time when
pollution was only a shadowy spectre, visible on the
horizon to only a few Rachel Carsons." Coady spoke of
organically fit soil, for Sir Albert Howard's
composting methods, of "devitalized foods like corn
flakes." (Coady quoted in Laidlaw 1961:159) and in
comments that have a tragic significance today for
the economically shattered communities so recently
dispossessed along with huge, ruthlessly clear-cut
areas of Canada's forests, Coady spoke of the

234

inexhaustibility of intelligently handled forest resources. "We cannot," said a stern Coady (quoted in Laidlaw 1961:149), "sin against nature and hope to win."

In another place he strikes a chord with today's generation when he spoke out for peace and against the dangers of technology when it is allied to war's demands instead of to mankind's betterment but, being Coady, his mind searches beyond the warnings to suggest a blueprint to achieve peace. "If we don't put to good use," wrote Coady (quoted in Laidlaw (1961:204), "the scientific knowledge and machinery that the genius of man has discovered and invented, then they will be used for evil ends. Everything of a scientific nature, from botany to bombs, will be turned into the killing business of war. Peace can come only when people are satisfied with their world, when they have (a life) in harmony with their dignity as human beings."

His blueprint for peace, through unity and brotherhood, listed "Technological Unity" first, a concept where his thoughts are still ahead of most people even today. He urged the sharing of all technological advances with all the world's people. "It is the right of all the people of earth", Coady wrote in the December 1952 issue of The Canadian Messenger, "to have access to this knowledge ..." Next considering "Economic Unity" and "Political Unity", Coady then moved to "Social and Educational Unity".

> All the peoples of the earth should put their faith in the power of ideas and knowledge rather than in the coercion of external force. The whole human race must be lifted out of illiteracy and must have access, not only to the educational institutions that will enlighten their minds, but also to the social and cultural institutions that will look after their souls and bodies. (Coady 1952:3).

And this concern with men's souls as well as their bodies illustrates a Coady principle mentioned earlier: any ontological ordering of human needs must put the spiritual in pre-eminent place.

In curriculum terms, Coady's vision of adult education appears to have been far ahead of his time as well. More than a quarter-century before the explosion of Romanticism shattered the certainties of the educational world in the mid-1960s, Coady had been advocating principles and implementing

235

practices that were remarkably similar to these "new"
ideas, hopes and expectations. Labelled the
"Romantic Curriculum" in contrast to the traditional
or "Classical" curriculum by those who studied these
ideas in the 1970s (see Jenkins 1972, Lawton 1973,
Griffin 1978, and others), the new curriculum echoed
Coady's emphasis on the learner instead of the
content or material to be learned. Certainly the
whole "study club" or "discussion circle" technique
that Coady (143:66) described illustrates the
learner centredness of the Antigonish approach.
Similarly both Coady and the later Romantics were
concerned with creativity, originality, discovery,
awareness and the value of experience in contrast to
the traditional or Classical model's concern with
skills, conformity, information handling, obedience
and the value of instruction.

Coady's achievements were all the more
remarkable since they occurred in an era when
society's traditional boundaries, their form and
structure, were much more dominant, much more firmly
in place, than those faced by the later Romantics. In
the later era, as Martin (1981:15, 25) writes, there
was "a whole new cultural style, a set of values,
assumptions and ways of living ... exemplified (by)
... a setting of freedom and fluidity against form
and structure."

Coady's technique of beginning the education of
his adults with real life problems and concerns, of
involving the learner in his own education, and of
choosing co-operation as a solution are all
forerunners of the 1960s Romantic approaches (see
Lawton 1973:22-24) and contrast sharply with the
Classical position. The latter presented the student
with traditional subjects to study, offerred those
didactically and encouraged competition among the
students. Even more fundamental are the purposes
evident in each of the contrasting curriculum models.
For the Classical enthusiast, the acquisition of
knowledge appears to be the purpose of education
while Coady, and later the Romantics, seem to be
saying that the development of attitudes and values
that encourage the individual to develop to the
utmost limit of his capacities must take precedence.
This aim, expressing one of the Movement's six basic
principles, encapsulates, according to Keuscher
(1970:6), the Romantic curriculum philosophy.

While there may well be echoes of the great John
Dewey and Progressive education in the Antigonish
Movement and, of course, in the much later Romantic
curriculum, Coady's great achievement was that he

actually put his ideas, theories and principles into
practice. He discovered and acted upon some
remarkable insights into the nature of the adult
learner.

In areas well beyond education, Coady's mind –
and tongue – ranged widely. "With prophetic
foresight," records Laidlaw (1961:13), "he called on
sisters in religious orders to come out of their
convents, to mix in the workaday world of ordinary
men and women – shortly after his death there were
nuns marching at Selma." In another place he had
scolded Americans on "the scandal of believing on the
one hand in the equality professed in the Declaration
of Independence and on the other denying to blacks
the full rights of citizenship." (Coady quoted in
Laidlaw 1961:189). Further, Coady warned, it was
infinitely bad foreign policy to be allied with "the
big boys of business and finance (who) are the real
source of trouble" (Laidlaw 1961:189) for

> in too many cases the powerful vested interests
> have taken over and exploited for their own
> advantage the natural resources of other
> peoples, especially in the undeveloped sectors
> of earth. If we add to this the arrogant
> insistence on white supremacy, backed up as it
> often is by force and supreme contempt for the
> coloured races, the situation gets still more
> serious. This cannot go on forever ... Some day
> we will reap dividends of wrath for so stupid a
> policy. If we were wise we would help the people
> everywhere to get the good and abundant life by
> a proper development of their own natural
> resources. (Coady quoted in Laidlaw 1961:121-
> 122)

Perhaps because Coady had been advocating "the
application of adult education and cooperative
organization to the underdeveloped world" as long ago
as 1939 (MacEachen 1979:12) and perhaps because he
had been warning against the excesses of unrestrained
capitalism for even longer, there were times,
particularly in his final years, when he seemed to
succumb to discouragement. Perhaps that is why, just
five years before he died, he wrote to a friend of
many years in bitter disappointment:

> There is not much hope for the world because the
> economically and politically powerful people of
> the Western democracies – and this goes also for
> the religious leaders of all denominations, at

237

least a great percentage of them - will stop
short of doing the whole job. Their philosophy
is: we will go far enough with reform to ward
off the present danger, but we must not allow
reform to interfere with the privileged status
quo. That's just it in a nutshell. The rank and
file of the world's people have a sixth sense by
which they can unerringly detect this fatal
duplicity. They are not going to be fooled any
longer, and when the right time comes they will
put up new guillotines to cut the stupid heads
off the leaders in Church and State who are
incapable of seeing where the real danger is and
who lack the courage to apply an adequate
remedy. (Coady, quoted in Laidlaw 1961:208).

Reflection

But it is not as a momentarily embittered idealist
conscious of failures that Coady is remembered.
Indeed, if Coady is in any sense a failure it is only
in that special sense of a man's actual
accomplishment falling short of his Utopian dreams.
Coady spoke and believed in the millenium, in that
special time when all the world would achieve social
justice, brotherhood and peace. It is perhaps this
poignant sense of the unfulfilled that Tom Lovett
(1980:163) discerned when he wrote that "Antigonish
is now a lost dream."

For almost all other commentators, Coady and the
Antigonish Movement have been a boundless success.
"Recognition came quicky", wrote Laidlaw (1961:91),

... and to an extent that could hardly have been
anticipated. The world at that time was
feverishly searching for a way out of the Great
Depression; here was a program that went from
theory to practice in a relatively short time,
that struck at the most serious problems of the
time - the economic ones, and that still
preserved, and indeed fostered, the democratic
ideals which peoples in other parts of the world
were surrendering for security.

With increasing prosperity the times changed
and just as the initial impetus of the Movement was
slackening, Antigonish was discovered by concerned
and thoughtful leaders from the Third World.
Increasingly, visitors were drawn from Asia, Latin
America, the Caribbean and Africa during the post-war
period. As MacEachen (1979) writes, they found at

tiny, relatively obscure St. Francis Xavier, a proven method of economic self-help allied to adult education that used very minimal resources, mobilized the local population, and used straightforward techniques that poor people with limited education could learn readily. "Moreover, the techniques were ... aimed at meeting immediate needs - marketing, credit, housing." (MacEachen 1979:13). Further, the philosophy of the Movement appealed to these developing countries as they moved to independence. Their "leaders held high hopes that self-determination could be given real substance through a transformation of political, economic, and social institutions. They remained wary of the competing ideologies of capitalism and state-socialism .. The co-operative approach" as formulated by Coady, "stressed self-reliance, the development of local leadership, broadly based education, and a peaceful redistribution of economic benefits." (MacEachen 1979:13)

These requests for help re-invigorated the Movement and only a few months after Dr. Coady's death in 1959, the Coady International Institute was established to train people from over one hundred countries in adult education methods, community development and the philosophy and techniques of co-operative organization.

Those who analyse Coady and the Movement's success do have important reservations however. First, they insist, it is important to distinguish between its philosophy, its programs and its techniques. "This differentiation must be made because it is unlikely that the social pattern of a particular social movement can be replicated in different social circumstances and in different time periods." (MacDonald 1979:159) It is obvious, then, that techniques have to vary to suit the new circumstances. Indeed, even in Maritime Canada, the Movement's birthplace, the old techniques no longer suffice in these days of good communications and relative prosperity, of good roads and reliable vehicles, of satellite television receivers, and radios and telephones in every home and office.

While the usefulness and applicability of the Antigonish co-operative program appears to be more readily accepted by the policy makers in developing countries than does the adult education program, "it is not so evident," argues MacDonald (1979:161), "that they recognize or accept the human development possibilities of the cooperative program." They don't appear to realize that the second objective of

239

an Antigonish co-operative program is the increased development of human capacities through such methods as participation in decision-making and choice by the members. Similarly many in translating the Movement into their own terms miss the essential significance of the adult education element. To Coady and the Movement, social reform - permanent institutional reform - could only come about through adult education. But in the hearts of many of the policy makers gratefully accepting the Antigonish program of economic development, there may well be little commitment to "allowing man's capacities to be released through education on the social institutions which are primarily responsible for underdevelopment." (MacDonald 1979:159)

Ultimately, the success or failure of Coady and the Antigonish Movement can only be judged in terms of their own philosophy. If the people themselves become preoccupied with things economic and fail to use the opportunity to learn how to master their social and political realms, then Coady, as he would be the first to admit, and the people themselves have failed. Indeed, the people's own economic accomplishments, no matter how substantial, are in jeopardy if they haven't learned how "to manipulate the forces that control society", if they haven't learned to become "masters of their own destiny." (Coady quoted in Laidlaw 1961:109)

Bibliography

Boyle, G. 1953, <u>Father Tompkins of Nova Scotia</u>, New York P.J. Kenedy & Sons

Campbell, D.F. 1985, "Tompkins, James John" in <u>The Canadian Encyclopedia</u> Edmonton, Alberta Hurtig Publishers Ltd

Coady, M.M. 1939, <u>Masters of Their Own Destiny</u> New York and London, Harper & Brothers Publishers

Coady, M.M. 1943, <u>The Antigonish Way</u> Antigonish, Nova Scotia St. Francis Xavier University

Coady, M.M. 1945, <u>The Social Significance of the Co-operative Movement</u> Antigonish, St. Francis Xavier Extension Department

Coady, M.M. 1952, "Unity and Brotherhood" in <u>The Canadian Messenger</u> December 1952

Corbett, E.A. 1953, "Dr. M.M. Coady" in Harriet Rouillard, ed., <u>Pioneers of Adult Education in Canada</u>, Toronto, Thomas Nelson & Sons (Canada) Limited

Crane, J.M. 1983, "The Antigonish Movement: an Historical Sketch" in <u>International Journal of</u>

Lifelong Education Vol. 2, No. 2
Faris, R. 1975, *The Passionate Educators: voluntary associations and the struggle for control of adult educational broadcasting in Canada 1919-1952* Toronto, Peter Martin Associates Limited
Freire, P. 1972, *Pedagogy of the Oppressed* Harmondsworth, Penguin Books Ltd.
Gordon, K. 1979, "The Coady in Development" in *Human Development Through Social Change* Antigonish, Nova Scotia Formac Publishing Co. Limited
Gremillion, J. (ed.) 1979, *Human Development Through Social Change* Antagonish, Nova Scotia Formac Publishing Co. Limited
Griffin, C. 1978, *Recurrent & Continuing Education – a Curriculum Model Approach* Nottingham University of Nottingham
Hernon, J. 1960, "The Humble Giants" in *The Atlantic Advocate*, February 1953 pp.67-72
Jenkins, D. 1972, "Romantic and Classic in Curriculum Landscape" in *Curriculum Philosophy and Design* Milton Keynes, Open University Press
Keuscher, R.E. 1970, "Why Individualize Instruction" in Virgil M. Howes (ed.), *Individualization of Instruction: A Teaching Strategy* New York, The Macmillan Company
Kidd, J.R. 1960, "Foreword" to Laidlaw, A.F. *The Campus and the Community: The Global Impact of the Antigonish Movement* Montreal, Harvest House Limited
Laidlaw, A. 1961, *The Campus and the Community: The Global Impact of the Antigonish Movement* Montreal, Harvest House Limited
Lawton, D. 1973, *Social Change, Educational Theory and Curriculum Planning* New York, Hodder and Stoughton
Lotz, J. 1977, *Understanding Canada: Regional and Community Development in a New Nation* Toronto, N C Press Ltd.
Lovett, T. 1980, "Adult Education and Community Action" in Jane L. Thompson (ed.), *Adult Education for a Change* London, Hutchinson & Co
MacDonald, A.A. 1979, "A History of the Antigonish Movement" in *Human Development Through Social Change* Antigonish, Nova Scotia Formac Publishing Co. Limited
MacEachen, E.A. 1979, "Canadian Approaches to Co-operation" in *Human Development Through Social Change,* Antigonish, Nova Scotia Formac Publishing Co Limited
MacPherson, I. 1979, *Each for All: A History of the Co-operative Movement in English Canada, 1900-1945* Toronto The Carleton Library No. 116 Macmillan of

Canada in association with the Institute of Canadian Studies, Carleton University

MacSween, R.J. 1953, "The Little University of the World" <u>The Universities Review</u> XXV, No. 2 February 1953 pp. 91-98

Martin, B. 1981, <u>A Sociology of Contemporary Cultural Change</u> Oxford, Basil Blackwell

Milner, P. 1979, "Preface" in <u>Human Development Through Social Change</u> Antigonish, Nova Scotia Formac Publishing Co. Limited

Ward, B. 1979, "I cannot tell you how sad I am ..." in Gremillion, J. (ed.) <u>Human Development Through Social Change</u> Antigonish, Nova Scotia Formac Publishing Co. Limited

Wasserstrom, R. 1985, <u>Grassroots Development in Latin America & the Caribbean</u> New York, Praeger Publishers

Chapter Twelve

HORTON OF HIGHLANDER

John M. Peters and Brenda Bell

I can't sleep, but there are dreams. What you must do is go back, get a simple place, move in and you are there. The situation is there. You start with this and let it grow. You know your goal. It will build its own structure and take its own form. You can go to school all your life, you'll never figure it out because you are trying to get an answer that can only come from the people in the life situation (Horton, 1983a:30).

When Myles Horton wrote this note on Christmas night in Copenhagen in 1931, he captured the long and promising future of his work as a radical educator. He had pursued an education by conventional means, studied independently, travelled, and experimented in search of "something to offer" his would-be students in the Southern region of the United States. These efforts helped shape his beliefs regarding the interaction of education and social change, which underpinned his future with what he referred to as "the only instrument I ever learned to play", the Highlander Folk School. The school, or more accurately the idea or philosophy, was to be filled with controversy, failures and successes, as well as involvement with the most important social movements of twentieth-century America. Notes such as the one above also foretell the essence of Horton's approach to adult education.

No analysis of Horton's approach to adult education can be made without reference to Highlander, whose history has been ably chronicled by Aimee Horton (1971), Adams (1975), Glen (1985) and others. Horton has not published as much as most adult educators discussed in this book. Most of what he has said about adult education has been expressed through the medium of practice at Highlander. Although Horton is the first to point out that his ideas and those of others who have practiced at Highlander have not always been the same, his approach and what has come to be known as the "Highlander Idea" are practically synonymous. We therefore begin this chapter with a brief sketch of Horton's life and development prior to Highlander, then provide an overview of Highlander's activities since its inception in 1932. We finish with our interpretation of the major features of Horton's thinking as it shaped and was shaped by Highlander and the events of the century. While examples and quotes selected for the first half of the chapter do not begin to paint the whole Highlander portrait, they are included for what they reveal about the man and his thinking. Readers are thus encouraged to consider them in forming their own interpretation of the complexities of Horton's approach to adult education, a task that has proved both rewarding and difficult for the authors.

Before Highlander

Horton's childhood in small West Tennessee towns was shaped by his parents' strong belief in the value of education and by his family's involvement in the Cumberland Presbyterian Church. The church was "rational rather than revivalist, and placed emphasis on good works in this world rather than salvation in the next" (A. Horton, 1971:13). Both of his parents were school teachers at the time of his birth in 1905, but later farmers and share croppers. They believed that "the only way to get out of poverty was to be assertive and to go to school, and to be of use in the world without being so poor" (Horton, 1985).

But in school or church Horton found few challenging educational experiences and came to place greater value on experiential learning outside these formal institutions. Aimee Horton (1971:14) wrote:

> Working in a grocery store after school, he learned something about the social structure of the small southern community - about the Negro sharecropper families whose crops were "owned" by the landowner until their bills were paid and who were systematically over charged for inferior goods; about the white business and church leaders who paid the bills for Negro

women and their lighter-skinned children. Working in a local box factory in the summer, he learned something about the spoils system in southern industry where several hundred "grateful workers" were paid two dollars per day for producing thousands of wooden boxes which were sold to farmers for twice what they cost to make. And the cost ... was passed along to poor families in town who paid for the boxes with potatoes.

The workers who made potato boxes were eventually organized by Horton to strike for, and attain higher wages. Horton (1985) "didn't know about unions at the time", but his principled attitude toward worker rights even as a teenager was not coincidentally the same framework he followed during his later involvement with unions during the second quarter of the century. The insights Horton formed through such early work experiences would also help shape a personal philosophy of education and social change that kept company with some of the world's greatest philosophers.

Horton's youthful sense of morality and social justice matured during his college years at Cumberland College in Lebanon, Tennessee, where involvement with the student YMCA brought him into closer contact with other races and nationalities. "Civil rights" was not a label nor a social issue at the time, but Horton, as a college freshman, demonstrated his opposition to infringement on individual rights by organizing his classmates and successfully resisting the traditional practice of freshman hazing. Later, after hearing a paternalistic, anti-union speech by the owner of a local woollen mill, Horton responded by going to the mill to talk to the workers about their rights. The mill owner was on the Board of the college, and Horton felt his wrath. Horton recalls that again he was not thinking in terms of labor unions; he was responding to the mill owner's suggestion that, because he owned the factory, he could make determinations about people's lives. "That just hit me as an immoral way of thinking - such a crude, crass way of thinking. The arrogance. I'd always been on the worker's side - I knew only working people" (Horton, 1985). His display of a sense of justice was accompanied by a strategy that came to typify much of Horton's later active involvement in labor and civil rights activities. He set up the meeting at the mill under the pretense of holding a religious service. "The

245

real purpose was to get the people together. It took
a religious form, because that was something I was
familiar with" (Horton, 1985). It was also a bit of
gamesmanship.

In the years that followed, Horton was to
reflect upon that experience and begin an extensive
and largely self-directed study of unions and
unionism, especially the British labor union
movement, which proved influential in his
formulation of the Highlander idea. The writings of
the Fabian Socialists especially broadened his
conception of trade unionism to include elements of a
social movement. The Fabian vision of a political
democracy in which "economic power and priviliges of
individuals and classes (will be) abolished through
collective ownership and democratic control of the
economic resources of the community" (Cole,
1961:338), must have appealed to Horton as he
formulated his idea of an educational program to
individually and collectively empower poor adults in
the South. He later recalled this impetus for "our
work on political action, our work with communities,
and our work with farmer-labor cooperatives"
(Horton, 1985).

The Ozone Experience

Under the auspices of the Presbyterian Church and
during the summer prior to his senior year in
college, Horton organized vacation Bible schools in
Ozone, a small village in rural East Tennessee. The
experience led Horton to conclude that the Church and
other organizations were not helping people deal with
their problems of poverty, unemployment, and living
with a countryside devastated by logging and mining
practice. Without a formal plan, he asked parents of
Bible school students to come to the church to talk
about their concerns. They came and talked, and to
Horton's amazement, they were not disappointed in his
inability to answer their questions or to "teach
them" something they didn't know. He discovered that
these adults could articulate their problems and look
for answers in their own experiences. Adams (1975:4)
later wrote:

> He had learned that the teacher's job was to get
> them talking about those problems, to raise and
> sharpen questions, and to trust people to come
> up with the answers. Yet, he could not wholly
> trust the people or this way of learning.

In spite of appeals by his "students" for his further work with them, Horton decided not to return to the area after graduating from Cumberland because he wanted to come back only when he "had something to offer" the mountain people. He was to realize six years later that his first experience with community education in Ozone would provide the anchor for the Highlander idea.

A Search for Something to Offer

Following graduation and during a job as YMCA field secretary, Horton began to read widely, searching for a model of a community school for adults. He was strongly influenced by the writings of William James and John Dewey, but continued to read. A Congregationalist minister, sympathetic with Horton's interests, gave him a copy of Harry Ward's Our Economic Morality (1929), and encouraged him to go to Union Theological Seminary to study with Ward, a professor of Christian ethics.

Union Seminary in the late 1920's was a place of great intellectual ferment. Encounters with the religious thinkers at Union and the progressive educators nearby at Columbia challenged Horton's inquiring mind. The ideas of the Christian Socialists aided in uniting his sense of morality and justice with his concern for economic problems. Ward, a founder and first Chairman of the Board of the American Civil Liberties Union, staunch union advocate, and a supporter of Marxist thought, sent his students into "real-life" situations with specific questions to be answered (Link, 1984). Reinhold Niebuhr, professor and socialist, became a mentor for Horton and a strong proponent of his idea of a community school. Niebuhr's most widely-known book, Moral Man and Immoral Society (1932), was written while Horton was at Union under his tutulage. Niebuhr continued to be an influence on Horton's work after Union.

While in New York, Horton talked with Dewey and Eduard Lindeman. Horton found Lindeman to be a "fresh breeze", as he "made sense out of adult education, and I was moving more in that direction without knowing it. I saw adult education, through Lindeman, as a way of dealing with some of the problems (of working with poor southerners)" (1985).

Horton left Union in 1930 to study at the University of Chicago under sociologist Robert Park, whose theories of conflict and of mass movements added to Horton's growing understanding of the

processes of social change. Concurrently, he was
influenced by Lester Ward's Dynamic Sociology
(1883), which argued that education is action, and
that dynamic action is the foundation of social
progress (A. Horton, 1971). While in Chicago, Horton
spent time at Hull House, learning from Jane Addams,
and was encouraged by a Danish-born Lutheran minister
to visit the folk schools of Denmark. That
recommendation was to become another major phase in
Horton's search for meaning.

Denmark

Horton's study of Danish Folk Schools produced mixed
results. He was disappointed in the "newer" folk
schools for their lack of spirit and their loss of
earlier vitality, but found in the history of the
older schools some examples that were to become
useful to his vision of a community school in the
U.S. According to Adams (1975:22-23):

> He found that many of the directors were
> unconventional educators. They were men on fire
> to correct injustice, to awaken the peasants to
> the misery restricting their lives. The
> schools, each (had) ... a distinct purpose ...
> made wide use of poetry and song ... and sought
> to develop feelings and will more than memory
> and logic (emphasis ours).

Hart (1926:23), who influenced Horton's thinking,
had written earlier:

> A folk school in America, as in Denmark, would
> probably center about a personality of some real
> teacher, a man who is capable of learning, and
> who can teach, not so much by his teaching, as
> by his capacity to learn ... we have very few
> (people) who can teach their own capacity to
> learn (emphasis ours).

Purpose, a personality, a capacity to learn,
song, feelings, and will vs. memory and logic - these
were concepts that served to flesh out Horton's idea,
and to characterize his process of adult education -
concepts he also identified with Bishop Grundtvig,
founder of the Danish Folk High School movement.
Social interaction in non-formal settings, freedom
from State regulation, non-vocational education, and
peer learning were other features of the Grundtvig
approach with which Horton identified. (Horton,

1983:29). While Horton "... did not slavishly copy the Danish Folk School ... the present needs (in the Southern U.S.) were totally different from those of Denmark's" (p.30), Highlander was to feature many of the same concepts and activities as the early Grundtvig schools. The note on Christmas night in Copenhagen, written at the end of Horton's study in Denmark, tied Grundtvig to Ozone.

Highlander

Though his history is uniquely his own, at the time Horton and Don West (a graduate of Vanderbilt Divinity School) started Highlander in 1932, Horton was but one of many young Southern intellectuals deeply affected by the political, economic, and social climate of the time. As Richard Pells (1973:44) observed, for many "the depression exposed for all time the fundamental unreality of the American dream, especially the fact that the quality of human life in a system dedicated to profit offered people no feeling of community or common vision". The call for a new social order was widespread, and political movements for change had strong appeal. Horton and a few of his fellow students at Union and other young Southerners studying at Vanderbilt Divinity School in Nashville were not espousing new ideas, but it was their insistence on applying the ideas, and putting them into practice that was significant (Dunbar, 1981).

It is important to begin an overview of the history of Highlander with the understanding that Highlander was not a series of schools, each marked by a major social movement, but a continuous and comprehensive single idea put into practice. "I've always thought of each ("school") as being a part of a larger whole, instead of being a labor school, a civil rights school, a school for mountain people" (Horton, 1985). While education is at the heart of Highlander's program, Highlander's involvement reaches into the realm of social activisim, into all forms of movements for a democratic society.

Horton knew for years that he wanted to work within the framework of education, but sought a broader focus for his efforts. As mentioned earlier, he had read widely, including the works of Dewey, Lindeman, Niebuhr, Marx, the Fabians, Grundtvig, Shelly, and Parks. Ideas from these and other sources, as well as values shaped during his formative years contributed to his thinking, but it wasn't focused thinking. However, he was forced by the advent of Highlander to "make a formulation" of his beliefs. He recalled that, by the time Highlander started, he was very clear on at least two matters (Horton, 1985). First:

> There is no such thing as neutrality. Neutrality is for the status quo. (The educator) can't be objective. You have to decide what you want to do and who you want to work with. You have to have a purpose.

The second came from his religious background. Horton grew up

> knowing that all the great religions judged nations by how they treated their poor. I accepted that. I wanted to work on the side of society that didn't live by owning. If you're going to have a democracy, that's the kind of people you build it on.

These principles provided a focus for Horton. "They synthesized my religious and ethical upbringing and my reading and thinking in terms of an analysis of society" (1985). Horton therefore had a kind of sociological and philosophical framework within which to operate, and he had ethical motivations. At Highlander, he could combine these and make them a part of the labor movement and other movements.

Highlander was opened in "one of the eleven poorest counties in the United States" (Adams 1975:30), in a home donated by a friend of a minister/supporter. The intent was "to provide an educational center in the South for the training of rural and industrial leaders, and for the conservation and enrichment of the indigenous cultural values of the mountains" (Highlander Folk School, 1939). The school's first fund raising letter, sent by Niebuhr, stated that the school proposed "to use education as one of the instruments for bringing about a new social order" (Aimee Horton, 1971:44) These intents combined to form the two central foci of Highlander: (1) the achievement of a democratic movement, initially among unions and eventually in society as a whole; and (2) leadership training. The latter was not atypical in its time, but the former served to distinguish Highlander from most other American adult education institutions.

Park's conflict/crisis theories were to be tested early, as Horton told of "being alert for places in the South where contention was rising"

(Adams, 1975:25). A coal miners' strike at nearby Wilder, Tennessee, a bugwood cutters' strike in Grundy County and a shirt factory strike in Knoxville were ready-made arenas for the young activist-educators. Significantly, Horton and staff participated directly in the organizing activities of the strikers. And they began to learn about the reality of conflict, with its attendant threats to the lives of organizers. Horton and others associated with Highlander were to endure physical beatings, jailings, and a closing of the school itself as a result of their organizing activities.

Horton and staff learned very quickly that their own academic experiences were a handicap, insofar as their attempts to teach strikers were concerned. "The staff and I had gone to school. We were motivated to do it. But, we wrongly assumed that poor people would do some of the same things we did. We failed to correctly analyze the fact they weren't motivated by the same things, weren't socialized to go through the formal school system as we" (Horton, 1985). They were teaching, and attempting to convert the workers to a way of thinking about democracy. But it wasn't working. The people were paying much more attention to their local informal leaders than to Horton and staff. During these early years, Horton concluded they would have to "teach within the experiences" of the local leaders. While the Highlander program looked traditional "on paper", the content was not. Like labor schools of the era, Highlander's course and workshop topics included labor history, cultural geography, social and economic problems, and literature. However, the subject matter at Highlander was determined by problems brought by students, and new learning experiences were integrated into students' lives by the use of such means as improvisational drama, song-writing, and singing. Students were given major responsibility for the daily operation of courses and workshops, and were usually involved in teaching other workshop participants before leaving Highlander. These features continue to the present time to characterize Highlander workshops and courses.

A **Transition in Movements**

Highlander's labor program, which grew steadily to include residential education for rank and file leaders, continued through the war years, though on a reduced scale. From 1944 to 1947 Highlander ran the Congress on Industrial Organizations (CIO) schools for union leaders from around the South. But just as it seemed that the relationship with the CIO was solidifying, it was also dissolving. Horton and staff were pursuing their goal of a workers' movement for change, through developing a farmer-labor coalition, focusing on the problems of black Americans, and seeking to maintain a broad vision of brotherhood and cooperation in its work with CIO unions. The CIO, however, beset by internal struggles of its own, was losing much of its former militancy and social vision. When the CIO asked Highlander to disassociate itself from any "Communist-led organizations," the Highlander board drafted a statement of purpose which declared its intent to "create leadership for democracy" (Aimee Horton, 1971:366). The CIO leadership was not satisfied and member unions were instructed not to continue working with Highlander. But some did maintain their relationship. For several years into the 1950's, Horton served as the educational director of the United Packinghouse Workers (while maintaining his Highlander staff position), implementing a broad-based education program with rank and file workers (Glen, 1985).

As their worker education program waned, Horton and staff increasingly worked with people whose concerns focused on Southern racial problems. As increasing numbers of blacks came to Highlander to participate in labor education programs, the school became known as an "affirmation" of the possibility for an integrated society. It was perhaps the only place in its time where people of different races met, ate, learned, and worked together in a residential setting - and not always legally! For the next decade, Highlander was a kind of "half-way house" for those involved in the civil rights struggle (Morris, 1984).

Highlander's Citizenship Schools started on John's Island, South Carolina, in response to a black community leader's wish to register his fellow Islanders to vote. To qualify to vote, all citizens had to read the State Constitution, but few blacks were able to read or write. Horton's strategy for the schools began with a personal six-month visit to the area to learn from the people involved, and extended to teacher training and fund raising for the civic and literacy education programs. Horton insisted that whites refrain from leading the program or teaching in the localized classes. Instead, Horton and the Highlander staff worked through popular black leaders on the Island, and trained black teachers selected on the basis of their acceptance by the students and their interest in teaching (Adams, 1975; Morris, 1984). When Highlander came under attack by Southern political leaders and was closed by the State of Tennessee in 1960, leadership of the Citizenship Schools was passed on to the Southern Christian Leadership Conference (SCLC), a leading civil rights organization in the 50's and 60's. By 1970, the SCLC estimated that approximately 100,000 blacks had learned to read and write through the Citizenship Schools (Adams 1975:118).

Dozens of meetings and workshops at Highlander were followed by civil rights activities that were to make major changes in race relations in the South. The Student Non-Violent Coordinating Committee (SNCC) was the last group to meet at Highlander before the State closed Highlander.

Groups and individuals involved in sit-ins and demonstrations in the 50's and 60's were students at Highlander. Rosa Parks, the black woman who sparked an historical protest when she refused to give up her seat on a bus to a white man, was at Highlander a few months prior to the Montgomery, Alabama incident. The Montgomery bus boycott that followed led to the early distinction of Dr Martin Luther King, himself a visitor to Highlander. Andrew Young, former United States Ambassador to the United Nations, would say that "For fifty years the Highlander Center has produced leadership ideas, and a spirit of freedom that changed the course of history" (cited in Horton, 1983:23).

The school's closing and the transfer of the Citizenship School Program to the SCLC marked another transition point for Highlander. Horton applied for and received a new charter for the school, this time to be called the Highlander Research and Education Center. While the civil rights movement was in full swing, Horton was analyzing again the situation of southern Appalachian mountain people, and beginning to work to build ties between black activists and poor whites. Horton's sights were on the same goal as before; "he dreamed of a massive social movement that would fundamentally alter America, and genuinely felt that the potential for such a movement existed" (Adams, 1975:179-80). Horton led Highlander into the Poor People's Campaign, the Community Action Programs of the late 60's, and into a renewed tie with the Council of Southern Mountains, a coalition of organizations concerned with economic and political problems in Appalachia. However, no "massive social movement" materialized, and Highlander found itself for the first time in its history without a movement to contextualize its educational program.

Currently, issues which bring people to Highlander for workshops and planning meetings include land use, control of toxic wastes, occupational safety and health, labor organizing, cultural work in local communities, and more recently, international issues involving such nations as Nicaragua, India, and South Africa. Significantly, Horton since retiring in 1973, has remained active in the affairs of Highlander. He is currently travelling to several points around the world, and not coincidentally to nations experiencing major social upheavals. A citizen of the world, Horton's thinking about education and social change clearly has no national boundaries.

Features of Horton's Thinking

Horton was stimulated very early in life to make his contribution to society through some form of educational process. He had examined the public schools and colleges in the interest of pursuing teaching as a career, but found these institutions lacking in their impact on the conditions of poor people, who in his estimate, had problems greater than any other segment of society. Education for social change of the kind Horton had in mind was rarely practiced in the U.S.

While Horton's lifetime commitment to social reform reflects noble vision and laudable contributions, broad aims do not easily convince the reader in search of specific new educational ideas. Ironically, the specifics of Horton's approach to education are found in the global context of his work. For example, his insistance that education be grounded in the learner's experiences and that the educator shun any appearance of authority in the teaching-learning situation are manifestations of his belief in democracy in all forms of human enterprise. His analysis of society is as important to his process as is his analysis of the experiences of a group of students. He uses questions to stimulate self-examination by students and he asks questions about the nature of the social system which is the target of change. These tie together when students begin to ask questions about their own assumptions about the social system. Horton's belief in the imperative of control over their lives and the means of production parallels his belief in control over a learning activity by a circle of learners whose experiences and problems are being discussed.

He argues equally convincingly that laborers need to develop confidence in their ability to direct change in their working conditions and to learn from their own experiences. Dependency on authority is believed by Horton to be antithetical to freedom of thought and expression, whether it is in labor-management relations or in the relationship between student and teacher. Horton's approach to education is a restructuring process that places more control and responsibility in the hands of the learner, not only for purposes of democratizing the experience, but also as intended practice for learners who are interested in achieving the same ends in other arenas of their lives. It is perhaps for these reasons that Horton cautions the observer to not think of Highlander as a method or technique. He regards these aspects of an educational process transient in nature, and far less important than the philosophy and purpose of an educational program. A review of selected features of Horton's philosophy, purpose and approach to adult education will constitute the remaining sections of this chapter.

Neutrality and Leadership Development

Earlier in the chapter it was pointed out that Horton decided prior to Highlander that he could not take a neutral stance toward the structure of society or be neutral in his approach to education adults. The issue of neutrality, or objectivity, in education is not unfamiliar to adult educators, although more adult educators espouse neutrality than practice it. On the view that adult education must not be neutral, Horton lines up closest to Friere, and next to Lindeman, and probably furtherest from the likes of Paterson (1979) and Lawson (1975). Horton's view parallels those of great philosophers of education who have treated education as a branch of politics - Plato in his Republic, Aristotle in his Politics, and Dewey in his Democracy and Education. (Brubacher, 1977:14).

Neutrality in education does not necessarily mean that the educator takes an "objective" versus a "subjective" content-centered approach to educating adults. The distinction might better be made between positions that actually support the status quo and those that would deliberately alter the social order. On this point, Horton takes a critical, analytical approach to society.

Horton made an important choice of goals when he paired his aim of contributing to social movement with the aim of leadership development. The former is clearly aimed at a restructuring of a capitalistic society toward a more socialistic form, while the latter is a much more measurable, conventional, companion to the broader aim. Horton admits that the "movement" aim would be more difficult to achieve and measure, if and in whatever form it occurs. The leadership development aim, however, has been measured by Highlander staff in a surprisingly conventional manner. "We tried to reach an 80 per cent success rate in the leaders we worked with", says Horton (1985), and success meant that former students became key leaders for change in their community or beyond, or achieved new goals if they already held leadership positions. The conventionality ends, however, when the "multiplier factor" in Highlander's approach to leadership development is considered. Horton decided early that working with one local union or one isolated civil rights group at a time was not the route to broader social change, and neither was his work as an organizer of union and civil rights groups. Instead, he concentrated on working with leaders from several organizations or communities at a time. His assumption was that these leaders would take what they learned at Highlander and, with help from the staff when needed, work with other actual or potential leaders, and let the influence of Highlander multiply over larger numbers of people. However, few leaders could effectively do that without an understanding of their own social system, larger systems, and intended changes in them. If leaders were to learn to change a system, their learning experiences had to include a critical analysis of that and related systems.

Social Analysis
Horton believes that both the learner and teacher need to understand society in order to change it, or at least in order to cope with its demands. Two forms of analysis are important to Horton: (1) a long-range analysis of the overall social and economic structure of society, and (2) an analysis of the local situation facing the learner seeking change. Of learners, Horton says:

> They aren't operating in a vacuum. They are operating in a given period in history under a given economic system (e.g. capitalism). You have to know where we are in history, in terms of ideas (e.g. democratic ideas, authoritarian

ideas). You have to know how they have been carried out by politicians and industrialists, for example, and what the system has done in the way of structure to affect the people with whom you are working. You have to know what stage of development the people are in, relative to the situation. If you want to maximize the control people have over their lives then you need to know what control they don't have and why. Therefore, you need to understand the economics, the politics, the culture. This is an objective understanding. Anything you do has to be done in relation to this knowledge of the situation in which you are working. The educator must know this first, in order to know what learners don't know (1985).

Once educators are clear in their analysis and beliefs, they are able to help students carry out their own analyses, which are prerequisite to collective action. Horton does not hide his analysis from workshop participants, but neither does he impose it. Optimally, the process is a dialogue between equals, in which the facilitator and students exchange ideas and learn from each other:

You get the learners to know about their situation by asking questions. And then you share what you know. You draw information from them and supply information they don't have. You supplement what they need (to complete the analysis). There may be technical things they don't have because they haven't had the opportunity to learn them. The educator doesn't tell the learners what to do or give advice, but just shares facts. The learners decide what to do with the facts. (Horton, 1985)

Horton does not claim that he has no influence in workshops. "I have a vision (and analysis) which I can share. I do share my understanding of what is right and makes sense, so if they wish, they can learn from it, as I do from them" (1985). Following Hart's admonition, Horton is in this manner "teaching his own capacity to learn." There is also in this quote a sense of respect for the learner's own experiences, perhaps the keystone of Horton's approach to adult education.

Experience, Learning and Social Meaning

Like most adult educators, Horton believes that the extent of people's initial understanding of new ideas is in part a function of their own past experiences. Horton also believes that people's <u>ability to learn</u> <u>from experience</u> is a crucial factor in their subsequent ability to bring about social change. "I try to get people to understand that they have the makings of solutions to their (work or societal) problems in their own experiences. But they have to learn how to learn from their experiences and from other people's experiences" (Horton, 1985). Horton's near-term objective is for individuals to develop meaning from their own experiences and from experiences of others in a learning group. His longer-term objective is for the learner to develop "social meaning" (meaning that generalizes to others' experiences) that will form a basis for social change. Social meaning therefore begins with the learner's own reality.

In agreement with Kierkegaard, reality for Horton is a function of one's own acts, and truth exists as the individual produces it in action. Action becomes the basis of the individual's experience and the percursor of meaning. "Experience produces knowledge, and knowledge leads to meaning" (Horton, 1985). Action and experience are therefore critical factors in Horton's model of learning and social change, for at least three reasons: (1) Past actions and the actor's interpretation of them can serve as the object of reflection and analysis in a learning experience; (2) The act of learning itself can be the focus of an analysis; and (3) further action is the goal of learning. According to Horton, "one cannot act on learning if he cannot make it his own experience" (1985). This rules out learning by memorizing or other means which are independent of the learner's own experiences.

Community and organizational leaders who come to Highlander with problems to solve and goals to reach bring their action experiences with them (This becomes the "curriculum" at Highlander). They engage in another form of action when they share their experiences with other leaders, and project further actions on the basis of what they learn from one another. Reflection follows these actions, and reflections becomes the basis for further action. In this way learners begins to theorize about action from action experience, and frame their approach to social change. Theory flows from action toward action.

In Horton's model, collective action, essential to social change, begins with the individual and develops through group learning experiences. Individual community leaders develop their collective action skills in a kind of "collaborative learning" experience (Cunningham, 1983), which they begin in a Horton workshop and continue in their efforts to effect social change. They develop social meaning in the ultimate sense when and if a social movement is started. Horton's aim is to nurture a movement through widening circles of influence, beginning with the efforts of leaders working at Highlander in a democratic learning environment.

Horton's approach to establishing a democratic learning environment has been described by others as "popular education" or "education for empowerment". According to Heany (1982:161):

Education for empowerment - liberatory education - seeks to develop a pedagogy that emphasizes mutual responsibility for learning and teaching, shared critical reflection on the social order, and collaboration in action. Liberatory programs are those that facilitate the development of independent, critical, and politically aggressive makers of history.

Cunningham (1982:78) argues that the goal of empowerment education is "... to assist the learner to free him or herself from (societal) oppression, to demystify knowledge, and to allow the prevailing social reality to be redefined by the student ... to apply a critical analysis to society". In another article (1983:64) she cites Reed's "four principles of the empowering process":

1. Use the learners' values and social interests to determine the purpose, character, and direction of the learning process;
2. Use the social experience of the learners as the basic content, the raw material of the learning process, since there is no such thing as neutral knowledge;
3. Link the learners' practice to the historical development of society; and
4. Draw on the lessons and experiences of persons having similar social values and faced with parallel social conditions in order to improve the learner's own practice.

259

These principles come closer than most to Horton's own assumptions about adult education.

Leaders coming to Highlander for assistance are almost always in a minority position relative to the larger society or organization in which they live or work. Their perception of their ability to bring about change is usually restricted by their assessment of experiences in their local community or workplace, and does not necessarily extend to the larger society, to larger organizations, or to other people's experiences. They are usually unaccustomed to framing their local actions in terms of generalizable concepts such as collective action and democracy in the workplace. Moreover, they usually have not "learned how to learn" from their own and others' experiences, a limiting factor in any attempt on their part to make a difference in larger groups. Horton's approach is designed to help leaders overcome this limitation and develop their capability to learn from experience. "Acknowledgement of the people's experiences which otherwise were thought by them to be of little value, gives them the feeling that their experience is of value and that they can learn from their experience, make judgements about it ..." (Horton, 1985). Respect for learner experiences is essentially a matter of valuing an individual's uniqueness and not disregarding his or her individuality or right to self-determination. On this principle Horton argues that, while educators can make contributions of their own experiences to a group of learners (once accepted as a part of the group), he/she should never do so as <u>authorities</u>. An authoritarian approach conveys a message to learners that they cannot solve problems by themselves, that the authority-teacher is solving their problems for them.

Dialogue, also central to Horton's approach to education, "can not occur when there are superiors and inferiors in the same situation ... For dialogue to work, you must have genuine respect for each other's experiences" (1985). Mezirow seems to agree with Horton's idea, as he explains his own "conditions for ideal discourse". According to Mezirow (1985a:5)

> Participants in an ideal discourse would have a mutual goal of arriving at a consensus based upon evidence and the cogency of argument alone. They would have accurate and complete information to the topic discussed, and participants would have role reciprocity –

equal opportunity to interpret, explain, challenge, refute, express themselves and speak with confidence.

Mezirow's (ibid:7) conditions for dialogue are essential to the process of helping learners become "critically conscious of the reasons for their needs and to help them understand how their reality has been shaped and influenced (by traditional social practices and institutional arrangements)". He maintains that "education for social action" is not possible without "... a strong and unequivocal sense of solidarity with (learners)" (1985b:149), and that these are essential conditions for transformation of meaning perspective to occur.

Summary and Assessment

Horton's goal is to contribute to the development of a society in which the dominant ethic is humanism, a society of justice and equality. Like Friere, Horton believes that people living in unjust situations can change their lives through their collective actions. He would have people who are struggling for justice become conscious of their own power and ability to effect needed changes in society. Horton works toward a "complete" democracy in all sectors of a society; economic, political, industrial, and family.

One of the unique features of Horton's approach to change is the common application of change strategies to both societies and learning environments. His approach to learning and social change could be called "restructuring", to use a term selected by Walter and Marks (1981) to describe a deliberate or planned reorganization of some aspect of a social structure that affects individual behavior. It is an acknowledgement of the power of such dimensions of social systems as norms, rules, status and roles in the shaping of individual lives. In formal educational settings, the rules of conduct are supportive of an authority-subordinate relationship between teacher and learner. Horton argues that the structure of formal education, at least in the U.S., is not conducive to learning as he defines it. As discussed earlier, learning for Horton involves internalization of knowledge and meaning, which can result only from analysis of experience and a commitment to action. If the role of the teacher is primarily that of information-giver, and the teacher and content are perceived as the sole authorities in the experience, then learning in this sense can not

261

occur. The relative status of teacher and learners in the traditional sense actually promote learner dependency on the teacher, not control by learners over their own experiences and actions. Learners in such a position do not easily generalize their experiences beyond the classroom to the realities of social change.

According to Walter and Marks, restructuring can be pursued by the authority "in power" or by persons "out of power." The change strategies vary, depending on whether change is advocated by in power or out of power persons. Horton clearly works with people who are out of power.

Whereas legislation, policy, and incentives are used by in power agents to enforce change (especially constitutional-procedural restructuring), protests, disobedience, and competing ideology characterize strategies used by persons out of power. The civil rights movement in the U.S. involved such strategies. In terms of organizational change, authorities in power may choose reorganization, shift from product to function orientation, consolidation, centralization, and other shifts to influence individual performance, while out of power groups would rely on strikes, or other forms of protest. Moreover, "A common thread among change efforts (by out of power groups) is a personal code of conduct based on the highest moral principles of the culture, which serves as moral and quasi-legal proof of the legitimacy of change" (Walter and Marks, 1981:99). The principle here is that "the highest truth, not the greatest power", is the ultimate criterion. Gandhi and King are names synonymous with this principle. In organizational change, disruptive strategies are designed to make the organization inoperable or ungovernable, in the interest of effecting greater participation by and benefits of the worker. At the time of this writing, Horton had just visited South Africa, and concluded that blacks in South Africa are, through their protest, making the country ungovernable.

The strategies of change are numerous and varied, but for Horton, the Fabian strategy (Cole, 1961) made most sense and continues to underpin his thinking. For learning and social change to occur along the Horton model, the relationship between ideology and shared principles must be clear and consistently employed by participants in the process. The crucial operating principles in a learning experience include a clear goal, shared experience, respect for individual and collective experience, trust in the learner, action, and empowerment of the learner. These factors are constantly in play during a Horton workshop, and are anchored both in his vision of a democratic society and his concept of a democratic learning process. Only under these conditions, Horton would claim, can learning for social change occur.

References

Adams, F. 1975. Unearthing Seeds of Fire: The Idea of Highlander. Winston-Salem, N.C.: John F. Blair

Bell, B. and F. Ansley 1974. "East Tennessee Coal Mining Battles." Southern Exposure, v. 1, No. 3-4

Brubacher, J. 1977. On the Philosophy of Higher Education. San Francisco: Jossey-Bass.

Cole, M. 1961. The Story of Fabian Socialism. Stanford, Ca.: Stanford University Press.

Cunningham, P. 1982. "Contradictions in the Practice of Non-traditional Continuing Education", in Merriam, S. (ed.) op. cit.

Cunningham, P. 1983. "Helping Students Extract Meaning From Experience." in R. Smith (ed) New Directions for Continuing Education: Helping Adults Learn How to Learn, no. 19.

Dunbar, A. 1981. Against the Grain: Southern Radicals and Prophets, 1929-1959. Charlottesville, Va.: University of Virginia Press

Egan, G. 1975. The Skilled Helper: A Model for Systematic Helping and Interpersonal Relating. Monterey, Ca.: Brooks/Cole

Elias, J. 1982. "The Theory-Practice Split" in S. Merriam (ed) New Directions for Continuing Education: Linking Philosophy and Practice, no. 15. San Francisco: Jossey-Bass

Glen, J. 1985, On the Cutting Edge: A History of the Highlander Folk School, 1932-1962. Ph.D. dissertation, Vanderbilt University.

Hart, J. Light from the North: The Danish Folk High Schools - Their Meanings for America. New York: Henry Holt & Co., 1926.

Heaney, T. 1982. "Power, Learning, and 'Compunication'" in D. Guelette (ed) Microcomputers for Adult Learning: Potentials and Perils. Chicago: Follett Publishing Co.

Highlander Folk School. 1939. Highlander Folk School: The Story of an Educational Center for Working People. Pamphlet, in Highlander Library.

Horton, A. 1971. The Highlander Folk School: A History of the Development of Its Major Programs Related to Social Movements in the South, 1932-1961.

Ph.D. dissertation, University of Chicago.

Horton, M. 1983a. "Influences on Highlander Research and Education Center, New Market, Tennessee, USA" in The Danish Institute (ed) Grundtvig's Ideas in North America - Influences and Parallels. Denmark: The Danish Institute.

Horton, M. 1983B. "Bill Moyer's Journal: An Interview with Myles Horton." Appalachian Journal, v.9 no. 4.

Horton, M. 1985. Interviews conducted by the authors

Lawson, K. 1975. Philosophical Concepts and Values in Adult Education. Nottingham, England: Barnes, Numby, Ltd.

Link, E. 1984. Labor-Religion Prophet: The Life and Times of Harry F. Ward. Boulder, Co.: The Westview Press.

Merriam, S. (ed.) 1982. Linking Philosophy and Practice. San Francisco: Jossey-Bass.

Mezirow, J. 1985a. "Social Commitment in Adult Education." Paper presented at the First Annual Conference of the International League for Social Commitment in Adult Education, Ljucskile, Sweden, July.

Mezirow, J. 1985b. "Conceptual Action in Adult Education." Adult Education Quarterly, v. 35, no. 3, p.142-151.

Morris, A. 1984. The Origins of the Civil Rights Movement Black Communities Organizing for Change. New York: The Free Press.

Paterson, R. 1979. Values, Education, and the Adult. Boston: Routledge and Kegan Paul.

Pells, R. 1973. Radical Visions and American Dreams: Culture and Social Thought in the Depression Years. New York: Harper and Row.

Reed, D. 1981. Education for a People's Movement. Boston: South End Press.

Tjerandsen, C. 1980. Education for Citizenship: A Foundation's Experience. Santa Cruz, Ca.: Emil Schwarzhaupt Foundation, Inc.

Walter, G. and Marks, S. 1981 Experiential Learning and Change. New York: John Wiley and Sons.

Chapter Thirteen

PAULO FREIRE

Peter Jarvis

Paulo Freire was born into a middle class family in Recife, Brazil, in 1921 and initially read law and philosophy and qualified at the bar. However, it was during this period that his interests broadened and he began to read sociology and education. Perhaps the latter is no surprise since his wife, Elza, was a school teacher. Consequently, Freire abandoned law and assumed the position of a welfare officer, later becoming director of the Department of Education and Culture in the State of Pernambuco. It was during this period that he made contact with the urban poor, although it was not until the next phase of his career, when as Director of the Cultural Extension Service of the University of Recife, that he began to implement his well known literacy campaign. However, Freire did not act in isolation in Brazil, so that it is necessary to understand something of the historical background in that society during this period.

The Historical Situation
There was a very important influence upon Freire's intellectual development at this time: the rise of radicalism in the Church of Rome in Brazil. This development has been recorded in the writings of Emanuel de Kadt, and it is from his essay in Landsberger (1970) that this historical background is discussed here. Although de Kadt points out that Freire arrived at his view independently, there can be no denying that working within the same religious and cultural milieu his own development was in some way related to what was happening in the Church of Rome in Brazil. As early as 1929 Catholic Action was founded in that country, and it rapidly established its own university groups, (Juventude Universitaria

265

Catholica), but initially this was not a radical organization. However, a number of factors in the 1950s contributed towards a swing towards radicalism, so that by the early 1960s the movement recognised that university reforms in Brazil had to be part of the Brazilian revolution. Such a movement towards a Marxian, rather than a Marxist, radicalism incurred disfavour with many of the ecclesiastical hierarchy, which was a lesson that a second movement, Ação Popular, was to note. This movement began informally during 1961, was officially launched on 1 June 1962, and rapidly gained a middle class, radical and intellectual following. The movement was explicitly non-Marxist, but neither was it officially bound with any ties to the Church of Rome, although a theological position was implicit within it from the outset. Indeed, de Kadt suggests that it was a para-Christian movement and underlying its position are the writings of Teilhard de Chardin, Emanuel Mournier and Pope John XXIII, especially the latter's 'Mater and Magistra'.

For this movement, the development of history was not merely a simple evolutionary process but a dialectic one in which human struggle plays a significant part. This dialectic struggle gives rise to a historical consciousness (consciência histórica) which is 'a critical conscious reflection about the historical process' (de Kadt in Landsberger 1970:210). This consciousness only arises when the individual begins to examine the world in a critical manner in order to act upon it and transform it. Such transformation is called humanization. The end-product of this historical struggle is the creation of utopia, a concept rather like Christ's 'Kingdom of Heaven' or Marx's 'classless society', but one that must lie outside of historical time. However, in order for the process of humanization to proceed individuals must have the opportunity to develop their potential and this can only occur when the yoke of oppression is removed. Emanuel Mournier claimed that:

> Man must strive in co-operation with others to create a society of persons, a society which will rest on "a series of original acts which have no equivalent in any part of the universe". Such acts would include efforts to put one's self in the position of others, to understand them, and to make one's self available to them ... (cited in Landsberger 1970:213)

Mournier was fully aware that for as long as humanity exists there will be a struggle of force rather than a static utopia and it is within the context of this struggle that the person makes choices. Through these choices the person demonstrates authenticity and becomes edified. Since humanity has no essence apart from existence the person develops in and through these choices. But the restrictive structures of society often prevent the mass of people from making free choices, so that the social structure often inhibits the development of the person. Hence, the movement is faced with a dilemma: Ação Popular must inform the mass of people about the problems involved in building the new society without restricting their freedom. Mournier called the individual realisation of these problems conscientization (conscientização). Yet in order to help people to realize that they were inhibited by the social structures the idea of the dominant and the dominated was introduced. This clearly relates to the idea of the human struggle but it also reflects the Marxist dialectic.

It was these ideas that were being worked out and put into practice in just a few areas of Brazil, such as Pernambuco, before the Coup in 1964, after which Freire was arrested, imprisoned and, finally, he went into exile. Indeed, it was against this background and within this cultural milieu that Freire worked out his own ideas about education. His literacy campaign was gaining recognition, indeed it was known as 'Método Paulo Freire'. But with the overthrow of Goulart's government, these radical activities were halted by the new, dictatorial regime. In his enforced exile Freire wrote 'Education: The Practice of Freedom' in 1967. Other books followed and were translated into English, so that Freire was able to move from Chile to Harvard and from there to become a consultant to the World Council of Churches in Geneva. It was during this period that he worked with the government of Guinea-Bissau and 'Pedagogy in Process' followed in 1978. By 1980, the regime in Brazil had changed and Freire, who had expressed a longing to return to his native land (Freire 1978:67-8), was able to return and assume the posts of Professor of Education in both the State and the Catholic universities in São Paulo. In 1985, his 'Politics of Education' appeared and Freire's intellectual position had changed little, so that the following paragraphs contain a brief analysis of some of the main themes that occur in these five books.

The Context of Freire's Writing

Freire's ideas were clearly developed within the context of Ação Popular but, as Mackie (1980:93-119) points out, he has been influenced by a variety of writers, so that he is something of an eclectic. Perhaps he is best understood from within the realms of Christian activism, demonstrating a socially dysfunctional prophetic position, rather than any other. But Freire has also been influenced by Marxism, although no more than by other systems of thought, so that it would be unwise to classify him simply as a Marxist.

Even so, it must be recognised that there are similarities between Mournier's struggles between the dominated and the dominant and Marxist dialectics, so that as most of his writings have been written from the context of the oppressed they do appear revolutionary to those who have adopted a dominant perspective. Clearly, Freire (1972b) has adopted a revolutionary perspective in which he sees education as liberating and utopian. Stanley (1972:42-46) focuses upon this as one of the problems in Freire's thought since he does not really consider the possibility that even the educated may not seek liberation but rather accept a benign authoritarianism and while this may be a just criticism it is clear that Freire does not necessarily expect all people to accept the position that he espouses, as will become clear when his educational method is discussed in greater detail. Yet Freire (1972b:40-1, 71-83) remains utopian, having faith in people to recreate the social world and establish a dynamic society.

The only one of Freire's major works that has not been written from the context of the oppressed is 'Pedagogy in Process' (1978), written while Freire was advisor to the government of Guinea Bissau in its post-colonial period. Here, Freire (1978:14) calls for a radical transformation of the colonial educational system, rather than a mechanical assumption of control over whatever existed prior to independence. Even so, education is still expected to create a critical awareness in the people:

> In the revolutionary perspective, the learners are invited to think. Being conscious, in this sense, is not simply a formula or slogan. It is a radical form of being, of being human ... (it) involves a critical comprehension of reality. (Freire 1978:24)

However, this form of education must be part of the
state plan because in the new democratic society all
participants should be critically aware of their
reality. Education is not politically neutral but
rather it always has political implications.
Therefore, education must be in accord for this state
plan for society, which he contrasts to a more
traditional society's policy:

> Policies carried out by a rigid bureaucracy in
> the name of the masses to whom they are
> transmitted as order are one thing; policies
> carried out <u>with</u> (his emphasis) the masses are
> quite another thing - with their critically
> conscious participation in the reconstruction
> of society, in which the necessary directions
> never become slogans. (Freire 1978:101)

The Nature of Education

Most of Freire's writings concentrate upon literacy
education which is not surprising considering the
context in which he wrote. Even so, he (1978:100)
claims that neither literacy nor post-literacy
education are separate processes but they are two
moments in the same process of formation. Basically,
for Freire education has one major aim, to help the
participants to put 'knowledge into practice' and it
is this combination of reflection and action that he
calls 'praxis'. But he is clear that education is a
human process (Freire 1972b:51) and a revolutionary
one because its outcome will be that authentic human
beings will be able to transform the world and
humanize it. However, it has been suggested by Berger
(1974:136) that Freire is more concerned with
political revolution than with literacy:

> The political themes are not dragged in to help
> with literacy training. On the contrary,
> literacy training is but a useful tool for
> expansion of political consciousness and for
> political activation of the individual.

Such a claim, phrased in the way that it is,
demonstrates Berger's own unfamiliarity with
Freire's writings, which is somewhat surprising
since some of Berger's own significant contributions
to knowledge have been in the field of sociology of
religion. Yet in his unsympathetic discussion on
Freire he fails to detect the influence of the
Christian prophetic tradition, one which is more

Paulo Freire

concerned with the humanization of the world than
with the retention of the status quo and the
oppression of the masses. Clearly Freire is concerned
with creating a better world, he is concerned with
the development and liberation of people and he does
see education as one means by which individuals can
acquire confidence as authentic human beings. But
these are simultaneous processes rather than
separate and discrete ones as implied by Berger.
Freire (1972b:21) refers to humanization, one of the
fundamental doctrines of Açao Popular, when he
writes: "This, then, is the great humanistic and
historical task of the oppressed: to liberate
themselves and their oppressors as well." Hence,
Freire recognises here that both the dominated and
the dominant are in their different ways imprisoned
within the structures of society and that both need
to be liberated. Clearly the oppressed are apparently
more ignorant of the social processes that create for
them a culture of silence and through education, by
which they can become critically aware of their
reality, can they discover themselves and look to the
future to play their part in transforming the world.
The oppressors also need to be liberated and it is
probably harder for them than it is for the
oppressed, claims Freire (1972a:36-37), so that
liberation must begin with the latter. Indeed, 'it
would be a contradiction in terms if the oppressors
... actually implemented a liberating education'
(Freire 1972a:30).

Among the other aims of education is
conscientization, another concept that Freire shares
with Açao Popular. For Freire (1972b:51n)
conscientization 'refers to the process in which men,
not as recipients but as knowing subjects, achieve a
deepening awareness both of the socio-cultural
reality which shapes their lives and of their
capacity to transform that reality'. It is
specifically and exclusively a human process and it
is one which Rivera (1972:56) likens to rebirth or
religious conversion. It is perhaps one of the
concepts more closely associated with Freire than any
other and yet recently he claimed that it is a term
that he no longer employs himself. (This claim was
made at a public meeting in Cecil County Community
College, Maryland, U.S.A. in February 1985).
However, it does occur in most of his publications,
including the latest one 'Politics of Education'
1985). But it is a concept that Berger (1974:139-145)
claims that Freire is mistaken about on both
philosophical and sociological grounds. Berger

270

regards conscientization as consciousness raising
and then goes on to suggest that this relates to the
Marxist concept of false consciousness, which in turn
implies a cognitive hierarchy. While the concept of
false consciousness does imply this cognitive
hierarchy, the idea of conscientization does not.
Berger again demonstrates his unfamiliarity with
Freire's work beause he fails to understand that
Freire's educational method is about problematizing
reality rather than imposing another 'superior'
reality upon that already held by the learners.
Hence, an aim of education is that because
individuals become more aware of the social processes
they are more able, if they so desire, to transform
the world.

Having thus far examined the humanistic aims of
education in Freire's writing, it is now necessary to
look at the methods through which he suggests that
these aims will be achieved. Freire's teaching
methods are perhaps best summarized by Goulet (Freire
1974:viii):

- participant observation of educators 'tuning
  in' to the vocabular universe of the people;
- (an) arduous search for generative words at two
  levels: syllabic richness and a high charge of
  experiential involvement;
- a first codification of these words into visual
  images which stimulate people 'submerged' in
  the culture of silence to 'emerge' as conscious
  makers of their own 'culture';
- the decodification by a 'culture circle' under
  the self-effacing stimulus of a co-ordinator
  who is no 'teacher' in the conventional sense,
  but who has become an educator-educatee - in
  dialogue with educatee - educators too often
  treated by formal educators as passive
  recipients of knowledge;
- a creative new codification, this one
  explicitly critical and aimed at action,
  wherein those who were formerly illiterate now
  begin to reject their role as mere 'objects' in
  nature and social history and undertake to
  become 'subjects' of their own destiny.

Goulet (Freire 1974:ix) goes on to suggest that
'Paulo Freire's central message is that one can know
only to the extent that one "problematizes" the
natural, cultural and historical reality in which
s/he is immersed. Problematizing is the antithesis of
the technocrat's problem solving stance' because

within the former the person is totally involved whereas in the latter the problem solver seeks to distance himself from reality in order to try to arrive at a solution. However, a very significant factor in Freire's teaching methodology is the recognition of two cultures, that of the teacher and that of the learner, and the realization that the teacher has to bridge the gulf between the two in order to offer a service to the learner. Theologically, this may be viewed as an incarnational approach by which the teacher seeks to identify him/herself with the learner in order to learn not only the vocabulary but also the thought patterns of the learner. Only when this has been achieved can the teacher help problematize reality for the learner. Freire (1972b:36) summarized this as:

> The educator's role is to propose problems about the codified existential situations in order to help the learners arrive at an increasingly critical view of their reality.

It should be noted that Freire is not suggesting that the teacher's view of reality should be imposed upon the learners, as Berger (1974) implied, but rather that reality itself should be regarded as problematic.

For Freire the teaching and learning transaction is a dialogue between those who are participants in the process. Rather like the ideal society in Freire's thoughts there must be human relationship between teacher and learner, so that the traditional teacher-learner relationship is transformed into a relationship of 'teacher-student with students-teachers' (Freire 1972a:53). Bee (1980:50) puts it another way when she notes that traditionally in children's education, children are made the object rather than the subject of their learning. For Giroux (1981:133):

> radical pedagogy requires non-authoritarian social relationships that support dialogue and communication as indispensible for questioning the meaning and nature of knowledge and peeling away the hidden structures of reality.

While Giroux regards Freire's pedagogy as radical, Griffith (1972:67) claims that Freire's 'assumptions about the relationship between teachers and students, are neither new nor particularly useful in bringing about an improvement in the process'.

Griffith goes on to cite many adult educators who have countenanced similar teaching techniques and he then criticises Freire for not having examined nor cited the works of adult education in which these approaches are discussed. It is perhaps significant that Griffith is an adult educator since adult education theory has frequently differed from initial education theory on this fact that the learners are adult human beings and should always be treated as such. That Freire does not cite those other adult educators who have espoused this approach is a fact but his background must be borne in mind when making such a comment. Freire's concern is adult literacy in the third world rather than an academic treatise upon the development of adult education theory. However, the significance of this discussion may perhaps be seen in the contrasting direction of the two sets of relationships. Recently, Jarvis (1985:48-50) has suggested that there are two distinctive curricular models in education that relate to these two sets of directions: 'Education from Above' is the more traditional approach whereas 'Education of Equals' reflects that which is more common in adult education, especially that approach adopted by Freire. However, Freire has also been criticised by Boston (1972:87-9) for his approach to relationships. Boston claims that Freire is too concerned with the dominant-dominated relationship and that he needs to examine other dimensions of relationship. He suggests that Freire's analysis is one-sided and that there are other styles of relationship in Latin America, one he suggests being intermediary and another which he regards as a bargaining relationship. However, bargains can only be struck within the limitations of power. By contrast, Boston suggests that intermediary relationship is one that the Roman Catholic Church serves in Latin America but it is perhaps significant to recall that it was Ação Popular that recognised the dominant-dominated relationship. That Freire contrasts a vertical with a horizontal relationship and that he wishes the teacher-learner relationship to be a horizontal one is in accord with adult education theory and also in accord with the ideal, democratic society for which Freire aspires.

What then is the content of Freire's teaching? To a very great extent the content is closely related to the methods that he employs. Freire has been concerned not merely to teach people to read and write but to understand and relate their learning to the reality of their everyday life. Hence, he does not start with meaningless words and phrases but, having attuned himself to the vocabulary and the social world of the learner, he focuses upon 'generative themes', that is themes that allow the learner to analyse that which they already understand and which will encourage the development of associated ideas within the discussion in cultural circles (Freire 1974:157). Yet the presentation of these themes may be through visual, tactile or audio methods, according to which might generate discussion, etc. However, only the theme is presented and never a solution; the theme acts as a problem-posing rather than a problem-solving situation (Freire 1972a:91-93).

In a sense it may be seen that he is not seeking to transmit either worthwhile or objective knowledge, since 'worthwhileness' by definition is ideological and objective knowledge is a questionable concept. This approach, which Freire rejects, he refers to as the banking concept of education but by contrast he endeavours to encourage learners to create knowledge and meaning as a result of a constant problematizing of their existential situations. For him (1972a:49) the banking concept ensures that the educator has a major role, but not one of which he approves:

> It follows logically from the banking notion of consciousness that the educator's role is to regulate the way that the world 'enters into' the students. His task is to organize a process which already happens spontaneously, to 'fill' the students by making deposits of information which he considers constitute true knowledge.

Hence, in traditional education the educator controls the knowledge and, to some extent, the perception of reality with which the student is presented. But the student already has a perception of reality, so that another perception might be rejected whereas through dialogue and problematization new knowledge and new meaning may be created. This is obviously no new debate within either the philosophy or the sociology of education, nor indeed of adult education, although it has been thoroughly reviewed elsewhere (Jarvis 1985:73-92) no further reference is made to it here. Suffice to note that through the relaxation of control by the teacher, Freire's approach encourages the creation of knowledge and meaning relevant to the social situation of the learners. Since it does relate to their own reality, which they learn to analyse critically, he expects that praxis will occur, i.e. that having thought about the ideas the learners will act in accord with their conclusions in order to transform the world. But in transforming the world the individual has to make choices which will not automatically produce beneficial results:

> The process of transforming the world, which reveals this presence of man, can lead to his humanization as well as his dehumanization, to his growth or diminution. These alternatives reveal to man his problematic nature and pose a problem for him, requiring that he choose one path or the other. (Freire 1972b:55)

But is Freire's approach successful? Certainly learners have become literate in a few weeks, because the topics relate directly to the social experience of the learners. Berger (1974:136), commenting upon this success rate, claims, without justification, that for Freire pedagogical results are no real justification for the method since it is only undertaken for political ends. Such a claim demonstrates Berger's inability to see that for Freire the human being and human society are central to his thinking and that the achievement of humanization is both an educational and a political act, so that it is necessary to assess his work not only in literacy but also in human terms. Freire (1972b:43-47) records the human success in literacy, success that makes no mention of political revolution.

Yet politics cannot be isolated from the education process, so that it might be asked whether Freire's approach to education, one which came out of a third world situation, has any validity for the remainder of the world? Boston (1972:91) is in no doubt, claiming that 'even an indirect translation of Freire is simply folly'. Even Giroux (1981:139), who is very sympathetic to Freire's approach, suggests that:

> It would be misleading as well as dangerous to extend without qualification Freire's theory and methods to the industrialized and urbanized societies of the West.

Yet Griffith (1972:67) claims that Freire offers nothing new to adult educators and London (1973:56) suggests that:

275

Freire's approach to education and social
change has important implications for our own
country (USA) and for most industrialized
societies, as well as for the newly developing
world.

Hence, it might be worthwhile to try his approach in
the West. Indeed, in the United Kingdom, radical
community adult educators have no doubts that
Freire's approach is applicable (Batten 1980:27-38;
Alfred 1984:105-114). Freire has offered a theory of
teaching and learning that is at the heart of much
adult education theory, so that there is not a great
deal with which many adult educators would wish to
dispute. However, the context within which he has
placed his theory and practice causes some educators
doubts. He has coupled his approach to education to a
theory of change that has political implications as
well as human ones and in this there are conclusions
that have caused some educators profound unease.

Freire's Contribution to Educational Theory
It is necessary to locate Freire within the emerging
field of study of the education of adults so that he
should be viewed from within this theoretical
context, although Freire's own intellectual mentors
were clearly not to be discovered from within this
discipline (Griffith 1972:68). This perhaps reflects
the need for an emerging field of study, such as
adult education, to recognise its roots in the more
established disciplines and to translate some of
their conceptual insights into the education of
adults. This, Freire has done to a very sophisticated
extent. While it is clear that he has added little to
the theory of teaching adults, since there have been
many adult educators who have espoused techniques
similar to those adopted by Freire, there have been
few who have contributed to the theory of adult
education from such a wide variety of disciplines.
However, it is in the areas of sociology, politics
and philosophy/theology of adult education that his
contribution is perhaps the greatest.
  Sociology of education underwent a major change
in the West in the early 1970s and it is often
equated with the publication of 'Knowledge and
Control' in 1971. This symposium, edited by Young,
highlighted a more radical and phenomenological
analysis of education and it is one that is similar
to the perspective discovered in Freire's writings.
Clearly many of the issues about both knowledge and

power were not new, many being traced back to Mannheim and Marx, their publication at that time had a profound effect upon sociological studies of education. By contrast, there was no highly developed sociology of adult education, although there were a number of sociological studies of the education of adults, so that Freire's analysis brought the 'new' sociology of education to adult education before it had even established a sociology of adult education.

Because adult education has been predominantly a psychological discipline, with emphasis upon adults learning, neither the sociological nor the political implications of learning had been developed or analysed, but these are issues quite central to the whole of Freire's work. Indeed, the recognition that knowledge itself is controlled and socially structured, while commonplace in sociology, had not really been developed in adult education, so that some of these radical and different ideas had not been discussed in great detail when Freire's writings became known to Western adult educators.

In his latest book, Freire (1985) reverts to a theme that is implicit in much of his writing and in which the history of adult education is rich - that of the involvement of the church. No history of adult education could be written that is true to history without recognition that the church's role has been long and honourable. However, in Freire's work it is the prophetic tradition of the church rather than the missionary one that takes precedence. Such a tradition has frequently been uncomfortable to the elite, so that it is unsurprising that his writings are not always accepted since the political implications of the prophetic tradition often inhibit unbiased analysis. Yet for Freire the humanization of society must have political, indeed revolutionary, implications and it is this he tried to practise in Brazil and Chile. Indeed, Gutierrez's (1974:91-92) study of Liberation Theology views Freire's approach as 'one of the most creative and fruitful efforts which have been implemented in Latin America'. Freire's emphasis upon liberating the learner to become an agent in the world is significant to the structure-agency debate in sociology (Giddens 1979), but it is also important as both a philosophical concept about the development of authenticity, and as a theological idea about the development of the human being.

Freire's work contains a profound humanistic philosophy of education that requires further analysis in the philosophy of adult education.

277

Perhaps its relationship to some of the ideas expressed by Dewey (1916, 1938) and by Bergevin (1967) need to be discussed. Bergevin (1967:30-31) suggested some of the major goals in adult education in terms of the meaning of life and the provision of conditions and opportunities for adult advancement, although he did not really relate these to a radical sociological analysis in the same manner as Freire.

Freire offers an implicit theology of adult education which has not yet been developed, despite the long history of involvement that the churches have had with the education of adults. This is an area that requires considerable analysis in the future.

Because Freire has written about specific cultures there is a sense in which he has developed only those parts of his theory that are relevant to the social situation in which he was working; consequently there is only a synthesis of perspectives on the education of the adult that relates to those areas of concern rather than is a fully developed sociology of, or philosophy of, adult education. What he has written is related to his conviction, rather than always being carefully argued within the confines of the more traditional academic framework. Even so, Freire has produced profound insight into the philosophy, politics and sociology of adult education, so that his work will need to be taken into consideration as the development of adult education theory continues. But above all, his work offers a hope and an idealism of what the human being can become and a role that education can play in that process.

Bibliography

Alfred, D. 1984 The relevance of the Work of Paulo Freire to Radical Community Education in Britain in <u>International Journal of Lifelong Education</u> Vol 3 No2

Batten E. 1980 Community Education: a case for radicalism, in Fletcher C and Thompson N (eds) <u>op cit</u>

Bee B 1980 The Politics of Literacy in Mackie R (ed) <u>op cit</u>

Berger P L 1974 <u>Pyramids of Sacrifice</u> Harmondsworth, Pelican

Bergevin P 1967 <u>A Philosophy for Adult Education</u> New York, Seabury Press

Boston B O 1972 Paulo Freire: Notes of a Loving Critic in Grabowski S M (ed) <u>op cit</u>

Dewey J 1916 <u>Democracy and Education</u> New York, The Free Press

Dewey J 1938 <u>Experience and Education</u> New York,

Collier Books

Fletcher C and Thompson N (eds) 1981 Issues on Community Education Lewes, The Falmer Press

Freire P 1972a Pedgagogy of the Oppressed (Trans M B Ramos) Harmondsworth, Penguin

Freire P 1972b Cultural Action for Freedom Harmondsworth, Penguin

Freire P 1974 Education: The Practice of Freedom London, Writers and Readers Co-operative (originally published in the United Kingdom as Education for Critical Consciousness) London, Sheed and Ward

Freire P 1978 Pedagogy in Process: The Letters to Guinea Bissau London, Writers and Readers Co-operative

Freire P 1985 The Politics of Education (Trans D Macedo) Massachusetts, Bergin and Garvey Publishers Inc.

Giddens A 1979 Central Problems in Social Theory London, MacMillan

Giroux H A 1981 Ideology, Culture and the Process of Schooling, Lewes, The Falmer Press

Giroux H A 1985 Introduction in Freire (1985) op cit

Goulet D 1974 Introduction in Freire (1974) op cit

Grabowski S M (ed) 1972 Paulo Freire: A Revolutionary Dilemma for the Adult Educator Syracuse University Publications in Continuing Education

Griffith W S 1972 Paulo Freire: Utopian Perspectives in Literacy Education for Revolution in Grabowski S M (ed) op cit

Gutierrez G 1974 A Theology of Liberation London, SCM Press Ltd

Jarvis P 1985 The Sociology of Adult and Continuing Education London, Croom Helm

de Kadt E 1970 J V C and A P: The Rise of Catholic Radicalism in Brazil in Landsberger H A (ed) op cit

Landsberger H A (ed) 1970 The Church and Social Change in Latin America University of Notre Dame Press

London J 1973 Reflections upon the relevance of Paulo Freire for American Adult Education in Convergence Vol 6 No 1

Mackie R 1980 Contributions to the Thought of Paulo Freire in Mackie R (ed) op cit

Mackie R (ed) 1980 Literacy and Revolution: the Pedagogy of Paulo Freire London Pluto Press

Rivera D M 1972 The Changers: a New Breed of Adult Educator in Grabowski S M (ed) op cit

Stanley M 1972 Literacy: the Crisis of Conventional Wisdom in Grabowski S M (ed) op cit

Young M F D 1971 Knowledge and Control London, Collier & Macmillan

Chapter Fourteen

ETTORE GELPI

Colin Griffin

Ettore Gelpi heads the Lifelong Education Unit of
UNESCO and his concern with lifelong education
reflects the global scale of today's social and
political issues and the internationalist perspective of the organisation itself. It also reflects a
view of education inseparably linked to the realms of
production and politics, and to the relations between
the developed and the undeveloped worlds, the Eastern
and the Western blocs, the countries of North and
South. But a crisis has occurred in UNESCO and the
reasons for this serve as well as anything else to
introduce Gelpi's own educational philosophy.

UNESCO was founded in 1946 with the objectives
of promoting peace and security through international collaboration in education, science, culture and
communications. Its ideals were therefore much more
to do with promoting the principles of harmony and
co-existence than with promoting trade in material
things, and as the last forty years have shown, this
is by far the harder road to choose. The origins of
the organisation were in a conference held in London
under the auspices of the British government.
However, Britain has now followed the United States
out of UNESCO, and they are currently trying to
persuade Japan to do the same. This is because of the
alleged 'politicisation' of its concerns. During the
years of its existence education, science, culture
and communications have indeed become more
political, and the pursuit of peace and security even
more urgently so. But what has also happened is that
the original 20 member-states of UNESCO have grown to
number 160. What began as an association of the
victorious Western allies now includes the countries
of the Third World, demanding since the 1960s much
more say in international diplomacy and challenging
the hegemony of the Western powers. This is what

really constitutes the 'politicisation' of UNESCO and which has brought about the present crisis in its affairs.

From the perspective of universal lifelong education therefore, Gelpi's writings address an immense range of issues in rather broad categories. Lifelong education is itself a very broad category, much more so than adult education as such. But lifelong educators are of necessity concerned with all stages of both life and education. Radical educational movements, especially those concerned with workers' education, have more often than not addressed themselves to the learning of children and adults, and of adults young and old. It is a professional division of labour and knowledge that requires specialisation into age-specific categories. From Gelpi's point of view, learning is implicated in systems of production as such, as these are experienced by landless peasants or unemployed industrial workers. Thinking in narrow categories, whether professional or national, can seriously inhibit our thinking about education. From the point of view of adult education it might be supposed that child education is accomplished. From a global point of view, nothing could be more mistaken. A recent publication (TUC 1985) reveals that an estimated 150 million children are currently being exploited as cheap or unpaid labour. Most are from Third World countries but even in Britain many children work, often for a pittance: a Low Pay Unit survey identified up to 40% of children in some schools as having jobs. It is simply not the case that children have no knowledge of the world of work, and not useful to construct categories of work and education that do not reflect this situation (see Bates 1984). Taking the picture world-wide, children actually constitute the most exploited group of workers. But in world-wide terms the picture of work and employment as a whole demands new categories of analysis. In the fact of multinational corporations, the concept of a national economy is becoming redundant; typically, Third World countries are nominally, that is to say politically, sovereign. But economically they are increasingly at the disposal of the multinationals in decisions about investment and employment. As a recent TV Channel 4 series in the U.K. has shown, the concentration of economic power far outweighs the puny national sovereignty of Third World countries. 80% of all foreign investment is accounted for by the top 500 companies. One-third of all world trade is accounted for by the top 100. It

is estimated that by the end of the decade over half
of the trade of the free world will be controlled by
the top 500 multinationals. No theory of development
which neglects the role of multinationals will in
future be adequate, either in the case of Third World
or industrialised societies, and their role in
relation to conventional development agencies poses
crucial issues for the relation between national
sovereignty and economic development. Gelpi's work
serves as a timely reminder that it is increasingly
against this background of wealth and poverty, work
and unemployment, that education has relevance for
the struggles of workers and women and ethnic groups
suffering national or international colonisation.

Consequent upon the international disposition
of capital investment, vast movements in the world
population of workers are afoot. It has never been so
evident that the division of labour and the
possibilities for employment and unemployment are
international in character. One of Gelpi's main
concerns has been with migrant workers and their
children. Whatever happens to work and unemployment
in any particular country, the market in jobs is now
global, partly at least in consequence of the global
pattern of investment and the relative autonomy of
the multinational corporations. Even more is it a
consequence of the distribution of wealth and power
in the world. As in the case of the forced labour of
children, this problem is only now being brought home
to a wider circle through the popular medium of
broadcasting. Thus a recent series of television
programmes called The People Trade (International
Broadcasting Trust 1985) has demonstrated the ways in
which increasingly companies are able to choose the
most advantageous sites and ready-made workforces in
both industrialised and Third World countries. Work
itself has become an international commodity, to be
bought and sold to the benefit largely of the
multinational corporations. The same market forces
propel labourers off the land in Mexico, into Mexico
City and finally into California (where their
children are exploited as cheap or unpaid labour as
orange-pickers, according to the TUC survey). The
prevalence of market forces has created free trade
zones in which the pursuit of profits on the part of
the corporations has become the main factor in the
international division of labour and wealth. As a
result, in both the developed world of the North and
the undeveloped world of the South, more than 900
million people are unemployed or underemployed. The
presenters of The People Trade project a rise in this

figure to over 1500 million by the year 2000. It is against this kind of background that Gelpi's concept of lifelong education has developed: the increasing scale of the trade in people and work, with all its consequences for poverty and unemployment, resistance by workers and governments, the marginalisation in production of major groups in society such as ethnic minorities, women, the elderly and incapacitated, the children themselves. That such groups could actually add up to a majority of the population is an indication of the scale of the problems which such tendencies project.

Gelpi's ideas about lifelong education have developed therefore against this background of the global trade in people and work and wealth, and of the profound divisions which mark off the rich from the poor nations of the world. No doubt the increasing consciousness on the part of Third World countries has constituted the process of the 'politicisation' of UNESCO which the rich nations complain of and which has brought the organisation to its current crisis.

Until the publication in 1985 of Gelpi's Lifelong Education and International Relations his work was best known in the two volumes called A Future for Lifelong Education, published in 1979 by the Department of Adult and Higher Education of Manchester University and which were translated and introduced by Ralph Ruddock. Here are contained papers on diverse topics with a bearing upon the development of his thought, rather than a systematic exposition of the concept of lifelong education. Nor will the reader discover in Gelpi any conventionally academic discourse upon adult learning. Instead, Gelpi offers a powerfully suggestive analysis of the significance of education in the international division of labour and in the struggles of workers and all marginalised groups in society against the forms which this division takes. However, as Ruddock says in his sympathetic and perceptive introduction, Gelpi is not to be labelled or identified with any single ideological position: his concern for popular struggles, and for the dialectical possibilities which lifelong education opens up, reflects a turn of mind unfamiliar perhaps to the Anglo-Saxon way of thinking. To this way of thinking his work may appear unduly abstract and generalised. In terms of his own experience of the consequences of the international division of labour and wealth such criticism may be dismissed out of hand. Nevertheless, it is paticularly necessary to impose some sort of

framework upon Gelpi's writing, even at the expense
of betraying its authenticity.

It is appropriate therefore, to think to Gelpi's
contribution not in terms of a theory of adult
learning and teaching, but rather as a policy model
according to which lifelong education becomes an
integral feature of the struggle against the
international division of labour and its
consequences for all those people who are in some way
'marginalised' by it. In his study of Gelpi, for
example, Timothy Ireland identified three areas of
special concern which either run through Gelpi's
writing or else represent a typical consequence of
his social and political analysis. These are workers'
education and the role of trade unions in it, with
special reference to migrant workers and the training
of young workers; the linguistic and cultural needs
of migrants and their children, and other linguistic
and cultural minorities; and finally the lifelong
education needs of the elderly, especially in
industrial society (Ireland 1978: 66-84). Gelpi is
not, of course, the first to have considered these
areas from a standpoint of educational policy, but
what distinguishes his particular contribution is
the range and consistency of the underlying analysis,
together with a vast practical experience of what he
is talking about. Much of his writing, in fact, is
concerned with specific lifelong education projects
and applications, rather than with the systematic
exposition of the underlying analysis around the
concept of the international division of labour.

The opening chapters of A Future for Lifelong
Education do provide an indication of Gelpi's
conceptual framework, as well as of the difficulties
of expressing it in the conventional categories of
Anglo-Saxon adult education discourse. For example,
a dialectical conception of theory and practice:

> Education for all, and at all ages; but with
> what objectives and with what means? "Lifelong
> education" could result in the reinforcement of
> the established order, increased productivity
> and subordination; but a different option could
> enable us to become more and more committed to
> the struggle against those who oppress mankind
> in work and in leisure, in social and emotional
> life. (Gelpi 1979, vol. 1:1)

Lifelong education is not one option but many: in
societies of whatever ideological order its
potential is both for liberation and repression: it

is at the same time both progressive and reactionary. According to our more familiar categories of reasoning, as the philosophical Bishop Butler said, "everything is what it is, and not another thing." But this is not the logic of the Continental tradition of philosophy in which Gelpi was educated, and he sees lifelong education as a universal potential for the autonomy of individuals and groups which is contradicted in practice.

The paradox of adult education in a climate both of developmental activities and financial constraint is easily understood in Gelpi's terms: what is being developed and what constrained? Lifelong education policies are not neutral. This statement, says Gelpi, is 'the point of departure for all consideration of it.' Why should there be an almost total international consensus on lifelong education policy alongside what he calls "a progressive reduction of self-directed learning"? The paradox is resolved:

> The repressive forces of our contemporary society are ready to increase the time and space given to education, but only on the condition that it does not bring about a reinforcement of the struggle of men and of peoples for their autonomy. (Gelpi 1979, vol. 1:2)

Policies for lifelong education which have the whole-hearted backing of the state are not likely to be advancing human freedom, in that they are unlikely to advance the cause of self-directed learning. The thoroughgoing application of the principles of andragogy, Gelpi seems to be saying, would actually threaten the social order. In our society, he argues, "it is found necessary to teach and to learn in order to protect the established order." It is also necessary to "adapt people to change" in consequence of the application of science and technology: it is easy to imagine governments of whatever ideology eager to embrace lifelong education on these terms. And of course, from a global perspective, the application of science and technology is hardly a neutral process. Rather, it is a process deeply implicated in the exploitation of the poor countries of the world by the rich. Lifelong education as self-directed learning therefore becomes an actual obstacle to lifelong education as 'education for adaptation' because it means 'individual control of the ends, contents, and methods of education.'

The struggle for lifelong education is the struggle for control which far transcends the boundaries of pedagogy and is concerned with far more than the psychological obstacles to adult learning. Its aim is nothing less than transformation, social change, a crisis of values and of authority in productive and educational life. Gelpi is critical of any educational progressivism which is not directed towards genuinely political objectives, and consistently distances his concept of lifelong education from alternative educational strategies such as deschooling, non-formal education, the OECD's version of recurrent education and so on (see Ireland 1978:11-13). Gelpi has developed his own concept along very different lines from that of lifelong education as conceived at the UNESCO Institute for Education, Hamburg (Dave 1976), which has continued to be dominated by traditional pedagogic categories. For Gelpi, education transcends not only educational institutions but local and national frameworks, and one of his most characteristic contributions had been to relate lifelong education to international organisation and co-operation. But given what he calls 'the planetary scale of the economic system' lifelong education may be an instrument of cultural liberation or dependency, of autonomous development or of new colonialism.

It is clear then that Gelpi's view of lifelong education is essentially one of a social and political process whose objective is to achieve individual and cultural autonomy: he sees lifelong education as an integral aspect of the struggle of marginalised people in all societies against the oppressive structures of the international division of labour. It is an attractive feature of Gelpi's writing that his concept of struggle is not a dourly political one but one that incorporates creativity itself: 'happily,' he says, 'the exploration of educational reality is always full of promise.' This holds true because such reality is 'composed of both control and creativity.' Not many writers on education celebrate its creative potential by breaking into poetry. Gelpi does not offer the kind of systematic and largely negative critique associated with much political writing on education and he cannot be associated with any particular ideological camp. Believing that education systems are relatively autonomous in any social system, he never loses sight of creative opportunities for development towards individual and collective autonomy.

Nevertheless he consistently argues that in all

social and political systems education is
inextricably linked with the structures and
processes of production. Work and education cannot be
other than clearly tied together: the discovery in
Britain and elsewhere of a so-called 'new
vocationalism' should not lead us to suppose that
education has not always, in some way or other, been
a reflection of the realities of the work system.
Education policies of industrialised and developing
countries alike are aimed at problems of unemployment
and under-employment. Whatever ideological form they
take, such policies are concerned as much with
containing social conflict as with experimenting
with new educational ideas such as lifelong
education. The very fact that countries with very
diverse political systems may adopt such a strategy
suggests its ambiguous character: fundamental
conceptions of work and production do not change much
as a result, any more than do judgments about the
value of academic work (Beraho-Beri and Gelpi 1983).
As an expression of the relations of work and
education, then, lifelong education may be a
progressive strategy for human liberation or a
repressive agency of state control. No one has
expressed the dialectical potential of lifelong
education better than Gelpi: most writers on the
subject simply, and simplistically, assume that it
could only be a necessarily desirable thing. As was
earlier suggested, this is not so much a matter of
ideology as a way of thinking philosophically about
education: a way of thinking about the contradictory
possibilities of things rather than of their analytic
categories. To subscribe to a view that lifelong
education could only be a good thing is to neglect
its truly contradictory possibilities:

> A lifelong education policy which reinforces
> the division of labour, a partial schooling
> which is in contradiction with itself,
> encouraging urbanisation and the unemployment
> that goes with it, impoverishes the natural
> resources of some third world countries even to
> the point of exhaustion ... These effects cannot
> be objectives for educational strategies
> designed to favour the interests of exploited
> groups, classes and countries. (Gelpi 1979,
> vol. 2:10)

These kinds of considerations hold true, though, for
all societies, and not only the neo-colonised
countries of the Third World. In industrialised

287

countries too, access to an education system does not of itself constitute a system of lifelong education aimed at liberation. In Gelpi's terms a genuinely progressive strategy of lifelong education would be an exercise in the politics of knowledge and production itself, one which asks who should acquire knowledge, and for what purposes or control, and how should knowledge be organised in society? These tend to be neglected issues in educational debate. In his discussion of political and social factors (Gelpi 1979, vol. 1: Ch. 3) he argues that educators and policy-makers prefer to deal in generalities 'rather than face conflicts and contradictions, or to attempt significant utopian projects.' The need for an analysis of the political, social and institutional framework at the community, national and international level is therefore urgent. This means in effect that educationists need to address problems of class oppression, rural and urban conflicts, the exploitation of the countries of the Third World. 'For too long,' says Gelpi, 'too many progressive educators have failed to take into account the world of production, which is in all reality so significant for personal and social development.' A progressive strategy of lifelong education needs to be addressed to the kind of educational inequality arising from what he describes as the dualism of elite systems: 'In all truth, the problems of quality in mass education is the first problem to be resolved in lifelong education.' The second is that of participation in the educational enterprise:

> If the extinction of the social and international division of labour and the achievement of participation by all individuals in decision-making within the economic, political, social and cultural fields are seen as the grand objectives for modern man, an active role for all within the educational process and in cultural activity is one of the conditions for the realisation of these objectives. (Gelpi 1979, vol. 1:31)

To understand what is meant by the international division of labour is to understand the political origins of the current crisis of UNESCO. In his most recent work Gelpi has brought out the main features of this idea:

> ... the international division of labour which is developing today is based on the exchange of

popular consumer goods manufactured by abundant
and cheap manpower in developing countries with
more sophisticated goods mainly incorporating
capital and an advanced technology from the
older industrialized countries. (Gelpi 1985:25)

This reflects an economist's categories of countries
and regions of the world, to which must be added the
specific social, cultural, scientific and technological conditions obtaining in different countries at
different stages of development. Gelpi would fill out
such categories further therefore with a
sociological analysis of the distribution of power
and the different forms taken by the struggles of
groups, countries and regions for social
transformation. The international division of labour
is imposed upon countries, and the international
labour market conditions economic policies for
reform and development, not to speak of the global
military necessities which determine the fate of
'marginal' nations. In short, the international
division of labour reflects the international
balance of power. Its consequences can be described
in terms of massive migrations of people and the
transformation of processes of production and
technology, together with the nature and
possibilities of employment for children, youths and
adults. The division between industrialised and
developing countries is made manifest in these terms.
Great disparities exist between these countries in
terms of gross domestic product, rates of economic
growth and so on: 'the general conclusion is
inescapable that much of the world's output is
produced and consumed by relatively few of its
people.' The growth of world trade, as determined by
the multinationals, will not benefit the majority of
the peoples of the world, and the industrialised
countries will experience greater and greater
competition. In all countries, however, education
will come to have greater and greater significance,
reproducing in its functions for production and
technology the international division of labour in
new forms.

In order to transform the division of labour and
bring about what Gelpi describes as a new world
order, it is necessary for lifelong education to take
the form of a struggle for cultural identity. This is
particularly the case where, as in most Third World
countries, the productive system itself is
defenceless in the face of the global movement of
investment, technology and workers as a result of the

operations of multinational corporations. Nor can
the rich and industrialised countries of the OECD,
the EEC and COMECON escape the competitive logic of
the international division of labour, as planners,
industrialists and trade unions strive to defend ever
narrower categories of economic interest, and more
and more vulnerable groups in society are pushed to
the margins of affluence. In his writings Gelpi has
paid much attention to the analysis of the situation
of people who are, in some sense or other,
marginalised by the international division of
labour. In particular therefore, he has addressed
issues of trade union education and workers'
education, of peasant culture and working class
culture and the problems of cultural identity, and of
the significance of language teaching for migrant
workers and their children (Gelpi 1979, vol. 2). In
his more recent work he has addressed problems of
urban and rural culture in comparative contexts of
migration and international relations (Gelpi 1985:
Part 3) and the role of education in international
relations between the countries and blocs and regions
of the world (Gelpi 1985: Part 4).

Clearly the concept of lifelong education as
developed in these scattered papers of Gelpi emerges
sometimes as more easy to grasp in its abstract and
dialectical nature than in its practice, despite the
fact that he spends his life practising it worldwide.
The practical asks for lifelong education he
envisages as follows:

1. The involvement of the widest possible
representation of the people in the management
of educational systems with open access to all
the necessary information in order to perform
the function effectively. The widest possible
education of the entire population with the
opportunity for them to acquire information
about the most complex tasks of contemporary
societies regarding production, social and
cultural life.
2. The realisation of educational reforms centred
on new relationships between the social system,
the production system and social and cultural
movements.
3. The experimentation and development of
educational structures capable of satisfying
the demands both of particular publics and of
the whole of the population, and capable of
being a meeting place between traditional and
modern education, formal and non-formal

education, institutional education and self-directed learning.

4. The utilisation of 'space' in, for example, educational institutions, workplaces, daily social life, and time and leisure, to encourage individual and collective self-directed learning and the creation of new knowledge and understanding.

5. The association of creative workers in different aspects of educational activity, from the perfection of educational methods and contents to their diffusion by means of mass media and teaching.

6. Initial and continuing education of educators in liaison with research, creative and productive activities.

7. The definition of methods and contents aiming at individual and collective fulfilment; full intellectual, manual, sensory, aesthetic, linguistic expression; psychological self and interpersonal equilibrium; identification with living, creative culture.

8. Establishment of schemes for the evaluation (chiefly educational) of knowledge acquisition, with more attention to the development of individuals and societies than to the mere internal coherence of educational institutions. (Gelpi 1985:14)

In considering the practical tasks, however, the dialectical nature of lifelong education needs always to be borne in mind:

The new world order, as well as the new international order of education, is at once a concrete objective and an ideal to be attained. The transition from the old to the new order appears to be both difficult and contradictory since the development toward the new world order is not strictly a linear one. (Gelpi 1985:41)

The international context is as inescapable in terms of knowledge as it is in terms of production itself. 'The production and transfer of knowledge are among the most powerful instruments of new relations of domination or equality.' The contribution of education systems to the production of knowledge is diminishing in relation to other sources, such as the media. And broader conceptions of education itself, especially as linked to productive and cultural life, are emerging. Countries and populations are

291

beginning to 'reappropriate' their educational and cultural histories, and cultural creativity is becoming a major source of strength in the struggle against the national and international social hierarchies that the division of labour creates. At the same time, education systems continue to function to reproduce such hierarchies in both industrialised and developing countries. In the end, Gelpi trusts to what he describes as dynamic human creativity to frustrate the forces of oppression. As he says, 'history is full of surprises which enable men to be confident in their future.' Above all, Gelpi subscribes to a humanist belief for a new world order, envisaging a humanism that is 'anti-racist; sensitive to the different forms of human creativity; concerned with the individual and collective rights of men with respect to their objective and subjective existences; and, above all, active in the creation of an international society.' (Gelpi 1985:43)

Gelpi's writings are, it has been said, a scattered and cumulative achievement rather than a systematic elaboration of the concept of lifelong education. The main features of his contribution to our thinking about education are, however, easy to identify:

1. He is a dialectical rather than an analytic thinker, concerned with the contradictory potential of policies rather than with abstract distinctions of theory and practice which tend to characterise Anglo-Saxon thinking about these things. Lifelong education is at the same time both a source of liberation and oppression: from Gelpi's point of view it is useless to talk of progressivism in pursuit of freedom without taking into account the social, political and cultural realities of people's lives.
2. Gelpi is consistent in his insistence upon the link between education and production. There is no point in talking about progressive education except in relation to systems of work and production, which constitute the basis of the social, political and cultural realities of people's lives, and are at the heart of their experience of powerlessness and inequality.
3. There is no point in talking about systems of work and production without regard to the new forms being taken by the international division of labour. Thus educational work in relation to unemployment or under-employment, or in relation to workers' struggles, cannot be

adequately conceptualised in national or regional terms alone.

4. In relation to adult education, lifelong education is obviously very much concerned with adult learning projects. Equally obviously, Gelpi does not see much resemblance between lifelong education and adult education as it generally exists. For one thing, as it exists, adult education continues to reproduce social hierarchies as well as offering opportunities for liberation. 'Adult education can play an important role,' he says, 'only if it is not content to be merely a compensatory instrument.' (Gelpi 1979: vol. 1:47)

5. Against the backdrop of the international division of labour, and the realities of work and production, it is unhelpful to conceptualise education in the narrow, age-specific categories of traditional adult education theory, which all too often projects ethnocentric concepts of adulthood and individual need. In Gelpi's terms, progressive education theory is as likely as not to contribute to the kind of cultural imperialism against which lifelong education, properly conceived, is an instrument of struggle.

6. Adult education as social policy, rather than as theory, is also challenged by Gelpi's concept of lifelong education. Such policies, as addressed to national issues, such as unemployment or poverty, are transformed by the realities of the international division of labour. In Britain, for example, adult education as a form of social policy is dissipating into forms of special provision for the special needs of special target groups of people. All such groups, according to Gelpi's way of thinking, experience the common effects of the division of labour, and their common experience of marginalisation must constitute the heart of any adult education policy if it is to be really effective in meeting their needs, rather than simply another officially inspired strategy to contain social conflict.

7. Ettore Gelpi is a humanist and a utopian. The struggle which he finds at the heart of the lifelong education project is not revolutionary, but one arising out of the contradictory possibilities for freedom which exist in the repressive structures of the international division of labour. Self-directed learning

alone could never bring into existence the new, humanistic world order which he anticipates, only the analysis of the social and political realities of people's lives, and the possibilities these present for transformation.

Bland theoretical formulations would never have precipitated the 'politicisation' crisis of UNESCO. Gelpi's concept of lifelong education can only be fully grasped against this background. The biggest slice of UNESCO's budget goes to education: almost 37%. With this kind of money between 1979 and 1983, fifty million people were brought to literacy. But it is estimated that 889 million people are illiterate still, 60% of them women. And over 100 million children between six and eleven in Third World countries do not attend school. How should we theorise about adult education then? As Gelpi's life and work testifies, the rich countries of the world reject as 'politicisation' the utopianism of the UNESCO enterprise and adopt instead the neo-colonialist postures of trade-and-aid. In the light of this he must have the last word of hope for the future:

> The new world order is closely associated with the construction of this new humanism, which will develop through often desperate struggles for respect for human dignity against the direct or indirect physical and moral violence inflicted on humanity. Struggle and non-violence should not appear as antithetical modes of action but, on the contrary, as equally necessary means for creating social contexts within which human creativity and dignity will be reinforced. (Gelpi 1985:43)

Bibliography

Most of Gelpi's work is written in languages other than English. The following references are to all of his writings, and writings about him, that have so far appeared in English.
      The two main references cited in the text, and from which all the quotations are taken are as follows:
Gelpi, E. (1979) <u>Future for Lifelong Education</u>. Vol. 1: <u>Principles, Policies and Practices</u>. Translated from French by R. Ruddock, Manchester, University of Manchester, Department of Adult and Higher Education.

Ettore Gelpi

Vol. 2 <u>Work and Education</u>. Translated from French by
R. Ruddock, Manchester, University of Manchester,
Department of Adult and Higher Education.
Gelpi, E. (1985) <u>Lifelong Education and Internation-
al Relations</u>, London, Croom Helm.

<u>By Gelpi</u>:
1969 "Structure and functions of Italian
universities" <u>Education in Europe</u>, Proceedings of
the European Seminar on Sociology of Education,
Mouton. pp. 241-246
1973 "General and vocational education for workers"
<u>General and Vocational Education</u>, Report of an
international seminar, Sankelmark/Flensburg, 23-
25/10/73, Cologne, German Commission for UNESCO.
pp.72-76
1974 "European Renaissance and Reformation" <u>History
of Education</u>, Encyclopaedia Britannica. pp. 343-348
1976 <u>Human Settlements and Education</u>, Paris, UNESCO
1977 "Science education and society" <u>Education in a
Changing Society</u>, eds. A. Kloskowska and G.
Martinotti, London, Sage. pp. 109-117
1979 "Creativity, contemporary civilization, the
future of mankind" <u>Dialectics and Humanism</u>, no. 1.
pp. 99-103
1979 "Lifelong education policies in western and
eastern Europe: similarities and differences"
<u>Recurrent Education and Lifelong Learning</u>, World
Yearbook of Education 1979, ed. Tom Schuller, London,
Kogan Page. pp. 167-176
1979 <u>A Future for Lifelong Education: principles,
policies and practices</u>, Manchester University of
Manchester Department of Adult and Higher Education,
Manchester Monographs 13, Volume 1
1979 <u>A Future for Lifelong Education: work and
education</u>, Manchester, University of Manchester
Department of Adult and Higher Education, Manchester
Monographs 13, Volume 2
1979 "Lifelong education: suggestions for an
evaluation of experiences" <u>Lifelong Education: a
stocktaking</u>, ed. A.J. Cropley, Hamburg, UNESCO
Institute for Education, pp. 50-62
1980 "Politics and lifelong education policies and
practices" <u>Towards a System of Lifelong Education:
some practical considerations</u>, ed. A.J. Cropley,
Hamburg, UNESCO Institute for Education and Pergamon
Press. pp. 16-31
1981 "The meaning of life and the meaning of history
in some contemporary cultures" <u>Dialectics and
Humanism</u>, Volume VIII, no. 3, pp. 21-25

1981 "Emerging cultural and educational needs of young adult learners" Policy and Research in Adult Education, first Nottingham International Colloquium, University of Nottingham Department of Adult Education. pp. 98-107

1982 "International division of labour and educational policies" Dialectics and Humanism, Volume IX, no. 2. pp. 5-10

1982 "International division of labour and educational policies" Education with Production, Volume 1, no. 2. pp. 64-76

1982 "Education and work; preliminary thoughts on the encouragement of productive work in the educational process" International Journal of Lifelong Education, Volume 1, no. 1. pp. 53-63

1983 "Teaching" Encyclopedia of Occupational Health and Safety, Geneva, ILO

1983 "Learning for a lifetime" UNESCO Courier. pp. 4-7

1983 (with I. Beraho-Beri) "Work and education: ideological impasse or hope for an educational alternative?" Education with Production, Volume 2, no. 2. pp 49-53

1983 "Culture in the city" Dialectics and Humanism, Volume X, no. 1. pp. 183-188

1983 "Intercultural cooperation in higher education" Higher Education by the Year 2000, Proceedings of the IVth International Congress of the European Association for Research and Development in Higher Education, Frankfurt am Main, 5-10/9/83, pp. 138-152

1984 Educational and Cultural Realities: creative struggles for development, University of Surrey Department of Educational Studies. Mimeo

1984 "Lifelong education: opportunities and obstacles" International Journal of Lifelong Education, Volume 3, no. 2. pp. 79-89

1984 "Encounters and confrontation in education" Scottish Journal of Adult Education, Volume 6, no. 3. pp. 5-12

1984 "International relationship, lifelong education and adult education" Education and Society: focus on Asia and the Pacific, Kowloon, Hong Kong, Asian Students Association, pp. 92-100

1985 "Lifelong education: trends and issues" Encyclopedia of Education, Oxford, Pergamon Press

1985 "Lifelong education and international relations" Lifelong Education and Participation, papers presented at the Conference on Lifelong Education Initiatives in Mediterranean Countries, 5-7/11/84, Malta, University of Malta Press, pp. 16-29

1985 Lifelong Education and International Relations,

London, Croom Helm
1985 "Education, work and the young: creativity and hopes" <u>Vocational Training</u>, no. 17. pp. 20-23
1985 "Problems of educational research" <u>International Social Science Journal</u>, no. 104, UNESCO. pp. 149-156

On Gelpi:
Cross, J. (1981) "A rediscovered unity" <u>Times Educational Supplement</u>, 5/6/81
Griffin, C. (1983) "Gelpi's view of lifelong education" <u>Curriculum Theory in Adult and Lifelong Education</u>, London, Croom Helm, pp. 172-200
Ireland, T.D. (1978) <u>Gelpi's View of Lifelong Education</u>, Manchester, University of Manchester, Department of Adult and Higher Education, Manchester Monographs 14
Ruddock, R. (1981) "A trilogy of extracts: the material issues (Ettore Gelpi)" <u>Evaluation: a consideration of principles and methods</u>, Manchester, University of Manchester Department of Adult and Higher Education, Manchester Monographs 18. pp. 94-101
Suchodolski, B. (1980) "Ettore Gelpi on lifelong education" <u>Dialectics and Humanism</u>, no. 1. pp. 155-160

Other References:
Bates, I. <u>et al</u>. (1984) <u>Schooling for the Dole? The new vocationalism</u>, London, Macmillan
Dave, R.H. ed. (1976) <u>Foundations of Lifelong Education</u>, Oxford, Pergamon Press for UNESCO Institute for Education
International Broadcasting Trust (1985) <u>The People Trade: an IBT study guide</u>; by Paul Gerhardt, Stuart Howard and Pratibha Parmar, London, International Broadcasting Trust
Trades Union Congress (1985) <u>All Work and No Play</u>, London, Trades Union Congress in collaboration with United Nations Children's Fund

Part Six

CONCLUSION

Chapter Fifteen

TOWARDS A DISCIPLINE OF ADULT EDUCATION?

Peter Jarvis

This book has commenced with a thesis about the development of knowledge, especially adult education knowledge, and then proceeded to examine the work of thirteen thinkers about the field this century. Each of the thinkers has made a major contribution to the body of knowledge about adult education, and so it is necessary to re-examine the thesis in the light of contents of this book. In addition, this chapter seeks to draw out some of the recurring patterns that have emerged in these chapters, such as the influence of religious belief and the concern for better society that have motivated adult educators during much of this century. Additionally, and related to this, it is possible to see that for some of the early thinkers of the century, the provision of education for adults was a major pre-occupation, so that there are within their writings some profound attempts to justify adult education provision which provide a basis for philosophical thought. In contrast, other thinkers, such as Thorndike, developed their ideas from the basis of their own academic work so that the concerns of Mansbridge, for instance, play little part in their writing. Hence, it may be seen from the outset that adult education knowledge is a unique combination of elements of knowledge from the varying backgrounds and concerns of the different thinkers, whose work has contributed to the body of knowledge, that may now be called adult education knowledge.

This chapter, therefore, has a number of sections; the first returns to the thesis of the first chapter and seeks to reformulate it in the light of the subsequent discussion. Thereafter, the chapter examines the influence of religious thought on the development of adult education, discusses the issue of idealism and reflects upon the idea that, in the United Kingdom at least, adult education was regarded for a long time as a social movement, which may be one of the reasons why it is finding it quite difficult at times to come to terms with increasingly instrumental elements of continuing education. Finally, the chapter raises some questions about the extent to which the study of adult education may be regarded as an academic discipline.

The Development of Adult Education Knowledge

It will be recalled that the thesis presented in the first chapter was that as the division of labour occurs there is a subsequent division in the body of knowledge, but that this is not a simple and mechanical phenomenon since there are some thinkers who straddle a number of the new occupations and branches of knowledge and synthesize them. Additionally, it was pointed out that since the power structures of society are slower to change, there will be recurring themes in different times in history about the place of education in the social development of the world. There will, consequently, frequently be an idealistic, or utopian, element that extols the time when there will be a better world and this will provide a philosophical foundation for the education of adults, since for many adult education may be seen as one of the instruments by which this new society is created.

It was also shown, using examples of Lindeman and Freire, that it is possible to demonstrate the basic validity of the idea that a new body of knowledge may be created through the fission and fusion of knowledge through social change. However, it may be asked if all knowledge is dependent upon social conditions in this way and, clearly, from an analysis of the writings of these thinkers and answer must be in the negative. It would be difficult, for instance,to reconcile totally the research of Thorndike with the social conditions that prevailed at the time. At the same time it would be possible (Snyder, 1973) to claim that a great deal of funded academic research must be dependent upon the funding agency, so that academic researchers are not as free as many would like to regard themselves. Even allowing for the fact that funding organizations might well determine the direction of a great deal of academic research, it must be pointed out the new knowledge developed as a result of the social conditions need not necessarily relate to the fission and fusion of the structures of society through the division of labour. Hence, it must be pointed out that the thesis of the first chapter needs to be extended slightly in this respect.

Might it not be possible to claim that some academic research follows the logic of the discipline, rather than the demands of society? This is, obviously, the more idealistic interpretation of the development of knowledge. Some researchers and theorists might well develop ideas that have not been dependent upon the demands of funding agencies and so it must be recognized that there is a possibility that this will occur, although it is doubtful whether it occurs as frequently as is often supposed. But are they actually free of the social conditions? Obviously, no person is totally free of these and so the initiating factors in the generation of new ideas and knowledge may stem from questions that occur as a result of the researcher's own experiences and the subsequent ideas that arise. Indeed, elsewhere (Jarvis, 1987) it has been shown that such questions might arise from the disjuncture between an individual's biography and present experience which stimulates the desire to learn something that has previously been unknown. It is also claimed there that one of the bases of the creation of new knowledge for an individual is the synthesis of knowledge from divergent experiences. Hence, thinkers with wide experience will seek to combine their learning from different branches of their life and create new ways of understanding. This is in accord with the thesis argued in this book, that new knowledge emerges as a result of the fusion of the branches of knowledge that have themselves been created through the process of social change and differentiation.

It may, therefore, be claimed that adult education knowledge has developed in a number of different ways and that the thesis in the opening chapter outlines only one of these. The thesis in the first chapter is basically that new knowledge is created through synthesis of existing knowledge and ideas and this may well illustrate one of the major elements in creativity. Nevertheless, it must be recognised that some pure research may develop in the field of study which really develops already existing knowledge. Therefore a number of thinkers, such as Thorndike and Knowles, whose work has been discussed here do not necessarily need to be viewed as synthesizers. However, the fact that Thorndike was a psychologist raises the additional question of the relationship between adult education knowledge and psychological knowledge. Obviously, it is not possible to demarcate the areas of knowledge and claim that a single phenomenon may only be interpreted from the perspective of a single discipline. There must be some overlap between the disciplines and this is a question to which further reference will be made in the final section of this chapter.

While the basis thesis of the opening chapter has substance, it has been shown that there are other ways through which adult education knowledge is generated. However, the questions raised also point to the fact that the use of knowledge from other disciplines is important in the growth of the body of adult education knowledge, both because of the nature of social reality and of its interpretation. However, this raises questions about the extent to which it is possible to claim that adult education is a discipline, or a sub-discipline of education, and this will also be a focus of the last section of this chapter. Before this is undertaken, it is necessary to look back at the thinkers whose work has been discussed in this book and to examine other influences upon their thought.

The Influence of Religious Belief upon the Growth of Adult Education

A recurring theme throughout the above chapters has been the religious belief of the thinkers whose work has been discussed; this is as true for the thinkers in Britain as it is for those in the Americas. Perhaps the most significant thing about this belief is that its outworkings are totally social; it is an element of the social gospel of Christianity, epitomised in a high doctrine of the human being. From Mansbridge to Coady, from Tawney to Freire, there is a consistent pattern of religious belief being a motivating factor in their lives. At the same time it must be recognised that the outcome of the belief varies form one thinker to another. Mansbridge, for instance, enlisted the help of the establishment in order to propagate his ideas, while Freire has been much more revolutionary, adopting the prophetic role and confronting the power structures of his country. But this difference should not be regarded as surprising since the Christian religion has always produced a variety of different responses to social inequality. Yet, in different ways, there are a number of recurring themes that may be discovered in these chapters: concern for the poor and the working classes coupled with indignation at social inequality; idealism and the belief that the education of adults can help provide a base for a better world; belief that people can learn throughout their lives and that education should, therefore, be a lifelong provision. Each of these themes will now be briefly discussed individually.

Social Inequality: A recurring theme in nearly all of the writers is that the poor and the working classes have not had sufficient opportunity to be educated and to enjoy the fruits of knowledge. This is not something that is new to the twentieth century, as is well known, and which may be illustrated from the work of the Christian Socialists in Britain in the previous century (Gibson, 1986). Even so, this tradition may be seen a great number of the thinkers discussed in this book: Mansbridge founded the Workers Educational Association, Coady and Horton have both been involved in workers' movements, Tawney was concerned about the conditions of the poor, Freire enraged by the exploitation of the poor by the upper classes in Brazil, Knowles and Kidd both had a period in their careers in adult education working with the Young Men's Christian Association and much of Lindeman's academic career was in social work.

It is perhaps not surprising that in the light of the above statements that, in their different ways, these writers expressed their Christian belief in their philosophies about adult education. In many of the writers there is a great concern for the equality of teacher and learner relationship which has become a fundamental tenet of some philosophies of teaching in adult education. Freire takes this argument even further by pointing out that the teaching and learning interaction is not a teacher-student relationship but a teacher/student-student/teacher relationship where each learns from, and teaches the other. This relationship which, in part has also found a place in the writings about andragogy, certainly has ideological undertones and it is perhaps significant that in many situations it is recognised as also being conducive to the teaching and learning situation. However, the teacher-learner relationship is really no more than an example of the ideology of equality worldwide that pervades the writings of these thinkers, and which certainly resulted in Kidd's work in founding the International Council of Adult Education.

Education is also regarded as a means to a good

life, which is something that should not be the prerogative of the wealthy and the leisured classes. Perhaps the claim in the famous 1919 Report on Adult Education in Britain summarises a great deal of this concern:

> That the necessary conclusion is that adult education must not be regarded as a luxury for the few exceptional persons here and there, nor as a thing which concerns only a short span of early manhood, but that adult education is a permanent national necessity, an inseparable aspect of citizenship, and therefore should be universal and lifelong. (1919 Report, para 5)

Mansbridge, Yeaxlee and Tawney all served on that committee, so that it is hardly surprising that these words do reflect this major concern of the early thinkers.

It is also significant to note that from a less religious perspective this same concern for the working class, especially the immigrant labourers, in the contemporary world has been the subject of considerable concern by Gelpi. In many of his works that have been written, or translated, into English there are the recurrent themes of the right to work and the relationship between education and work. In a sense, Gelpi's concerns appear different from those of thinkers in the earlier part of this century, although there are similar ideological elements in the concern for the dignity of the human being, but then social conditions have changed greatly and so this is to be expected. The education of adults with which Gelpi is concerned does perhaps relate more directly to the world of work than that which was pioneered by some of the early thinkers, who were concerned that the working classes should have the benefits of a liberal education. Even so, the early thinkers were not unaware of the economic benefits to the nation of an educated work force, for the 1919 Report continues to specify that the sound economic recovery of the nation, after the 1914-18 War, was dependent upon an educated workforce (para 7).

For the majority of these writers, their overriding concern was that this social inequality should be overcome without disturbing the social structures of society. They were clearly reformist in their orientation rather than radical (Jarvis, 1985 pp. 8-14), although it might even be correct to classify some of them as more liberal than reformist in which case they viewed education as the force for

development of the individual, as individual, who was
then free to act as an individual agent, in any way
that the person chose. It is perhaps significant that
few of the early writers on adult education this
century actually regarded adult education as
constraining people and perhaps acting as a hegemonic
force, which also reflects the liberal and reformist
ideologies that they espoused.

Adult Education and a Better World: One of the major
themes of Christian theology is that in the fullness
of time the world will be re-created into a more
perfect place. Indeed, this is not only a concern of
Christian theology, Marxist thought is also keenly
concerned with the creation of the utopian classless
society. Whether, religious or secular, looking
forward to a time when the world is a better place
than it is today has been a constant hope, and it
must be borne in mind that the creation of a better
world is actually a different aim in education to
that of generating the good life, that was the
concern of the liberals and of some the reformists.
However, the manner in which this hope is to be
realised has differed, some have believed that in the
fullness of time this would be a divine gift, or
intervention, whilst others have believed that they
have had to try to facilitate the conditions for this
to happen.
    In the case of Freire, he has proclaimed a
revolutionary perspective based upon the idea that
people's thought processes are ensnared within the
hegemonic culture into which they are born and
socialized, so that liberation through conscientization is his theme. However, the liberation is
meaningless unless, thereafter, people who have been
freed seek to recreate the social world in which they
live. Freire recognized that the oppressors were also
trapped within their world, few would lay down the
reins of power voluntarily and so there is a
revolutionary perspective within his ideology.
Horton, working in slightly different conditions,
also embraced the cause of the exploited, but this
time it is through labour unions. The adult educator
has to assist those whose education has not already
equipped them to assert themselves, negotiate with
their oppressors and, if necessary, to use the forces
at their disposal – such as the withdrawal of labour
– in order to create better working and living
conditions for and with the people. Others have
recognised that through learning adults can be freed

to act upon the structures of the world, although they do not necessarily include it within their writings. Knowles, for instance, tells a story of how some Brazilian officials attended one of his workshops and adjudged that what he was doing was revolutionary because people were being exposed to a process of learning which could also be liberating. Other thinkers, like Gelpi, have taught that people have the right to work, so that their lives may be enriched, and they have the right to be educated for work. Nearly, ever thinker included within this book has recognized that the provision of education throughout the lifetime can result in an enriched life but some have taken a more sociological perspective and recognized that ultimately the standard of living for all depends upon the social structures and since these are at present the basis of social inequality, they have to be replaced with more egalitarian structures. In a real sense, most of the thinkers would see education as a significant means to a desirable end, rather than as an end in itself (Dewey, 1916, p.50).

It is perhaps significant to note that adult education has long regarded itself as a movement, and it still refers to itself as a service, which reflects the ideology of these thinkers from the earlier part of this century. It is perhaps this commitment that has been quite crucial to the development of adult education. However, it is an adult education service and as such adult educators in the United Kingdom, at least, appear more easily able to incorporate the work with the unemployed into their programmes than they do vocational education. The division between adult education and further education is qute clearly reflected here, with the latter being more firmly incorporated into the educational institution of society. Even so, both are part of the education of adults, which itself is a major element in the provision of lifelong education.

Lifelong Learning and Lifelong Education: The distinction between lifelong learning and lifelong education should be recognised from the outset, although there has been a tendency to confuse the two concepts in some adult education literature. Elsewhere (Jarvis, 1986), it has been argued that education may be regarded as the institutionalis-ation of learning. But there is a recurring theme amongst these early writers that was specified in the 1919 Report, that adult education is not a luxury for the few, but it is something that should be provided for all people throughout their lifetime. Few of these early thinkers would have regarded this as imprisoning, in the manner that Illich and Verne (1976) have suggested, but rather the opposite - the chance to improve the conditions of life for all. Yeaxlee (1929) was the first to examine the idea in depth and many of the problems upon which he focused are as significant now as they were at the time when he wrote about them.

But it is also important to recognise that there was also a conviction among the early writers of this century, despite the findings of many psychologists, that adults could continue to learn effectively throughout their lives. This belief is common to many of these writers, both those who have adopted a more radical perspective and those who have been less concerned with the politics of social change. Indeed, it has been shown here that Dewey's work implicitly presupposes a theory of lifelong education, although it was Yeaxlee who was the first to offer a developed treatise upon it.

Thus it may be seen that perhaps the most potent motivator for many of these exponents of adult education was their religious belief and, even more significantly, whilst their ideology has become secularised it would be true to say that the humanistic perspective that many contemporary adult educators adopt is in accord with these beliefs. However, has the result of their endeavours resulted in the creation of a new academic discipline or in a field of study?

Towards a Discipline of Adult Education?

In order to clarify this discussion it is necessary from the outset to define the concept of discipline, from within the framework of knowledge. Hirst (1974, p.46) makes the point that distinct disciplines are forms of knowledge, and that these are sub-divisible. He also focuses upon the idea that there are theoretical and practical fields of knowledge. Hirst's forms of knowledge are: mathematics, physical sciences, human sciences, history, religion, literature and the fine arts, and philosophy. From within this perspective, it might be possible to argue that education is a sub-division of the human sciences and, therefore, a separate discipline. But the problem with this approach is that educational knowledge, as may be seen from the theorists discussed in the above pages, comprises a synthesis of branches of knowledge from a variety of other sub-disciplines, etc. Hence, it is not an intrinsically a single form of knowledge and, therefore, it cannot be regarded as a discipline.

Clearly, adult education is a field of study, so that it would be wiser to begin to examine it from the second perspective adopted by Hirst, that of practical and theoretical fields of knowledge. However, it must be recognized immediately that the field of study is itself so complex that it may be impossible to demarcate it. Peters (1966: pp 23 ff), for instance, claims that education has become too complex to define and so it cannot be demarcated but, by contrast, Boyd and Apps (1980, pp 1-13) attempted to do just this when they produced their three dimensional model of the field of study of adult education. Obviously their approach was over-simple, but it still might be possible to produce a complex model of the field of study if the criteria of selection were initially agreed upon. Hence, for the purpose of the remainder of this chapter, it will be assumed that it is possible to demarcate the field of study that might be called adult education, or the education of adults. Immediately, it will be seen that there is a confusion of terms, since the latter appears to be wider than the former, and while this distinction has been explored elsewhere (Jarvis, 1983), it will be assumed here that the wider term is more meaningful within this context and so the remainder of this discussion will focus upon the education of adults.

To what extent is the education of adults a theoretical or a practical field of knowledge? Bright (1985, pp. 173-179) argues that adult education, which is the focus of his paper, does not at present constitute a theoretical field of knowledge, although he allows for the possibility of this developing and points to one example where it might be occurring. Clearly, many of the thinkers referred to above actually utilized the perspectives of other disciplines with which to discuss the education of adults. In many of these writers there are philosophical, historical, psychological and sociological perspectives about adult education. Indeed, it is of relevance to note that it is possible to examine many manifestations of the education of adults and to interpret them from any combination of these disciplines simultaneously. Hence, it is possible to have a philosophy of, or a sociology of, the education of adults.

To what extent, however, is it possible to have

an adult education psychology, etc? This is clearly much more problematic, which supports Bright's contention that the education of adults should much more realistically be regarded as a field of practical knowledge. Indeed, even if there were adult educational psychology, it would comprise psychological knowledge applied to the practicalities of the adult education situation, which would merely be a distillation of psychological knowledge for specific purposes. Therefore, it must be recognized that the knowledge that is utilised in the education of adults is, fundamentally, knowledge from other disciplines which is applied to the field of the education of adults. Hence, the unique combinations of sub-disciplines utilised by most of the writers included within this book may be seen to constitute one approach to the construction of a body of knowledge about the education of adults. Thus this body of knowledge appears to be a combination of branches of knowledge applied to a specific situation. The implication of the above branches of other disciplines or sub-disciplines, rather than a discipline in its own right.

However, there are many courses in adult education now, some at post-graduate level and others specifically created for intending teachers of adults and, it might be asked, how these courses relate to the above argument? Is there not a subject called adult education? Naturally there is a subject, in as much as a subject relates relevant knowledge to a field of study and in this instance the relevant knowledge is that combination of knowledge considered by those responsible for the preparation of teachers of adults to be relevant to that course of preparation. Hence, it is an integration of branches of disciplines, rather than a discipline in its own right.

Knowles has used the word andragogy to refer to the study of adult education and the use of this term merely provides a term that seeks to delimit the field of study. Kidd (1973, p.23), for instance, also employed a term - mathetics, which is the science of the pupil's behavior while learning just as pedagogy is the discipline in which attention is focused on the schoolmaster's behavior while teaching.' Both of these terms seek to convey the same thing, the emphasis on the learner rather than the teacher and in some ways Kidd's term avoids some of the problems of the concept of andragogy, but neither of them do more than provide a focus for the combination of sub-disciplines which constitute the body of adult

311

education knowledge. Perhaps this is best illustrated by the work of Thorndike, referred to earlier in this chapter, a psychologist whose research was considered to be relevant to adult education and whose work was, therefore, widely read.

Conclusions

This book has attempted to demonstrate how the body of knowledge that might be called adult education knowledge has begun to emerge. There is no single systematic approach, nor is there a single discipline. Different thinkers have brought their own approaches to the field of practice and of study and have reflected upon it and have produced their theories about it.

Adult education knowledge is not a seamless robe of integrated knowledge but rather a variety of combinations of sub-disciplines and those thinkers who have contributed most to the construction of this amorphous body of knowledge have drawn from a variety of sources and applied their findings to this complex field of study, which is the education of adults.

Bibliography

Boyd, R.D. and Apps, J.W. et al (1980) Redefining the Discipline of Adult Education San Francisco, Jossey Bass Publishers Inc.

Bright B.R. (1985) The Content-Method Relationship in the Study of Adult Education in Studies in the Education of Adults. Vol. 17 No. 2 pp. 168–183

Dewey, J. (1916) Democracy and Education. New York, The Free Press

Gibson, G. (1986) Thought and Action in the Life of F.D. Maurice, with particular reference to the London Working Men's College in The International Journal of Lifelong Education Vol. 5 No. 4

Hirst, P.H. (1974) Knowledge and the Curriculum London, Routledge and Kegan Paul Ltd.

Illich, I. and Verne, E. (1976) Imprisoned in a Global Classroom. London, Writers and Readers Publishing Co.

Jarvis, P. (1983) Adult and Continuing Education: Theory and Practice London, Croom Helm

Jarvis, P. (1985) The Sociology of Adult and Continuing Education. London, Croom Helm

Jarvis, P. (1986) Sociological Perspectives on Lifelong Education and Lifelong Learning. University of Georgia. Dept of Adult Education Monographs

Jarvis, P. (1987) - forthcoming Adult Learning in the

Social Context London, Croom Helm
Kidd, J.R. (1973) revised edition How Adults Learn
Chicago, Association Press
Peters, R.S. (1966) Ethics and Education. London,
George Allen and Unwin Ltd.
Remmling, G.W. (ed) (1973) Towards the Sociology of
Knowledge. London, Routledge and Kegan Paul Ltd.
Snyder, R.G. (1973) Knowledge, Power and the
University: notes on the impotence of the
intellectual in Remmling, G.W. (ed) op.cit.
Yeaxlee, B.A. (1929) Lifelong Education London,
Cassell and Co.
The 1919 Report. (1980) edition. Reprinted by Dept of
Adult Education, University of Nottingham.

NOTES ABOUT THE AUTHORS

David L. Alfred: David Alfred is a tutor-organiser for the South Eastern District of the Workers' Educational Organisation. Graduating in Government from Exeter University in 1963, he has taught Liberal Studies and Sociology in colleges of further education, and many social science courses as a part-time tutor for the WEA (in conjunction with Oxford's Delegacy for Extra-Mural Studies) and the Open University. A WEA workshop in Hastings which he convened wrote and produced in 1982 The Robert Tressell Papers: Exploring 'The Ragged Trousered Philanthropists'. His article on 'The Relevance of the Work of Paulo Freire to Radical Community Education in Britain' appeared in The International Journal of Lifelong Education in 1984. As part of the MSc degree in Educational Studies which he was awarded by Surrey University in 1985, he wrote a dissertation on Political Education in the British Army 1941-1945.

Brenda Bell is a consultant to Highlander's labor program, and has led and participated in workshops at Highlander. She once served as Regional Coordinator of the Amalgamated Clothing and Textile Workers Union Humanities Education Program, and has taught on the Southern Summer School for Union Women, and has work experience in the areas of labor education, social work, and community education. She has served as editor of Motive magazine, a special issue of Southern Exposure on labor history, and is the author of several articles on Southern U.S. labor. Included in her publication list is Pregnancy and Mining: A Handbook for Women Miners. Ms. Bell holds an M.S. in Adult Education from The University of Tennessee.

Stephen Brookfield is Associate Professor of Adult and Continuing Education and Associate Director of the Center of Adult Education at Teachers College, Columbia University, New York City. He has been national chair of the Adult Education Research Conference of North America (1985) and currently serves on the editorial boards of Adult Education Quarterly and the Canadian Journal for Studies in Adult Education. He was a founding member of the International League for Social Commitment in Adult Education and has served on the national executive committee of the Association of Recurrent Education (U.K.). He has been professor of adult education at the University of British Columbia, British Vancouver, Canada and was formerly research officer for the Advisory Council for Adult and Continuing Education (England and Wales). His books are: Adult Learners, Adult Education and the Community (1984), Self-Directed Learning: From Theory to Practice (1985) and Understanding and Facilitating Adult Learning (1986).

John M. Crane is a graduate of the University of Saskatchewan (1962, B.A. and B.Ed.) and of the University of Surrey, U.K. (M.Sc. in Educational Studies in 1982). He has had a long involvement with adult basic education and has been interested in its background. In addition, he has a particular interest in self-paced, individualized learning, which was the subject of his dissertation. He has published a number of articles on adult education and he is currently an instructor on a self-paced, individualized learning program in Camosun College, Victoria, Canada.

Angela Cross-Durrant started her working life in National Health Service, and began teaching in 1971 at an Institute of Adult Education in Bristol. This was followed by a period at Soundwell Technical College, also in Bristol. Three years afterwards she moved to Twickenham College of Technology, later Richmond-upon-Thames (tertiary) College, where she now works as a Senior Lecturer.

She looks upon herself as a 'lifelong learner', as she studied in her own time for her A-Levels, various teaching qualifications, and her first degree (in English Literature) which she undertook as an External Student of the University of London. (She had previously completed a Cert Ed on a Sandwich

Course under the auspices of the same University). In 1985 she completed an MSc in Educational Studies on a part-time basis at the University of Surrey. Her interest in Lifelong Education was formalised during this latter period of study.

She has had published a number of papers on the education of adults.

Barry Elsey entered adult education as a mature student after leaving school without any qualifications. First by part-time and then full-time study, he went on to university. He entered university adult education as a research fellow and then to a lectureship at the Universities of Liverpool and Nottingham. He has wide experience of university extension work and professional training programmes in adult/continuing education. His research and writing in adult/continuing education has reflected a personal interest in adult students, volunteer tutors, 'second chance' education for adults and the application of social theory to policy and practice in adult/continuing education.

Colin Griffin. Lecturer in Sociology at Hillcroft College. Studied philosophy, sociology and politics at the University of Birmingham and the London School of Economics, and took the Diploma in Adult Education at the University of London.

Worked as an Assistant Librarian at the L.S.E., Senior Lecturer in Sociology at Kingston Polytechnic, Senior Lecturer in Education at St. Mary's College, Cheltenham, and as a Senior Counsellor with the Northern Region of the Open University. For many years an Extension Lecturer for the University of London.

More recently, course tutor for the Diploma in Adult and Continuing Education at the University of London Department of Extra-Mural Studies, tutor for the Open University's E355 course on Education for Adults, and Associate Lecturer in the Department of Educational Studies, University of Surrey. Also associated with the assessment of experiential learning project at the Policy Studies Institute.

Publications in the area of recurrent and lifelong education, and in curriculum theory and social policy of adult education, in Adult Education, International Journal of Lifelong Education, etc. Curriculum Theory in Adult and Lifelong Education published by Croom Helm in 1983. Currently writing on social policy and adult education for publication in 1986. Translations of various papers by Ettore Gelpi, including several chapters of his <u>Lifelong Education and International Relations</u>.

William S. Griffith. William S. "Bill" Griffith has been Professor of Adult Education in the Department of Administrative, Adult and Higher Education at The University of British Columbia in Vancouver, Canada since 1977, and had been Chairman of the Adult Education Special Field Committee at The University of Chicago for 15 years. Beginning his professional career in agricultural extension, he subsequently earned his Ph.D. in adult education at the University of Chicago. In addition to serving as Senior Editor of the eight-volume <u>Handbook of Adult Education in the United States</u>, he has been Chairman of the Commission of the Professors of Adult Education and a member of the Steering Committee of the Adult Education Research Conference. In 1980 he was given the Research to Practice Award of the Adult Education Association of the United States. As a Fulbright Senior Researcher he spent the 1972-73 academic year in Australia where he investigated the organization and coordination of public adult education. With the support of the British Council, he visited selected university adult education departments in Great Britain in 1982. His areas of interest include adult basic education and the coordination of adult education provision inter-organizationally.

Peter Jarvis is currently senior lecturer in the education of adults at the University of Surrey, U.K. He has written numerous articles and several books. His latest book is entitled: <u>Adult Learning in the Social Context</u> and is also published by Croom Helm. He has taught and lectured about adult education internationally. He is editor of the Croom Helm series on 'International Adult Education' and also the Croom Helm series on 'Theory and Practice of Adult Education in North America.' In addition, he is joint editor of <u>The International Journal of Lifelong Education</u>, and he serves on the editorial board of <u>Adult Education Quarterly</u>.

John M. Peters is Professor of Adult Education at The University of Tennessee. He has taught at Cornell University, North Carolina State University, and The

University of British Columbia. He has conducted seminars and presented papers at The University of Surrey, U.K. Professor Peters is the Editor of Building An Effective Enterprise of Adult Education (1980), and numerous articles and chapters on adult education. A former Secretary of the Adult Education Association of the U.S.A. and Executive Committee Member of the Commission of Professors on Adult Education, Professor Peters is active in international organizations of Adult Eduction.

William A.B. Smith Graduated from Georgetown College, Georgetown, Kentucky with a double major in Psychology and Sociology, 1968, B.A. degree.

Graduated from Southwestern Baptist Theological Seminary with a major in Religious Education, 1972, (M.R.E. degree).

Graduated from Southwestern Baptist Technological Seminary with a double major in Psychology and Foundations of Teaching, 1978 (Ed.D. degree).

Has served in the following capacities: Minister to the Deaf, and trainer for deaf ministers. Teacher of children with learning disabilities. Served local churches as Minister of Education for 10 years.

Serving now in the following capacity: Associate Professor of Foundations of Education on the faculty of Southwestern Baptist Theological Seminary, teaching since 1978. Has authored and co-authored publications in creative methods of teaching, leadership training of volunteer teachers, and curriculum design.

Alan Miller Thomas Born Toronto, Canada, 1928. Educated at Upper Canada College, University of Toronto, (English and Philosophy) B.A., 1949; Teachers College, Columbia University, (History of Education) M.A., 1953; (Social Psychology), Ph.D., 1964. Served as Executive-Director of the Canadian Association for Adult Education, 1961-69. Elected President of that organization, 1972-78. Taught at the University of British Columbia, 1955-1961, where he inaugurated the first full-time graduate program in adult education in Canada (1958). Second Chairman of the Department of Adult Education, Ontario, Institute for Studies in Education (1971-1979). Served as executive-assistant to Federal Minister of Communications, 1970-71. Served on OECD review team for Finland, 1981. Major interests are policy matters

318

in adult education. Completed studies in Canada of adult education in industry, labour education, education in prisons. Recently completed a book; <u>Principia Mathetica: The Politics of Learning</u>.